D0203594

DISCARDED

WIDENER UNIVERSITY

CROATIA

MID-WEST UNIVERSITY

Political Anthropology, Volume 7

OUTWITTING THE STATE

Edited by
Peter Skalník

With a foreword by
Henri J. M. Claessen

Transaction Publishers
New Brunswick (U.S.A.) and London (U.K.)

Copyright © 1989 by Transaction Publishers.
New Brunswick, New Jersey 08903

All rights reserved under International and Pan-American Copyright Con-
ventions. No part of this book may be reproduced or transmitted in any
form or by any means, electronic or mechanical, including photocopy,
recording, or any information storage and retrieval system, without prior
permission in writing from the publisher. All inquiries should be addressed
to Transaction Publishers, Rutgers—The State University, New Brunswick,
New Jersey 08903.

Library of Congress Catalog Number: 88-36945
ISBN: 0-88738-274-6
Printed in the United States of America

Library of Congress Cataloging-in-Publication Data

Outwitting the state / edited by Peter Skalnik.
     p.   cm. — (Political anthropology ; v. 7)
  Includes bibliographies and index.
  ISBN 0-88738-274-6
  1. Political anthropology.   2. State, The.   I. Skalník, Peter,
1945- . II. Series: Political anthropology (New Brunswick, N.J.)
; v. 8.
GN492.P62   vol. 8
[GN492.2]
306'.2—dc 19   88-36945
                                                           CIP

GN
492.2
.097
1989

WIDENER UNIVERSITY
WOLFGRAM
LIBRARY
CHESTER, PA.

Contents

Foreword

When Peter Skalník some years ago invited me to write a foreword to his collection volume, *Outwitting the State*, I did not hesitate to accept the invitation. We had been working together closely for some years, editing two books, *The Early State* (1978) and *The Study of the State* (1981), and though our views were not identical, we held many views in common. Since, however, we became separated by thousands of kilometers and—as will be apparent from the pages that follow—also by divergent views. Skalník is inclined to be rather critical with regard to the past works, and I have continued working in the same direction. As a consequence there are views in this book and in the introduction that I do not share. Before going shortly into our differences of opinion, I hasten to say that I have no problems with the thesis that some groups or peoples succeed in "outwitting the state." It is only realistic. The idea that states—modern nation-states included—should have a monopoly of force or control is so far from reality that it is only surprising that it took so long before it became recognized by anthropologists (cf. Sahlins 1968). Yet already Wittfogel (1957: 109, 113) pointed to the existence of a "beggars democracy"—the phenomenon that even in the most absolute states, people can escape control. On the one hand this is connected with the fact that there is a limit to control: that what is thought or spoken between trusted people will escape control. On the other hand, there is a realization on the part of government that investments to achieve complete control after a certain moment no longer produce results justifying the costs. The essays in this volume show that the escape of state regulations is not restricted to small numbers of people, but that whole groups or peoples can succeed in doing so. The first idea that comes to the mind in this respect is the inability of states to suppress revolts and rebellions: France of the 1980s is not able to control Corsica; England is not able to control Northern Ireland; the Soviet Union cannot cope with ethnic rebellions in Azerbaidzhan. Efforts to express such forms of resistance in more general formulations are greatly needed. It must be noted, however, that the chapters of this volume are concerned not so much with people fighting the state, but with groups who try to maintain their own style of living, their own culture, notwithstanding the fact that these are in conflict with the views held by the government.

Apparently these groups succeed in countering state power with another form of power. At least this is the way in which Skalník states it. There are, in his view, several types of power, and who would argue with that? Moreover, power is always a kind of a relationship, a dyadic relation between someone who exerts power and another who suffers from it (or submits to it, et cetera). Without the existence of the second person or group, there is no possibility to exert power. Some scholars state that politics, power, and state form a kind of continuum (a "semantic overlap" as Skalník characterizes this approach). Swartz, Turner, and Tuden (1966:14ff) coined the two ends of such a continuum *coercive power* and *consensual power*. Basic to all the forms of power included in the continuum is that it enables the holder "to limit the behavioral alternatives of other people." This occurs— regardless of the fact that the one in power uses the barrel of the gun or that his followers believe his words to be truth. They do what he wants them to do. When this view of power is accepted, the "semantic overlap" becomes doubtful. There is more, however. Power in terms of the application of force is certainly not limited to state governments. Whatever definition of power applied, nobody will contend that, for example, leaders of Mafia groups succeed in enforcing their decisions; they exert power (exemplified in Mario Puzo's *Godfather*; cf. Maas 1969).

Though in *The Early State* some pages were devoted to the problem of the origins of the state, the book was not conceived with that goal in mind. The main goal of the volume was the establishment of a type, a structure, the early state, the predecessor of the modern state. That the concept was well suited to be used in an evolutionary framework is true, but the concept of the early state, however, was not "designed especially to support evolutionist typological theories." Moreover, the view of evolutionism as only the construction of a series of stages is no longer tenable. The volumes I coedited with Pieter van de Velde and Estellie Smith (*Development and Decline* in 1985 and *Early State Dynamics* in 1987) show that the typological approach, characteristic of evolutionary anthropology in the 1960s, no longer is relevant. So why beat a dead horse? Let us be clear about one more thing. The fact that most early states were preceded by polities that qualify as chiefdoms—in whatever definition (Mann 1986; Johnson and Earle 1986; Champion et al. 1984; Hagesteijn 1985; Eisenstadt et al. 1988)—does not imply that each chiefdom automatically did develop into an early state; the majority did not. The same holds for the mature state; only some early states developed into mature states (Claessen 1985; Claessen and Van de Velde 1987, especially the chapters by Shifferd, Bargatzky, Tymowski, and Van der Vliet). And, continuing the line of history, only some mature states developed into modern-industrialized-capitalist states (see, e.g., Smith 1986; Wilkinson 1973; Braudel 1974).

There is no automatism implied and neither a kind of inevitability. The development toward a more complex type can be explained in each case (in general, as well as in specific terms) as the result of a complex interaction of a series of factors. The modern capitalist industrial state did not develop out of nothing; it was a logical successor to previously existing forms. That this development took place in Western Europe only was the consequence of specific historical constellations and developments (Romein 1954; cf. Wilkinson 1973; Weber 1958). There is no reason, however, to consider Tawantinsuyu, the realm of the Aztecs, Maurya India, the Mongol empire, Javanese Majapahit, or the Roman empire qua political structure as something qualitatively different from, say, France, Spain, or England in the fifteenth century. They all were states, varying from early to mature.

But let us return to the chapters of this volume. They range from Micronesian Ponape to the Hausa of Niger, from Central Borneo to the Old Believers in Canada. This is a wide range of examples, and in bringing together these cases, Skalník places himself in the front ranks of current anthropological discourse. The approach used can be characterized by an increasing awareness of complexity, interaction, and time depth (cf. Belshaw 1988). Each of the analyses presented here demonstrates these characteristics. The relations between those who outwit the state and the state government are complex and intricate. It is not possible to explain the behavior of the participants in simple terms or in easy generalizations. For example, the Ponapean behavior had its roots in a long-standing cultural tradition, in which the communal interests stood central. They then became dominated by colonial powers—Germans, Japanese, Americans— each with a different political ideology, but all differing from the Ponapean views. By cleverly manipulating the American model of democracy, they succeeded in retraditionalizing their society. The developments in Ponape show a complex interaction of a variety of factors: ideological (in the sense of values, norms, political ideologies, et cetera), economical (the introduction of money, wage labor, et cetera), and demographical (considerable changes in the number of people in the course of a century [cf. also Petersen 1982]). Finally, the events in Ponape cannot be explained and understood without taking into consideration the past. Traditional views, means of subsistence, and demography continue to play a role in the present; the succession of the colonial governments cannot be left out of the picture. And to study Ponape without placing the island within the broader context of Micronesian cultures would make the analysis incomplete.

The characteristics of modern anthropology, as exemplified by the chapter on Ponape, are found to play a role in the other chapters, too. They all describe and analyze complex situations, in which a number of factors can be found to play a role, each of them interacting with the others. Without adding the historical background to the analysis many of the recent developments would be unintelligible. Naturally, the time depth varies per case. The problems of the Hausa in coping with the government-induced cooperative movements, as analyzed by Bäck, have only a shallow depth in time. However, by explaining the resistance of the Hausa as a consequence of their traditional culture, even here the past shows to be of direct importance in understanding the case in the present.

A consequence of the growing awareness of complexity, interaction, and time depth is the crossing of disciplinary boundaries. The anthropologist no longer can do without the findings of historians, archaeologists, linguists, or biologists. Boundaries between disciplines fade and cooperation with scholars working in other fields is increasing and necessary. From this it follows that anthropology has to cope with a bewildering growth of information. Each discipline we enter has a new stock of data and unfamiliar methods to handle them. The anthropologist not trained in these fields has to find ways to cope with the situation.

One of the means to cope with the growing complexity of data is the development of models. Models can be considered as a reduction of reality to its basic forms. A good model shows the structure of a phenomenon, the positions within the structure, and the relations between the positions. By introducing changes into the model, e.g., in the set of relations, a new structure can be constructed, et cetera. Complex social phenomena can be made understandable in this way. A good model not only represents the reality of a given moment, but has also the possibility to accommodate with changes over time—the time factor—by adding new positions or by changing the set of relations.

Outwitting the State is a fascinating volume, in which eight complex and intricate cases are presented against a historical background. They demonstrate the limitations of state power in a convincing way. Political anthropology is enriched with a new and fruitful concept, a concept well suited to be transformed into a model.

—Henri J. M. Claessen

References

Belshaw, Cyril S. 1988. Challenges for the future of social and cultural anthropology. *International Social Science Journal* 116: 193–202.

Braudel, Fernand. 1974. *Capitalism and material life 1400–1800*. London: Fontana/Collins.

Champion, Timothy, Clive Gamble, Stephen Shennan, and Alasdair Whittle. 1984. *Prehistoric Europe*. London, et cetera: Academic Press.

Claessen, Henri J. M. 1979. Introduction to *Political anthropology: The state of the art*. ed. S. L. Seaton and H. J. M. Claessen. The Hague: Mouton, pp. 7–30.

———. 1985. From the Franks to France: The evolution of a political organization. In *Development and decline: The evolution of sociopolitical organization*, ed. H. J. M. Claessen, P. van de Velde, and M. E. Smith. South Hadley: Bergin and Garvey, pp. 196–218.

Claessen, Henri J. M., and Peter Skalník, eds. 1978. *The early state*. The Hague: Mouton.

———. 1981. *The study of the state*. The Hague: Mouton.

Claessen, Henri J. M., and Pieter van de Velde, eds. 1987. *Early state dynamics*. Leiden: Brill.

Claessen, Henri J. M., Pieter van de Velde, and M. Estellie Smith, eds. 1985. *Development and decline: The evolution of socio-political organization*. South Hadley: Bergin and Garvey.

Eisenstadt, S. N., Michel Abitbol, and Naomi Chazan, eds. 1988. *The early state in African perspective*. Leiden: Brill.

Hagesteijn, Renée. 1985. Circles of kings: Political dynamics in early continental Southeast Asia. Ph. D. thesis, University of Leiden.

Johnson, Allen W., and Timothy Earle. 1986. *The evolution of human societies: From foraging group to agrarian state*. Stanford, Cal.: Stanford University Press.

Maas, Peter. 1969. The "canary that sang." London: Mac Gibben and Kee.

Mann, Michael. 1986. *The sources of social power: A history of power from the beginning to A.D. 1760*. Vol. 1. Cambridge: Cambridge University Press.

Petersen, Glenn. 1982. *One man cannot rule a thousand: Fission in a Ponapean chiefdom*. Ann Arbor: University of Michigan Press.

Romein, Jan. 1954. *Aera van Europa: De Europese geschiedenis als afwijking van het Algemeen Menselijk Patroon*. Leiden: Brill.

Sahlins, Marshall D. 1968. *Tribesmen*. Englewood Cliffs: Prentice Hall.

Smith, Anthony D. 1986. *The ethnic origins of nations*. Oxford: Blackwell.

Swartz, Marc J., Victor W. Turner, and Arthur Tuden, eds. 1966. *Political anthropology*. Chicago: Aldine.

Weber, Max. 1958. (1904/05). *The Protestant ethic and the spirit of capitalism*. New York: Scribner's Sons.

Wilkinson, Richard G. 1973. *Poverty and progress: An ecological model of economic development*. London: Methuen.

Wittfogel, Karl A. 1957. *Oriental despotism: A comparative study of total power*. New Haven: Yale University Press.

Preface

The editing of this book required time and energy. It can be said that it saw the light of day despite challenging teaching obligations at the University of Cape Town. But now it is here in your hands and it is with great pleasure that I offer this volume to the reader. Eight anthropologists from different countries and with various backgrounds have combined their efforts. Chapters 2–9 are the result of rewriting papers that were discussed at the symposium on responses of indigenous/local systems of authority to imported patterns of state power. The symposium, which I organized together with Jérôme Rousseau at Quebec in August 1983, was part of the Eleventh International Congress of Anthropological and Ethnological Sciences. Besides the eight papers the revised versions of which appear here, a ninth communication on the structure of Tanani Makhzan, an anti-state in preprotectorate Morocco, by Doyle Hatt of the University of Calgary, was presented at Quebec. I sincerely regret that Hatt's paper was never submitted for publication.

The revised papers were then retyped on a word processor and copies sent to all contributors. Since 1986 my introduction was drafted several times. A draft was discussed with Mike Aronoff when Transaction Publishers showed interest in the manuscript. It was finished after the agreement about publication was reached in May 1988. I am especially grateful to Mike Aronoff for encouragement and advice.

I would like to thank Hans Claessen for his skillfully played role of the discussant at Quebec and for his willingness to write a foreword to this volume. Chris McDowell prepared the index.

The work on the introduction and the word processing received financial support from the University of Cape Town. I received several smaller grants that helped pay the technical staff. Ida Thandiwe Goxo typed the whole manuscript in MS-Word program on a word processor, and Caroline Marsberg corrected typing errors and adjusted the style. Dr. Anne Sarzin corrected my language in chapters 1 and 9.

P. S.

1

Outwitting the State: An Introduction

Peter Skalník

> *A Copernican revolution is at stake . . . reflection on power must effect a "heliocentric" conversion*
> —Pierre Clastres

The history of humanity in the last few thousand years has been a history of expansion and conquest. The centrally organized societies have absorbed others that did not have sufficient means of defense and that were not organized hierarchically, equipped with armies, infrastructure, and centralized resource management. Many of these conquered human groups offered resistance, but they soon learned that they could not stand against the conquerors. The latter tried to impose their order on the indigenous populations. As a result, empires and new kinds of centralized polities emerged that combined elements of the old order with the new.[1] They were thus a kind of political compromise. Some survived for longer periods than others. In some areas such as India, sub-Saharan Africa, or the Middle East there were several waves of confrontation between foreign rule and local political order.

The European colonialism was preceded by a whole spectrum of centralizing processes that involved conquest, interpenetration, or alliances between autonomous groups. As a result, social orders of remarkable tenacity emerged. This to some extent concerns even Europe of the post-Roman and feudal periods where, through conquest, violence, and religious legitimation, bonds of subordination and superordination dominated the life of societies for many centuries. Probably as a result of conquest, the Indian caste system formed, seemingly, a sophisticated and enduring social contract arrangement.

In Africa centralized polities often emerged as a consequence of con-

1

quest. The violent beginning was gradually followed by ritual pacts or other forms of internalized consent with the new social order. Kings and chiefs had their guaranteed position, as did warriors, commoners, craftsmen, priests, or even strangers. Nobody was supposed to move from one social stratum to another, and indeed, no one thought of doing so. If usurpation of high office took place, an unusual occurrence, the usurper was quietly incorporated into the genealogy of the ruling house or line. Such social order rested on the belief shared by all participants that no element of the hierarchy could exist without the other. The situation, which outsiders could view as unequal, exploitative, or ridden with class antagonisms, appeared natural to the participants.

It appears that only with the emergence of the modern nation-state in western Europe and North America, simultaneous with the Industrial Revolution, the time came that archaic political orders would have to succumb to the all-embracing power of the state. As modern warfare requires destruction of the enemy (unlike von Clausewitz's dictum that war is continuation of politics by violent means), the nation-state model is expected to destroy all previous ideas and practices of people's coexistence. In the anthropologist Ronald Cohen's words: "... the state is the most powerful, continuously authoritative, and most inclusive organisation in the history of the species" (Cohen 1978:31).

I trust that I am not exaggerating if I state that a usual assumption is that politics is about power. Millions of people have been habituated to the belief that few have power and most do not. "You don't get power; you grab it," a multimillionaire oil magnate advises his son in the popular American television series "Dallas." Politicians, citizens, journalists, and social scientists agree on this point. They also seem to agree that the state, whether democratic or not, is a major legitimate wielder of power in society. Individuals or groups who gained prestige through nonpolitical means relate it sooner or later to state power. Most people believe that no one can escape the power of the state. A semantic overlap in concepts such as "politics," "power," and the "state" is taken for granted.

It is thus unusual in the extreme not to view the struggle for power as the main ingredient of politics or to question the supremacy of the state. Namely, political anthropologists have put forward such "eccentric" views and proposed a new look at the main political concepts.

The present collection of essays by eight anthropologists with different political and cultural backgrounds represents in my opinion a major step toward a radically new perspective in understanding of politics. The authors show how various people they have studied have been able to cope ingeniously with the power monopoly of the state. Unlike the very ethnological presentation of "primitive" South American Indians' struggle against the introduction of the hierarchical etatist logic as depicted by Clastres in his pioneering book *La société contre l'état* (1974), almost all the cases discussed in this volume are drawn from contemporary changing societies in which state power had already been imposed on people unfamiliar with it previously. The contributors to this volume argue that while these people are obviously "powerless" vis-à-vis the state power, unable to confront it directly, they nonetheless manage to *outwit* the state by applying strikingly different models of "power." These models challenge the concept of power as domination or command, i.e., power as we conventionally think of it. Theirs is not power of violence, threat of physical force, confinement of opponents into psychiatric wards, nor power of imprisonment, detention, or other forms of oppression, which are usually backed by laws of a particular state. The "powerless" have a more efficient "power" of knowledge, empathy, consensus, compromise, and experience, in other words the "power" of comprehensive participation.

The volume brings an abundance of evidence that social bonds in the archaic (i.e., nonmodern) polities[2]—whether expressively centralized or not—were comforting rather than oppressive (cf. Krader 1976, 1979), whereas in states these bonds were as a rule felt as oppressive. Such was the situation when both "stateless"[3] and "statelike" societies were subjugated by technologically advanced colonial conquerors equipped with modern bureaucratic, armed state apparatus. Without idealizing the states' opponents, the authors of essays in this book offer engaging case analyses of outwitting the state as original strategies of constructive coping with the imposition of state power.

If we accept for a moment the division into "stateless" and "statelike" ideal political types, the eight case studies in the present volume can perhaps be divided into roughly two equally large groups. The "stateless" group would comprise the Kreisha Bedouin (Jordan), Cree Indians and Russian Old Believers (both Canada). Indigenous chiefdoms or statelike polities of Pahang and Kelantan (Malaya), Ponape (Micronesia), and Maradi (Niger), as well as coastal sultanates and inland chiefdom's on Borneo, form the other group. The Nanumba and Konkomba of Nanun (Ghana) could be added to both groups, as the former is a centralized indigenous polity while the latter could be classified by some anthropologists as "acephalous tribesmen." The common denominator for both groups is the fact that they are analyzed in the situation of confrontation with an outside power, which in all but one case (that of Borneo) is the modern colonial or postcolonial state. These confrontations are resolved, temporarily or permanently, by outwitting the nominally stronger state through numerically and technologically weaker indigenous polity or "stateless" groups. Outwitting tactics differ from case to case.

The data examined in the various chapters, however, suggest that commonly accepted anthropological classification of indigenous archaic polities into two main types, viz. "stateless" and "state," is of little or no relevance to the basic mechanism of outwitting. Representatives of both types are incomparably weaker than real states, yet both succeed in outwitting powerful states that either conquered them or tried to do so.

Before defining or building a model of outwitting the state, I would like to introduce the reader briefly to every essay.

The Essays in a Nutshell

Let us begin with the longest essay in the book. The case of the Cree Indians in Canada well illustrates the points made above. The Cree political culture as presented by Colin Scott was egalitarian, based on consensus, which considered the use of violence as antinormative and the practice of magico-ritual services as more essential than the acquisition of material products. When faced with the violent and exploitative regime of the "Whiteman" as represented by the fur-trading Hudson Bay Company and the Canadian state, the Cree devised an outwitting practice of "luring" gifts from the traders. This showed that the Cree readily grasped their own indispensability vis-à-vis the traders. The Indians managed to impose the ideology of reciprocity on the white traders and limited thereby the rate of their own exploitation by these traders. They also used the "women force" for getting more military assistance from the whites. The Cree entered into exchange with the whites, but at the same time managed to insulate the domestic, political, and economic scene from exploitative practices. The cooperation of the Cree was commensurate with the support given to their own "traditional" leaders by the white people.

The Ponapeans, inhabitants of a small island in Micronesia, unlike the Cree were organized into a number of chiefdoms. Glenn Petersen demonstrates that their political culture was not based on centralized power monopolies like those of their successive colonial masters (Germans, Japanese, Americans), but on authority stemming from the community. Their concept of politics based on chief's honor as the embodiment of people's imagination was thus very different from Machiavellian quest for unshared power of "the prince" imposing his will on the community. Petersen persuasively shows that the Ponapeans, facing an Americanized model of self-government in the form of the Federated States of Micronesia, devised sophisticated outwitting tactics, which resulted in the retraditionalizing of their society and eventual emancipation from the imposed statehood model.

The Kreisha Bedouin of the western Arabian Peninsula lost their autonomy to the Jordanian state. From an independent elite they became an encapsulated minority. Joseph M. Hiatt traces the change of the Kreisha from a group that looked with suspicion and contempt at all features of sedentary life, including the state, to supporters of the state. Nevertheless, their acceptance of the Jordanian army and service in it was balanced by innovations that the army brought to them and especially by the guarantee of Kreisha survival as a cultural unit with its own honor and identity. In this case the initial disadvantage of incorporation was offset by the advantage of playing a crucial role in a state agency such as the army. The Kreisha have thus outwitted the Jordanian state by becoming an indispensable pillar on which the Jordanian state depends for its very existence.

The relationship between coastal sultanates and inland groups of shifting cultivators on Borneo is the only case presented in which confrontation with the European state does not enter into the picture. Jérôme Rousseau mentions the Dutch and British entry onto the scene only as a sequel to the relationship that he examines. This relationship evidently hinged on a stalemated balance of power: the coastal sultanates were unable to assert their rule in the interior of the island because they lacked the real state's power; the inland chiefs knew it, and if they felt disturbed by encroachments from the coast, they nonetheless refrained from trading with it. That in turn was undesirable from the point of view of sultans and traders, who were greatly interested in jungle produce. Therefore conciliatory gestures followed, balance was restored, and trade continued.

Malay *negri* polities, such as Pahang and Kelantan, which are subjects of William D. Wilder's analysis, exemplify structural features similar to those of coastal Borneo. They were not states in terms of action policy or monopoly of power or in terms of rule that would effectively involve most aspects of life. The ruler was the center of "contemplative" politics. Ritual was a dominant characteristic of these statelike polities. It can be argued that their apparent weakness made Pahang and Kelantan capable of "surviving" to this very day. It is obvious that these sultanates never were sovereign states nor ever intended to be. The question is what measure of group identity within Malaysia is derived from the Malaysian state and how much from these "traditional" polities. Historically, the same ratio can be examined between Siam and the sultanates and the British and the sultanates. Outwitting techniques helped Pahang and Kelantan to emerge from this test as successful polities. What is fascinating in their political culture is that authority stems from below, i.e., from peasants to the sultan, whereas culture from the top to the common people. That *negri* are not states in the modern conventional meaning of the term does not detract from the originality with which they are tackling the supreme question: how to create viable large (supravillage) conglomerations of people who are subjected to environmental and social circumscription, without excessive resort to oppression and violence? The answer in Pahang and Kelantan was the combination of authority and culture in a way that neither was allowed to predominate. These two ingredients are not normally distinguishable from each other.

The Russian Old Believers, *raskol'niki* or schismatics, are shown in a historical fashion. David Z. Scheffel examines the conflict between the state rulers, who decided on substantial religious reform in the seventeenth century, and those later known as Old Believers, who could not accept the change because their whole spiritual world would fall apart. The state viewed as criminals and madmen all those who did not accept the reform. On the other side, truly orthodox people saw antichrists in the representatives of the state. Characteristically, most of them exempted the sovereign, czar, from this accusation and believed that he was kept uninformed about what happened. On several occasions Old Believers hoped that uprisings and upheavals would prompt the czar to cancel the reforms. Frustrated, they retreated to distant areas of the Russian empire and eventually abroad. Their tactics consisted in the avoidance of any direct contact with the state for three centuries. This ensured the preservation of their socio-religious identity. In this century, after an interlude in China, a number of Old Believers arrived in Canada in the hope that they would be able to live there undisturbed by state intervention. When they realized it was impossible to escape the state's power even in an allegedly tolerant multiculturalist country like Canada, they devised outwitting strategies to preserve maximum freedom by participating in activities that they considered futile, but which brought them means to develop their community as independently from the state as possible. If their communal religious autonomy and identity were jeopardized directly, they were prepared to "go somewhere else."

The Hausa agriculturalists around Maradi in southern Niger were studied at the moment when cooperatives and other participatory development designs were imposed on them by the state. Lucien R. Bäck shows their very artful capacity for using "traditional" resources to interpret the innovations, so that they achieve opposite to those intended. The intentions of participatory development were: 1) to legitimate the Niger government in the eyes of the Hausa so that together with other ethnic groups of Niger a nation could be formed; 2) to build democratic cooperation institutions in a largely "traditional" social setting; and 3) to increase agricultural production of subsistence crops. The government passed legislation directing rural population into participation in the "cooperative movement." This decision from above was so imperative that all farming people were compelled to join the "movement." Subsequently, however, they managed to realize their "traditional" goals by outwitting the state policies. The *sarakai* (chiefs) and *alhazai* (powerful Muslims who emphasized their social position by pilgrimage to Mecca) "embraced" innovations like cooperatives and started to manage them on behalf of the people. The latter in turn saw in this elite more likely symbols of prosperity rather than in broad masses who were originally designed to run the cooperatives "democratically." As a result, the Hausa agriculturalists "retraditionalized" themselves under the leadership of neo-traditional dignitaries. The state-inspired development process was captured by the reactivated forces of the Hausa "traditional" society.

My research in Nanun established that the social forces that trace their origin in the precolonial past regroup under the imposed Gold Coast/ Ghana state domination and in their old-new guise continue to shape the destinies of people. The essay tries to explain why and how seemingly opposed political cultures, *naam* of the Nanumba and "regulated anarchy" of the Konkomba, skillfully use the relative power vacuum created by the economic and organizational weakness of the Ghanaian state for creating a political arena in which they are masters. This inevitably led to their armed conflict, because the colonial and postcolonial regimes did not recognize the validity of "traditional" rules that allowed settlement of members of one ethnic group in the territory of the other. Through misunderstandings combined with neglect by the state, many problems in Nanun were left unsolved and "overpowered" by the state policies promoting capitalism, development, and the etatist political and administrative practices. When these innovations were no longer backed by the state, the old and new grievances came rapidly to the surface. The people of Nanun, both Nanumba and Konkomba, realized that they could only rely on themselves and their political institutions. In the process a significant rapprochement between the two political cultures took place.

Outwitting Conceptualized

The phrase *outwitting the state* has so far escaped definition or further elaboration. I have only characterized the eight contributions and mentioned that in each of them the "powerless" people responded by outwitting to the imposition of state power. This section of the introduction argues that outwitting is a specific political strategy that occurs in specific, though widespread, social settings. It is not only present in each case of this volume. Outwitting the state not only represents a common denominator of these cases, but appears as one of the most common features of relations between societies and various groups within societies.

First we need a working descriptive characterization of the concept.

Outwitting the state means that the conventional hierarchical and re-pressive concept of power formulated by Max Weber as "the possibility of imposing one's will upon the behaviour of other persons" (Weber 1954:323; cf. Bendix 1960:290) is *transcended* by a different kind of power "providing identity for the community," as Pasquinelli (1986:79) and others recently tried to demonstrate.[4] The reader probably noticed by now that the con-cept of power as used here appears ambivalent unless a clear redefinition is undertaken. It is my contention that adding adjectives and specifications to the word *power* does not solve the conceptual problem.[5] Our discussion is therefore based on an important conceptual distinction between *power* and *authority*. Unfortunately, many authors use the two terms interchangeably, indicating that in their opinion it is more or less the same concept (cf. Clastres 1974). Weber's usage of the two concepts is in fact also syn-onymous because he conceives of *Herrschaft* (domination) as resulting from the process whereby power is legitimated into authority (Weber 1968 1:53,212–16; cf. Aronoff 1986). I wish to eliminate these ambivalences.

Power, in my conceptualization, should be understood primarily as state power. This means capacity for carrying out decisions and activities osten-sibly on behalf of a whole society by specific state agencies that have mo-nopoly of use or threat of use of organized violence. The brilliant sentence ascribed to Napoleon that one can do anything with bayonets except sit on them suggests that there is no other power than that which gets legitimized. Unless that happens, power ceases to be power. In that sense the distinction between power and authority is superfluous. Lenin understood domination as a direct result of power and therefore was able to define the state as a "machine for maintaining domination of one class by the other" (Lenin n.d., vol. 39:73).

There is, however, also another political order in which people's coexis-tence does not require state power and domination of some over others. Such an arrangement I call *authority*. Authority, in unambiguous contrast to power, is legitimate without the backing of power and is voluntarily recognized by all. It is so because authority is diffuse, truly residing in and exercised by the people (cf. Pasquinelli 1986 and Havel 1985). (Only in some exceptional cases discussed later can authority be wielded by a state organization without being backed by power.) If this substantial distinction between power and authority—in spite of its obvious schematism—is ac-cepted and its far-reaching consequences for social and political theory are realized, we will be able to understand why the "states" in ancient Europe, Asia, precolonial Africa, America, or Oceania, as well as the "chiefdoms" in recent and present time, were not really states and could afford to be so (cf. Skalník 1983, 1987). The ways in which such polities outwitted the real states demonstrate that very graphically.

Outwitting Tactics

The cases discussed in the volume display a variety of tactics of outwitting the state. *Collaboration presented as reciprocity* is one of these forms. Scott's interpretation of the Cree Indians' response to the white man's state of Canada suggests that the ideology of reciprocity, widely recognized as a major logic according to which relationships in archaic societies were structured, became a powerful means of legitimation of inequality between the Cree and the state. I would argue, however, that the Cree through consenting to collaboration presented to them in the form of reciprocal, simultaneously advantageous trade achieved considerable success. They thereby preserved their Cree identity. By locking themselves into collaboration, they created a situation in which they emphasized their indispensability to the white man's state by "luring" gifts and demanding better treatment.[6]

The Kreisha Bedouin of Jordan gained enormous influence in the Jordanian state by their acceptance of incorporation into the king's army. Their collaboration was certainly reciprocal. It can be even argued that they gained more than the state. Their cultural identity was preserved, *and* they gained economically as well. On the other hand, the Hausa agriculturalists in Niger had to collaborate with the state out of fear of harsh measures inflicted by the state.

The Hausa case was *collaboration through dependence*. Their "traditional" elites lost a long time ago against the centralizing power of the modern independent state. But now with the state imposition of development process, the people, feeling upset by the measures, chose to support the chiefs and *malams* who in turn changed the "cooperative movement" to their own advantage. That apparently seemed more acceptable to the agriculturalists than the prospect of entirely grass-roots movement. The outwitting took a form of retraditionalization. (See below.)

Malay *negri* Kelantan and Pahang were never independent in the Western sovereign sense. That did not prevent them from enjoying unity of people and their "rulers." Collaboration with the faraway stronger polities did not make much difference in the life of ordinary people. When they were nominally part of Siam the difference was not substantial, because Siam was another archaic polity. The British and Malaysian states could not prevent Kelantan and Pahang from doing internally what they wanted either, because the activities were not in the realm of active exercise of state power. When the party politics was imposed, the people either voted for a party that was pro-*negri* or responded with factionalism that effectively prevented the state from carrying out its policies in the area. The result was outwitting of these states by the continuity of *negri* political culture in both polities.

Rousseau mentions the use of conversion to Islam as a device tried by some central Borneo "aristocrats" to gain a powerful position in their areas. By conversion they hoped to ingratiate themselves to the coastal sultans and thus secure their support. However, the "power" of sultans was quite limited and they only sometimes could help their would-be allies.[7] Rousseau's contribution centers around another tactic of outwitting the state, which I call *balance of power*. The Borneo sultans in their turn tried to gain influence in the interior by exploiting disunity in inland areas, e.g., paying gambling debts for the upriver leaders. The less formalized social and political structures of the interior groups did not, however, allow the coastal states to exert lasting influence in central Borneo. The result was a balance of power. Rousseau calls it "stalemate." The encroaching of the coastal Malay preindustrial polities into the interior of Borneo with the intention of implanting their centralized political culture there did not succeed. Instead the people of the interior (often known as Dayak) managed to keep their independence without being lured into the trap of centralization. This can be explained by the warlike history of these groups, who practiced headhunting and slavery and in most cases prevented unification beyond village level. Trade, the main vehicle of communication between the inland areas and the coast, does not flourish *inter arma*. The need to trade coupled with structural weakness of coastal centralization, i.e., their being ideological polities, in addition to the mutual hostility among them, gave the inland groups outwitting "weapons" that they used against the sultanates. Sometimes the instability on the coast was more significant than the differences between the coast and the interior taken as wholes. Besides, every sultanate claimed much larger territory than it really was able to control. The apparent reason for this was the desire to control trade and to impose taxes on it. These claims were more rhetorical acts than reality. As long as the inland territories were not responsive to centralization or not prepared to pay allegiance to a sultan, they continued to reject it. Once a real state came in, in this case the Dutch colonial state and later the Indonesian state, these inland groups became involved effectively as state subjects, later citizens. Only remote areas could temporarily keep free from its power during the periods of weakness, such as the Japanese occupation during World War II, or periods of economic and political instability, which characterized the first two decades in the history of independent Indonesia. In those cases avoidance was the prime outwitting technique.

Contemporary developments in Malaysia's sultanates can also be interpreted as "balance of power" tactics of outwitting the state. Wilder shows that the *negri* (centralized "traditional" polity) has been in "balanced opposition" to the modern party politics. The peasants, a majority of the population, supported "their" *negri* not by openly traditionalist stance (which would have been crushed), but by joining the ostensibly modern democratic political life. By voting for a party that was opposed to the centralizing and homogenizing tendencies of the Kuala Lumpur regime, the peasants spelled out their dislike of making *negri* an organic part of a political bureaucracy. They realized that this measure would give (real) power to few and take any remaining authority and identity away from the villagers.

Another outwitting tactic is *avoidance*. The Russian Old Believers, as depicted by Scheffel in his partly historical and partly empirical study (he did his Ph.D. research in an Old Believer village in northern Alberta), were prepared to travel around the globe in search of places where they would be free or relatively free from state oppression. First, they decided to avoid supporters of the new state religion and vowed not to share anything with them (food, prayers, intermarriage, etc). Some even renounced priesthood, as in their eyes it became contaminated by the heresy of the church. They continued to live in historical Russia, and the state "tamed" them gradually. Those who followed the rebellious priests went to the periphery of the state, where they could both avoid the power of the state and enjoy the unlimited freedom of nature (*vol'nost'*). They maintained themselves as agriculturists and, undisturbed, became practically nonpolitical. When that freedom was jeopardized by the iron grip of Bolshevik state power in the 1920s, the Old Believers retreated first to China and then via Brazil to the U.S.A. and Canada. In Canada, as Scheffel shows, they can no longer practice avoidance in its full sense and have to combine it with some forms of collaboration. In their eyes, both are equal to outwitting the Canadian state.[8]

Petersen's case study of Ponape in Micronesia gives a clear example of another outwitting technique, which is *retraditionalization*. Ponapeans, "traditionally" organized into chiefdoms, were taught by their American protectors that they should embrace American principles of statehood and democracy. While Ponapeans (and other Micronesians) have embraced material advantages of being closely attached and almost united with the U.S.A., they gradually realized that their concept of politics did not coincide with the American one. No blend of indigenous political culture with the imposed state logic occurred. As Petersen shows, a tension emerged between the two. Today's Ponapeans believe that the only solution is through the reassertion of Ponapean political culture. And that also means that they are no longer prepared to cooperate in the larger conglomerates with other parts of Micronesia, each of which has its own concepts of authority and its own customs. Retraditionalization is the outwitting technique of the Ponapeans.

The Hausa of Niger also used this technique against a development model imposed by the state. Chiefs and Muslim dignitaries were trusted more than the state officials. The development movement was seen as an opportunity to reintroduce old hierarchical relations that were already weakened by colonialism.

Also, the Nanumba-Konkomba conflict in northern Ghana could be seen as outwitting through retraditionalization. The crisis that emerged from the conflict has emphasized the role of "traditional" leaders. The youth organizations could not really solve a problem that was viewed by most as a matter of "traditional" nature. The "chiefless" Konkomba finally realized that their needs can best be served by introducing the institution of chieftaincy among themselves. The Ghanaian state finally realized that it cannot stand against chieftaincy, because if it does, chieftaincy, enjoying the support of rural illiterate masses, would always be able to outwit it.

The various tactics of outwitting the state are not ideal types. They tend to change from one to another according to the context. The rule, however, is that a tactic is used that at the moment is considered most efficient. The discussion that follows puts the data from the eight case studies into broader contexts. Outwitting, as already suggested, is a widespread, in fact worldwide, phenomenon.

Outwitting in Broader Contexts

Anthropologists and historians have implicitly shown in many detailed studies published during last fifty years that archaic polities were not based on a monopoly of power and concentration of violent means in the hands of a few. The conceptual models of "chiefdom" (cf. Service 1962; Carneiro 1981) and "early state" (Claessen and Skalník 1978, 1981) in many respects summarize these findings. The main shortcoming of these concepts is not so much that they are ideal types, but that they are designed to support evolutionist typological theories. This suggests that there is a logical and historical connection between these types of archaic polities and the nation-state as we know it from Western political history. The present volume contradicts evolutionist theories and refutes the idea that "chiefdom" was a precursor of the state. It equally rejects the transformation of "early" states into "mature" states. It thus supports implicit findings of the Montreal symposium "The Early State and After" of 1983 (Claessen and van de Velde 1987). Our volume makes evident that *naam*, *negri*, or other archaic polities work according to a strikingly different logic than that of the states. Whereas centralization in them is incomplete and qualitatively less efficient than in the states and their dignitaries serve as both takers and givers, the level of central command in the states of European origin contrasts with the balance occurring in archaic polities. The latter do not contain the structural prerequisites that would usher them into states. They in fact developed mechanisms that prevent or do not allow the development of state agencies. And if they are subdued by and incorporated into states—as in the case of colonial conquest—these mechanisms strike back and outwit the state political culture.

This process is best observable in situations where an archaic polity was encapsulated by an imposed state. Such are the cases examined in this book. The state power and the alien political culture that arrives with it are so different and so powerful that outwitting is virtually the only possible response. Direct resistance soon proves to be unaffordable; passive accommodation is impossible as well. The most acceptable is some kind of collaboration that allows things to continue almost as before, with the idea that "we were here before them and we will be here after them." That sometimes works and allows the subdued population to select slowly elements from the foreign "civilizational packet," which they gradually incorporate into their indigenous political and social culture. But in many cases whole societies failed to devise ways of coping with the foreign supremacy and as a result were decimated (e.g., by the Khoikhoin, Guanche, North American Indians, Caribs, Tasmanians, some Siberian peoples).

To illustrate this point, the example of the Kingdom of Lesotho in southern Africa is, in my opinion, very interesting. In the first third of the nineteenth century, mostly Sotho-speaking refugees from the *mfecane/difaqane* wars united under the able leadership of Moshoeshoe in the unoccupied area of high mountains and foothills. The unification took the form of a relatively centralized archaic polity, with Moshoeshoe delegating male members of his Koena (crocodile) clan into various parts of the polity as *morena* (chiefs). When he was increasingly threatened from all sides, especially by the Boers, Moshoeshoe asked Queen Victoria to "accept him as a flea into her mantle," i.e., he wanted protection. This plea was heard in 1868, but the British first tried a direct rule from the Cape. When successful armed resistance of the Basotho proved to the Cape administrators that direct rule was futile and expensive, the British government took over and introduced indirect rule in the territory. The combination of inaccessibility and other priorities played into the hands of Moshoeshoe's successors. During several decades the Basotho polity, underestimated by the British, who viewed it as mere paramount chieftainship, consolidated itself and Koena chiefs were posted to almost every corner of the protectorate. In this way, under British state protection, the Basotho outwitted this very state. Migrant labor in South African mines and trading relations with the surrounding provinces of South Africa have acquainted the Basotho with the gamut of the South African power model and Western capitalist economy. Basotho leaders also outwitted the planned incorporation of their country into South Africa by skillful maneuvers that persuaded the British that they should grant it independence. When Lesotho became independent in 1966 and the paramount chief became king, the country was to a degree prepared for acceptance of power-based statehood. That, however, does not mean that Western style democracy could be effectively introduced. The maxim "a chief is a chief by the people" is still respected (Hamnett 1975:15). Assassination as a culturally acceptable way of gaining political influence was not eliminated. Nonetheless, the Lesotho case shows that a gradual merger of two contrasting political cultures into one is possible and that this transition may happen without excessive trauma caused by forceful imposition of a foreign political culture. The outwitting tactics of selective incorporation of etatist political culture have today been complemented by Lesotho's successful policy of wooing development aid from various technologically developed countries without allowing imposition of the political culture of the donor states.

Similar problems of the gradual and selective introduction of Western state political culture are faced by, for example, Swaziland, Morocco, Thailand, Nepal, Bhutan, Oman, Saudi Arabia, Tonga, Fiji, and other formally independent states in Oceania. These countries managed to prevent the forceful imposition of foreign political culture by various outwitting techniques and preserved to a considerable degree integrity of their original indigenous political cultures.

The experience of states like Ethiopia or Afghanistan where revolutions overthrew age-old political cultures shows that abrupt innovations may be doomed to failure. Iran with its recent fundamentalist revolution can serve as an example of extremist traditionalist reaction to the Shah's forceful style of imposition of foreign civilization models. The triumph of Muslim fundamentalism in Iran can be seen as another case of outwitting the state. The nonviolent methods that eventually persuaded the Shah to leave the country were, however, supplanted by forceful introduction of purist Islamic norms of political culture and sociocultural behavior. The internal political intolerance was exported to the outside world. The war between Iran and Iraq was only the tip of an iceberg of this intolerance with and hostility to the Western political culture. The problem is that waging such a war and introducing so forcefully the fundamentalist norms within the Iranian society requires use of a Western-style state power model and political culture. The means do not bless the aim, and it appears impossible to retraditionalize Iran by using antithetical methods of political domination.

Outwitting strategies could also be discerned in China, where several waves of imposition of European, Soviet, or generally foreign models have caused vigorous societal reactions of vast consequences. This process is, however, very complicated, because the original Chinese political culture does not exist anymore. There are only fragments of it scattered among eclectic political practices. China was subjected to several revolutions in this century. To some outside observers, the last so-called Cultural Revolution might have appeared to establish some kind of authentic Chinese values but without reference to the past, for example, the empire and its religious underpinnings. The reactions to it are current attempts at modernization of China, which may prove to be another case of uncritical imposition of foreign models. In the background of all this, the suppressed residua of Chinese political culture rebel and if not constructively taken into account may erupt one day in an open retraditionalization attempt. There are numerous examples of extreme or less extreme responses to the imposed external state power or whole foreign civilizational order. The common denominator is the outwitting of the imposed state and return to at least some values and practices of the old, "traditional" order.

In contrast, there are few countries in which the transition from "traditional" political order and culture to the state power model was achieved endogenously, as was the case of several European countries and of Japan. Most, however, needed revolutions to introduce the modern state and a concomitant political culture. It is a widespread fallacy that societies that have gone through revolutionary upheavals are successful. What is often forgotten is that these countries needed revolution because the political forces of the ancien régime acted in ways that did not promote innovations. These forces brought forth the least wished extreme: the revolutionary eruption that not only eliminated the old elite, but introduced another extreme in the form of ruthless dictatorships. France can be cited as an example. The French Revolution of 1789 and the few years that followed resulted in Robespierre's Terror and the imposition of extremist innovations such as the belief in Supreme Being, a substitution of Christian religion (Masaryk 1934). These extremes were crowned by Napoleon's megalomaniac attempt at violent imposition of the French revolutionary vision of the state and political culture on the whole world. Restoration of the monarchic political culture followed, and it cost several uprisings, coups, revolutions, and restorations, coupled with military defeat by Prussia in 1870, before a new French bourgeois democratic political culture could establish itself and allow for the rapid growth of economy and culture.

I believe it is perfectly consistent to argue that historically the most successful have been the societies that did not need revolutions and that did not radically destroy the political cultures and values of the "traditional" past, but managed to incorporate them into the new order. One could parabolically say that such societies effected the genuine, lasting revolutions. Japan and England come to mind in this connection. Both experienced minor political upheavals, and their revolutions were not aimed at the destruction of the existing political culture. Their major revolutions were in the field of industry and trade. The Netherlands, another example, has not experienced revolution in the conventional sense since the ousting of the Spanish supremacy in the sixteenth century. A political revolution was not necessary during the existence of the independent Netherlands, i.e., for more than four hundred years. Still the Netherlands is one of the most prosperous countries and the Dutch state administration the most efficient in the world. Switzerland and some of the Scandinavian countries do not have a revolutionary history but still rate among the best organized and wealthiest. The answer is the "evolutionary revolution," which continously introduces innovations in the political culture and broad social order and where leaders are responsive to the changing expectations of the people. Societies that did not experience abrupt, chaotic, and violent revolutions followed by periods of instability and suffering have developed a high degree of identification of the population—notwithstanding its class structure—with the state. In Japan, Great Britain (Northern Ireland excluded), the Netherlands, Switzerland, and Scandinavian countries people of all estates consider the state "theirs" and identify with the symbols of statehood. The Japanese even celebrate the "birthday of Japan as a state." Outwitting the state in such societies is not needed unless one realizes that evolutionary change of society and "its" state was outwitting the state as a malign excrescence of society, the state that tends to oppose society and become an instrument of oppression for the benefit of the few. Outwitted thus was the potential of the state to become the enemy of the people, machinery alienated from the people, in opposition to the nation (cf. Malinowski 1944). The state ceased to be the state de facto in these societies. This identity between people and the state has helped them to endure tremendous stresses, such as Britain's lonely war against Hitler's Germany or Japan's desperate fight in World War II. The Japanese also endured the postwar stress of political restructuring. Their defeat was interpreted by them as a strong indication that they should modify an otherwise unshattered basic identity between the state and the people.

Simone Weil suggested that modern states, i.e., states wielding a power monopoly, have inherent totalitarian tendencies (cf. Weil 1978:158). I would agree with her with the proviso that a few states have increasingly merged with the people's own authority and capacity to regulate their coexistence. Otherwise, there is a lot of truth in the Marxist idea that the state is an instrument guaranteeing privileges of the few and the oppression of others. However, even in the classical Marxist field of reference, i.e., capitalism, the state is not always primarily this kind of instrument. Whether Marx and his followers call for smashing of the state or argue for its inevitable withering away or its reabsorption within future restored egalitarian conditions (cf. Sayer and Corrigan 1987:75), this eschatological doctrine matters little to ordinary people who seek a decent life and some happiness here and now. Ordinary people actually witness that ostensible attempts at creating egalitarian societies end up in an uncontrolled expansion of the state in the countries governed by communist parties. The state, if unchecked by the ordinary people, tends indeed to totalitarianism and represents a lethal mutation.

Conclusion

The archaic polities, both decentralized and centralized, when conquered by the European states appeared helpless vis-à-vis the state power that subdued them. Most people living in modern societies equally experience powerlessness in facing the state that rules over them. They can only exceptionally identify with it and thus defuse state power. Their only way to preserve identity and integrity is by trying to outwit the state.

The archaic polities based on nonviolent "power," i.e., on the authority of wisdom of words and cultural concepts, have devised various ways of outwitting the state. The cases of outwitting the state as they are discussed in the contributions to the present volume show that people's authority is not only the antithesis of state power, but it is also more durable than any power in an instrumental, pragmatic sense. The cases examined in the book give evidence of the indestructibility of this authority and the transience of state power. The fact that such polities, founded on an expressive political culture based on authority and not on power, have been more balanced and stable than violence-oriented nation-states of the modern era amounts to a major discovery of political anthropology. From the Western maximization point of view, these polities were unsuccessful. But I would argue that it is possible and desirable to reverse the whole scene and realize that, seeing they were based on the illiterate, unurbanized masses, where "culture came from the top while power welled up from the bottom" (Geertz 1980: 85), they were extremely successful. The archaic polities were characterized by longevity, stability, and the capacity to turn a nominal defeat into victory over the imposed statehood. W. M. Macmillan's fifty-year-old words that "history demonstrated the ability of weaker cultures to adapt themselves to and triumph over their supposedly stronger conquerors" (Macmillan 1938:375) find eloquent confirmation in this book.

These societies and their political cultures were in fact not weaker; they were stronger than their opponents. Outwitting the state proved a more efficient way of facing power than violent resistance. The latter would only equal acceptance of the oppressors' "language" without any chance of winning. As outwitting is not identical with resistance, it cannot be subsumed under the heading of adaptation either. Outwitting the state is a strategy that uses the advantage of nonetatist political culture to actively offset the power of the state.

There is so far no satisfactory and generally accepted theory of transition from archaic to modern political culture. The existing theories are unsatisfactory because they operate from an uncritical etatist point of view. Eurocentrism is all-pervasive in evolutionist theories of state formation, culture growth, class struggle, etc. Nonetheless, anthropology is the only social science discipline that transcends the limitations of experience from only one kind of society—those dominated by the modern Western state. The present volume attempts to document and theoretically interpret the processes that lead to the rejection of the state power orders through outwitting. Its significance for the present and future consists, in my opinion, in that it explains the eventual failure of imposition of imported state power. That in turn opens the way to a viable theory and practice of alternative, "powerless," and truly "stateless" politics in an undivided society.

It is of the utmost importance to draw a comparison between the cases of outwitting strategies of Third World people and the movements of intellectuals and oppressed groups in the economically advanced countries of the First World and the Second World seems to me to be of utmost importance. These groups try to make sense of their lives in conditions of spiritual oppression imposed by state bureaucracies, oppression by alienating automatism of technological civilization, and oppression by totalitarian straitjackets of party dictatorships. The comparison helps us to realize that outwitting the state is a worldwide process whereby the powerless and the oppressed reach for their emancipation without being destroyed through direct confrontation with the state power. As a response to continuous repression or subjugation by foreign states, nations have developed their own outwitting strategies, which not only ensured their survival but even led to their prosperity and liberation. Gandhi's nonviolent philosophy and practice of civil disobedience (*sathyagraha*) could be cited as a famous case of outwitting that has succeeded.

I hope that the reader can learn from this book that anthropology is something other than a child or handmaiden of imperialism, helping to perfect exploitation, oppression, and domination. The anthropology of this volume is a humanistic discipline discovering ways that do not necessarily lead to concentration of power in the hands of few. The anthropologists who contributed chapters to this book are de facto concerned with the position of the underdog. The implication is that they debunk totalitarian tendencies in political centralization; they refute Michels's "iron law of oligarchy" (Michels 1962); they point out the people's genius in designing resourceful strategies for achieving political aims of the majority of people despite overwhelming power of the state.

Notes

1. My professor of African anthropology at the Leningrad State University, the late Dmitri A. Ol'derogge, liked to cite the example of England, which was conquered by the Normans under William of Normandy (later known as the Conqueror or William I) in 1066. "Are there any Normans and Saxons walking in the streets of London today? Of course not!" He wanted to stress that an effective merger of the conquerors with the conquered happened. Even the aristocracy of today's England cannot prove its Norman purity. The English people identify with British royalty and nobility. Commoners who are deemed to have contributed to the fame of the country—public figures like politicians, civil servants, businessmen, scholars, and artists—receive noble titles (Dame, Sir) from the sovereign.

2. I use the term *polity* as a general concept denoting any state, "statelike," or "stateless" unit. In a narrower sense I use *polity* where it is not appropriate to use *state*, that is, in cases that otherwise have to be adjectivized with *primitive, tribal, early, archaic, traditional, precolonial*, etc. (cf. Skalník, 1983, 1987).

3. *Stateless*, along with other adjectives like *acephalous*, should be used with utmost caution because of its negative implication.

4. The example of the dissidents in eastern Europe and the Soviet Union who have completely rejected violence as an instrument for emancipation of the oppressed majorities in their countries deserves a special mention. These groups renounced violence not only because it is impossible to win against the state machinery, which is heavily armed and supported by a vast omnipresent secret police, but mainly because they concluded that violent means can never be justified in attaining moral aims. Violence gives birth to violence ad infinitum. The "powerless" of the "second world" are learning that they have power to say no to the post-totalitarian states (Havel et al. 1985). The project of the "parallel polis" first proposed by the Czech intellectual Benda (1979), which has inspired the actions of eastern European dissidents, attempts to create alternative citizens' initiatives that have nothing to do with state reglementation. This has been successful in creating independent though underground publishing, independent universities and other forms of education, an unofficial economy of mutual help, independent trade unions, unofficial art, and alternative community life. In Poland, for example, the whole society today to a large extent effectively behaves as if there were no communist state. Eventually these attitudes may make the state truly obsolete. I do not need to stress that the parallel polis has nothing to do with what is commonly understood as anarchy. It could be, and is, accused of anarchy by the very state that it parallels and transcends.

5. I have shown elsewhere (Skalník 1983, 1987) that the concept of the "state" is

made sterile by adding adjectives like *early, segmentary, traditional*, or *primitive* to it.

6. This reminds one of similar outwitting strategies used in worldwide relations between the developed North and the underdeveloping South. The Third World, realizing its indispensability as a supplier of minerals, tropical produce, manpower, or simply prestige fodder for healing bad conscience of the former imperialists and colonialists, demands better prices for its produce, more development aid, and more loans. By extending loans to them, the developed countries today are to an extent at the mercy of the debtors. The Peruvian government, for example, simply announced that it will not pay back the loans as demanded by the creditors.

7. Two other illustrations of collaboration through dependence that resulted in outwitting come from the Soviet Union and Canada. Carrère d'Encausse's argument that Soviet Muslims accepted socialism not because of its intrinsic values, but because socialism was conceived by them as a historical by-product of Islam and thus aided the Muslims in pursuance of their own goals (Carrère d'Encausse 1981:240, 248). Controlled acculturation among the Hutterite religious sectarians in North America was achieved by collaboration for the sake of preservation of cultural identity and group survival (Eaton 1952).

8. It is useful for sake of comparison to note that the Russian state when faced with Old Believer dissidence in regard to the religious reform called all those who did not want to obey and show loyalty criminals and madmen. A similar situation can be observed in communist countries where the state used this totalitarian technique. All those who did not publicly show in a prescribed way their loyalty to the new regime were considered enemies. The result in both cases was avoidance in the form of internal and where possible also external exile of millions. Only in Hungary, after the suppression of the 1956 uprising, the Soviet-imposed Kádár regime tactically changed the slogan from "Who does not go with us goes against us" to "Who does not go against us is with us." Kádár stayed in power for thirty-two years and enjoyed a surprising degree of legitimacy in his country.

References

Aronoff, Myron J., ed. 1986. *The frailty of authority*. Political Anthropology, vol. 5. New Brunswick and Oxford: Transaction Books.

Benda, V. 1979. The parallel polis. *Palach Press Bulletin* (London).

Bendix, Richard. 1966. *Max Weber: An intellectual portrait*. London: Methuen & Co.

Carneiro, Robert L. 1981. "The chiefdom: Precursor of the state." Pp. 37–79 in *The transition to statehood in the New World*, ed. G. D. Jones and R. R. Kautz Cambridge: Cambridge University Press.

Carrère d'Encausse, Hélène. 1981. *Decline of an empire: The Soviet socialist republics in revolt*. New York: Harper and Row.

Claessen, Henri J. M., and Peter Skalník, eds. 1978. *The early state*. The Hague: Mouton.

_____. 1981. *The study of the state*. The Hague: Mouton.

Claessen, Henri J. M., and Pieter van de Velde, eds. 1987. *Early state dynamics*. Leiden: Brill.

Clastres, Pierre. 1974. *La société contre l'état*. Paris: Minuit. (English translation, New York: Urizen Books, 1977.)

Cohen, Ronald. 1978. "State Origins: A Reappraisal." In *The early state*, ed. H. J. M. Claessen and P. Skalník, The Hague: Mouton.

Eaton, I. W. 1952. Controlled acculturation: A survival technique of Hutterites. *American Sociological Review* 17:331–40.

Geertz, Clifford. 1980. *Negara:The theatre state in nineteenth century Bali.* Princeton: Princeton University Press.

Hamnett, Ian. 1975. *Chieftainship and legitimacy: An anthropological study of executive law in Lesotho.* London: Routledge and Kegan Paul.

Havel, Václav et al. 1985. *The power of the powerless: Citizens against the state in central-eastern Europe.* London: Hutchinson.

Havel, Václav. 1985. "The Power of the Powerless." Pp. 23-96 in Havel, V. et al.

Krader, Lawrence. 1976. *Dialectic of civil society.* Assen: Van Gorcum.

_____. 1979. *A treatise of social labour.* Assen: Van Gorcum.

Lenin, Vladimir I. n.d. *Sochineniia* (Works). Moscow.

Macmillan, W. M. 1938. *Africa emergent.* London: Faber.

Malinowski, Bronislaw. 1944. *Freedom and civilization.* New York: Roy Publishers.

Masaryk, Tomáš G. 1934 (1893). *Kult rozumu a nejvyšší bytosti.* Praha: Adolf Synek.

Michels, Robert. 1962 (1911). *Political parties: A sociological study of the oligarchical tendencies of modern democracy.* New York: Collier Books.

Pasquinelli, Carla. 1986. Power without the state. *Telos* 68: 79–92.

Sayer, Derek, and Philip Corrigan. 1987. Revolution against the state: The context and significance of Marx's later writings. *Dialectical Anthropology* 12(1): 65–82.

Service, Elman. 1962. *Primitive social organization: An evolutionary perspective.* New York: Random House.

Skalník, P. 1983. Questioning the concept of the state in indigenous Africa. *Social Dynamics* 9(2): 11–28.

_____. 1987. On the inadequacy of the concept of the 'traditional state' (illustrated with ethnographic material on Nanun, Ghana). *Journal of Legal Pluralism* 25 and 26: 301–25.

Weber, Max. 1954. *Max Weber on law in economy and society.* Cambridge: Harvard University Press.

_____. 1968. (1922). *Economy and society: An outline of interpretive sociology.* New York: Bedminster Press.

Weil, Simone. (1978). *Lectures on philosophy.* Translated by Hugh Price. Cambridge: Cambridge University Press.

2

Ponapean Chieftainship in the Era of the Nation-State[1]

Glenn Petersen

The locus of power—indeed, even its existence—in a society of the sort ethnologists call chiefdoms is an ambiguous matter. If one wishes to study the way in which such a society responds to externally imposed state power, however, it is necessary to at least try to establish the character of political organization that must respond to the state. This paper describes the responses of the people of Ponape, in Micronesia's Eastern Caroline Islands, to a century of colonial rule and analyzes them in terms of the indigenous Ponapean concepts of political authority that shape these responses.

An assumption widespread among ethnologists and prehistorians is that the hierarchical character of chieftainship and the authority of the chief are preconditions out of which such concepts as "the state" and "state power" evolve through a relatively simple process of intensification (Haas 1982). It is not clear to me, however, that the authority of chiefs (or at least of some chiefs) resembles the power of the state and can be transformed into it through intensification. As Ponapeans respond to the state imposed upon them by the United States, they modify not only their own lives, but the very character of the imposed government in order to have it function in a fashion that is more Ponapean than American (Petersen 1983).

If one tries to adopt a traditional theoretical approach in studying the Ponapean polity, it is easy to be misled into believing that the presence of paramount chiefs, who have enormous ritual status and *mana* (Ponapean *manaman*), and Nan Madol, a vast complex of monumental basalt structures, demonstrate that centralized political power is indigenous to the island. An archaeologist, Stephen Athens, has recently argued that Nan Madol gives clear evidence of this power: "The labor involved in Nan

23

Madol's construction is indeed staggering. Oral accounts leave no doubts as to the social differentiation between the ruler and ruled. The power to command the labor obviously existed" (1983:59–60). "The power to command the labor" did *not* obviously exist. The only thing that is obvious is that a great deal of labor went into building Nan Madol. If one chooses to rely on oral accounts, a large corpus of traditional narrative tells us that construction in the area was completed *before* there was a political hierarchy on Ponape (Bernart 1977:27–29). Competitive feasting on Ponape, according to both nineteenth-century descriptions and my own observations, mobilizes a great deal of labor on an essentially voluntary basis. And the gap between the authority modern Ponapeans ascribe to their chiefs and the authority I have in fact observed leaves me with grave doubts about the degree of "social differentiation" on Ponape.

It is essential that Ponapean concepts of authority be understood on their own terms if Ponapean responses to state power are to be interpreted. Indigenous Ponapean politics and colonial rule have not simply blended; they have created a tension that Ponapeans believe can only be resolved by the assertion of Ponapeans' culture. At the time of contact, circa 1830, there seem to have been three levels of sociopolitical organization on Ponape: the localized kin groups (*keinek*), which may have been either lineages or simple groups of people living and working together; the local communities (*kousapw*), known as sections or petty chiefdoms, with their chiefs (*soumas*); and the paramount chiefdoms (*wehi*), with their hierarchies of title-holders and paramount chiefs (*nahnmwarki*). After a half-century of trade, visits from whaling ships, and missionary activity, the Ponapeans became a colony of Spain in 1886. This regime was followed, in short order, by the Germans, the Japanese, and the Americans. During the last two decades the United States has introduced an electoral/bureaucratic system of government that is now largely run by Micronesians. Since 1979, Ponape has been part of the Federated States of Micronesia (FSM), which is supposed to become fully self-governing at the conclusion of U.S. trusteeship, an event that has been scheduled and rescheduled since the early 1960s. Detailed accounts of Ponapean social organization, contact history, and culture change can be found in Riesenberg (1968), McHenry (1975), and Petersen (1982: 1984a).

The Culture of the Ponapean Politics

It is my position in this chapter that for Ponapeans, politics entails a fundamentally different comprehension of the nature and exercising of power and authority than that understood in the modern Western intellectual tradition. There is nothing original in this contention. It has roots at least as deep as the opposition of some of Greek philosophy to Platonic dualism and can be traced through what Isaiah Berlin (1976, 1980) calls the "Counter-Enlightenment" work of Vico and Herder. It certainly represents one current in the development of modern (post–eighteenth century) anthropological thought. It is not my intention in this paper to argue this position from a philosophical or epistemological point of view, however. I am simply going to assert, on the basis of my two years' residence and participation in a Ponapean community (over the course of ten years), working as an ethnographer, that the fount of authority in a modern Ponapean community is the community itself, not a Machiavellian princeling, and that if one is to understand the operations of Ponapean politics one must understand how Ponapean culture establishes the context and forms in which individuals may tap and direct that power. I shall develop this theme in order to demonstrate how Ponapeans perceive and participate in the introduced electoral/bureaucratic system in their own terms, rather than in the political terms and categories of those from whom the system has been derived—that is, Americans. I am not, I should note, prepared to assert that what follows is the truth; it represents, rather, the direction in which years of reflection upon, analysis of, and continued questioning about the nature of Ponapean social life have taken me. I am aware of exceptions to what I say. Any attempt to generalize has to skip over particulars, particulars that survive and argue contrarily nonetheless.

There are two countervailing strains in Ponapean culture, as it is realized in individuals: one toward hierarchy and one toward individual autonomy. Ponapean chiefs are respected and revered; they are, as I have already pointed out, imbued with mana, which comes to them through the continuity of their matrilineages. Ponapean chiefs are also characterized by their *wahu*—their "honor." *Wahu* can be translated literally as "valley" and refers to the gulf that lies between chiefs and the other members of the community. Yet as one section chief reminded his people at a feast held to reintegrate the community after some of its people had split away to form a new section, "Everyone has honor ... honor inheres in one as a human and as a member of a community ... honor is like a fair wind: if it blows for us then we shall succeed" (Petersen 1982). The chief's honor, then, is not power. As one Ponapean aphorism has it, *"Ke sohte kak mihmi pahn emen"* ("you cannot live under another"), and another *"Ngehi me kin kaunda paliwarei"* ("I am master of my own self").

The entire shape of Ponapean culture and social life manifests these two interdependent pulls. Authority, though it draws upon rank, is by no means identical to it. Rather, individual authority derives from skill and ability and exists, in a sense, in its own negation. A politically effective man is characterized in most instances by humility. It is the wisdom or pragmatism of his suggestions, not their force, that leads to action. The Ponapean language includes a complex honorific or respect form (*meing*) that is used in all formal settings. People of high rank are referred to and addressed in linguistic forms that exalt them, and all others are spoken of in humiliative forms. But in using this language, one always lowers oneself in self-reference; all speakers, even the paramount chiefs, refer to themselves in the humiliative form. In formal political situations, e.g., at feasts, leaders do not assert themselves; the language does not allow for it. If orders are given, they are given by a lower-ranking individual acting as the chief's representative, known as the *auwenwehi*—literally the "mouth of the chiefdom" (and not the chief).

There is also a complex structure of secrecy woven into Ponapean social relations.[2] Two of the cardinal virtues Ponapeans urge each other to practice are *kanengamah* and *mahk*. *Kanengamah* can be translated as "patience," but its meanings have to do with holding things—in particular emotions—back. *Mahk* may be translated as "reserve" or "self-containment," though it is ordinarily used in a transitive sense: "I will overlook your affront; I do not deign to have you see how this affects me" might be one way of describing how it is used. Both of these qualities concern the holding back of one's self, a major means of preserving autonomy. Because Ponapeans routinely refrain from divulging their sentiments, they have enormous individual freedom from any need to meet others' expectations of them.

Daily patterns of activity are also affected by this emphasis on secrecy. Competitive production of feast goods plays a leading role in political advancement, and an element of surprise is critical to successful participation in the feasting. Ponapeans do not ordinarily enter upon others' land (openly, at least) except along recognized trails. Nor do they inquire of others about their crops or possessions. Given that most Ponapeans spend their entire lives within small, homogenous, and highly endogamous communities and thus know a great deal about each other, there is also a remarkable lot that they do not know about each other. Again, this secrecy serves to reinforce and protect personal autonomy. While gossip plays a major social role—as it does in every society—there is an explicit notion that a man's affairs are his own. All this is reinforced by the dispersed settlement pattern, the rugged terrain, and the dense vegetation. Ponapeans are physically as well as psychically separated from each other. Their life-style provides them with considerable interfamilial privacy.

In response to these centrifugal forces is the ceaseless round of feasting that calls Ponapeans forth from their isolated farmsteads. Feasts are focused upon chiefs. Quantities of food and kava are brought together and are possessed temporarily by the chief, prepared, and then redistributed.

The symbolism of a feast has the chief at its center, sitting, ideally, on a raised platform and looking down upon the people working below him.[3] (So central is this raised position in Ponapean political symbolism that the general term for chiefs or high-ranking people is *soupeidi*—"those who look down.") The highest-ranking chiefs may receive considerable quantities of tribute at these feasts that are not redistributed, though much—perhaps most—of what they retain is dispersed among their families, hangers-on, and the people who help them transport the goods home. It is not unusual for section chiefs, however, to contribute more to feasts than they retain in the redistribution.

One of my clearest recollections of my early encounters with the seeming contradictions of Ponapean political culture comes from a conversation I had with the wife of a man who was one of several eligible successors to a chief thought to be on his deathbed.

At one point in our talk she was praising the sensibility of American democratic politics. Americans, unlike the Ponapeans, she argued, did not foolishly have to give all that they possessed to greedy, demanding chiefs. A few minutes later she was maintaining that most of their community wanted her husband to be the next chief because of his generosity. She complained that her husband was an exceptionally generous man, who gave away all that the family possessed, and that Ponapeans expected great generosity of their chiefs. A bit more literal in those days than I am now, I attempted to show her the contradiction in her statements: chiefs who were on the one hand greedy, on the other generous. She did not understand my objection; nowadays neither do I. Men who acquire, on Ponape, are equally men who distribute.

Because Ponapean chieftainship rests both upon achievement and ascription, there is a clear note of hierarchy even while there is continual economic leveling. Accumulation serves only as preparation for distribution. And in the same fashion, the honor accorded to chiefs is merely a reflection of the community's esteem for itself. Feasts are the product of community effort and are in fact conducted in a surprisingly anarchic fashion. Few formal preparations or assignments are made in anticipation of a feast. Though there is a master of ceremonies, he is a coordinator or conductor who establishes the rhythm, rather than a supervisor who assigns the tasks. At extremely large feasts, which draw hundreds of participants, many of whom are relative strangers, there may be more conscious efforts made at organization, but under ordinary circumstances feasts unfold by themselves. Each participant decides for himself or herself what to contribute and what tasks to undertake. And when, as is often the case, a family is holding a feast to mark a life crisis event—a death, a wedding, a journey, a graduation—it is the chief who must, by his obligatory attendance, serve his people as their figurehead (cf. Clastres 1977). The chief's presence confers ritual status upon the event, though the ritual itself is not the chief's doing but the people's.

The decision-making, and -enforcing, powers of the chiefs are of much the same quality as the roles they play in feasting. The near-century of colonial rule has undoubtedly affected their powers, but it is difficult to determine just what degree of control nineteenth-century chiefs had over their subjects. If one applies the same sort of divergence between what Ponapeans today say about the nature of their political institutions and what the ethnographer observes to written accounts from the past, it may well be that Ponapean chiefs never had especially centralized control of their communities, despite their enormous ritual status. Or so I am inclined to believe. The authority of section chiefs seems exceptionally vulnerable today. They are continually obliged to tread a very fine line between demanding too much participation in community activities, thereby alienating their people, and calling for too little, thereby allowing the section to slip into torpor and disintegration. Sections can and do split apart as a result of population growth and disenchantment with the chiefs. In *One Man Cannot Rule a Thousand* (Petersen 1982) I treat this process at monograph length. Paramount chiefdoms have in recent years had their boundaries frozen by the charters that have made each a municipality within the state, the FSM, and the trust territory; and the paramount chiefs are less threatened by secession. In fact, they may at times actually encourage fissioning among the sections as a means of thwarting the rise of especially successful leaders or communities who might threaten their own hegemony.

Paramount chiefs in general rule through their section chiefs. There is not a great deal of ruling to be done, of course. Most aspects of Ponapean life are of a familiar and repetitive enough nature that tasks get done as part of the flow of life, rather than in response to a system of orders. Nevertheless, ritual events, celebrations, and the general structure of status are hinged upon the chiefs and instructions and orders are sometimes given. Individuals may be told what they are expected to contribute to certain feasts or to community efforts of one sort or another. But chiefs only occasionally make decisions on their own. Any sort of joint effort is preceded by discussions among holders of the highest titles. Some form of consensus—a reading of community opinion, in effect—is found. A formal announcement may sometimes be made: e.g., each family is expected to contribute one pig, one kava plant, or one large yam to a specific feast. Or nothing formal will be said at all, since the decision is no more than a reflection of what community members sense is proper participation or a proper contribution, and a family's decision to participate is based on many factors.

Performance and participation cannot be directly enforced. Ponapean chiefs no longer have powers of coercion (if indeed they ever did). It is the system of titles—the formal, public manifestation of individual status—that ensures participation. In a general way, community service is rewarded by advancement in the title system; the higher a man's title, the more is expected of him. There are individuals who seem to have little interest in advancement, and while they generally participate in community activities, they do not contribute much. These people are, however, in a definite minority and frequently the targets of mild teasing and derision. Failure to participate in or contribute to community events is the most frequently—in fact, it is practically the only—explanation given for the removal of titles. If a man or a family does not meet the standards set by the chief or community, titles might be taken back. Upon occasion titles are removed as a result of personal conflicts, I know, but this is not usually acknowledged; inadequate participation or tribute is invariably given as the reason. A title, then, is to a large degree a statement of one's status within the community. There are occasional exceptions to this, as when a title is removed because of personal conflict between a chief and a community member; I know of cases where this has occurred and the status of the man who lost his title was not seriously damaged. But this happens when an individual's status is so well founded within the community that an attack by the chief is not by itself sufficient to detract from the community's regard.

What this all means is that the true locus of authority in Ponapean communities is the community itself. An able chief is respected and listened to, but he founds his authority upon his own ability to listen. If pronouncements are made, they are liable to fall upon deaf ears or meet considerable disagreement. A generous chief can make demands and expect a degree of cooperation; having known no truly greedy chiefs, I cannot simply assert that they are inherently ineffective, but I assume that this is why they are not often encountered. Ponapeans continually complain about their chiefs, but they also admit freely that their complaints have little significance: *"Pihl en pahn mweli,"* they say, the "water under the boulders," which can be heard trickling but has no impact.

Ponapeans have, I believe, an enormous sense of controlling their own lives, precisely because there is no differentiated source of authority over them. They have a clear concept of hierarchy and speak of it often, but it is extremely difficult to find it embodied as authority. Ponapeans sometimes speak of things within their lives that cannot be located by an outside observer.

The Ponapean Electoral/Bureaucratic System

It is within this context—that is, the simultaneous acceptance and rejection of a hierarchy of authority—that the evolution of a new political structure on Ponape must be understood. The Ponapeans and the other Micronesian peoples have in part taken for themselves and in part had thrust upon them a political structure that reflects several millennia of cultural development in Europe (and the United States). The functioning of Western bourgeois democracy, with whatever degree of optimism or pessimism one views it, presupposes a number of cultural traits. Some of these grow out of a long and complex scholastic/philosophical tradition. Others derive from an important historical precondition: the absolute authority of the state, a hierarchy of power that is real and effective as well as apparent. With significantly varying degrees, modern democracies assume some popular control of government, but more critically, they assume governments that genuinely control the lives of the governed. Their religious, legal, economic, scientific, and artistic traditions all share this heritage in one fashion or another, a shared assumption of centralized, legitimate, and overarching authority and power. While earlier monarchy and autarchy have given way to bourgeois democracy, the quantum advances of modern technology have given contemporary governments far more control over individual lives than their predecessors ever had. It is a structure of government founded upon such presuppositions that has been introduced in Micronesia, where very different cultural underpinnings have evolved.

There is today on Ponape a system of government modeled after that of the United States. Within the five paramount chiefdoms and the island's one town—the municipalities[4]—there are elected executives (the chief magistrates), justices, and councils. There is a state legislature with representatives elected from each of the municipalities, a state court, and an elected governor. And there is the FSM congress, the FSM president, and an FSM supreme court. The U.S. systems of municipal, state, and federal governments and executive, legislative, and judicial branches are faithfully replicated. Constitutions and charters have been carefully deliberated on by Ponapean and Micronesian delegations, but they have been drawn up, finally, by U.S. (and in a few cases U.S.-trained Micronesian) attorneys. The memberships of the congress and legislatures are subdivided into committees; the executive branches are composed of a multiplicity of divisions, departments, bureaus, agencies, and authorities. At almost every level of government and in almost every branch, expatriate technical advisers and administrators can be found. But in the main, the governments of Micronesia are staffed and run by Micronesians.

Ponapeans, as I have explained, have notions of authority and government that differ fundamentally from those of the people who initially devised this form of government, and their performance within the government is significantly different than that of the people who designed it. One hears on Ponape constant shrieks of rage from expatriates who are thoroughly frustrated by the Ponapean process of governing. From my perspective as ethnographer, it is easy to say, given my preceding arguments, that this is how it should be. I cannot deny the likelihood that were I in an administrative or technical position in the Ponapean government, my own shrieks would be heard as well.

I am going to use two kinds of examples to illustrate the problems currently being encountered in Ponapean government. The first is the product of Micronesia's colonial history and presents immediate problems for the development of efficient, responsive government on Ponape. The second is of a much deeper nature and represents basic philosophical differences between Ponapean notions of actions and American notions of principle. I will then go on to explore the wider implications these kinds of problems hold for the growth of an effective electoral/bureaucratic system of government and the ways in which I perceive the Ponapeans already at work adapting the actual functioning of their government to their own system of politics. Finally, I address an issue that arises out of this very process—the problem of federation among far-flung islands.

Present-day Ponapean government and apparently Micronesian government in general are confronted with an immediate problem of organization that is directly attributable to the U.S. administration's colonial legacy. U.S. rule in Micronesia has been for the most part autocratic. I am not necessarily charging it with heavy-handedness but pointing, rather, to the very centralized powers held in their time by the high commissioners and their district administrators. The various island legislatures acted throughout most of their histories as forums for discussion; district administrators always held veto power over them. The congress of Micronesia was likewise subject to the high commissioner's veto. Budgetary decisions were entirely executive functions: in the early days it was a process of allocating scarce resources; in more recent times it was the almost frantic search for ways in which to channel the flood tide of funding. As Ponapean political consciousness grew throughout the sixties and seventies, the Ponape District Legislature found itself at times functioning squarely in opposition to the administration. At other times it appears to have simply accepted its semi-impotent status and concerned itself primarily with internal matters. The legislature was in no way perceived by the administration as a partner in government.

At the same time, however, Ponapeans were entering the administration and learning executive tasks. By the early 1970s Ponape had its first Ponapean district administrator and departments in both the trust territory and Ponape district governments were being headed by Ponapeans and other Micronesians. The training and experience they gained were in the administration's autocratic tradition. Governmental decisions either came from Washington, D.C., through the high commissioner's office in Saipan or were made in the district administrator's office. These Ponapean administrators were, like their superiors, beholden to Saipan and Washington, not the legislature.

Today the Ponapean government is able to make many, perhaps most of its own day-to-day decisions and has an important voice in long-term planning. But the government is staffed largely by men who were trained in the U.S. colonial system and who continue to perceive government as essentially and primarily an executive operation. They have no experience in cooperating with a legislative body that is, technically, an equal partner. And the legislature, having a tradition only of opposition or irrelevance to the administration and receiving no sign or indication that the executive branch is interested in cooperation, continues to perceive itself as set against the governor's office and charged with striking an independent course. At a time when the government has been restructured to permit the cooperative effort absolutely necessary to the achievement of the creative solutions Ponape's immediate future cries out for, it remains instead bogged down in the unfortunate struggle that is part of America's colonial legacy.

Now such competition for preeminence is a fundamental part of any dynamic political system that is not monolithic; the traditional Ponapean polity depends upon the ceaseless interplay between the two parallel lines of chiefly titles for its own vitality. But at present the Ponapean government is constrained by it. The ultimate solution to this dilemma lies, I think, not in a series of workshops to reeducate Ponapean politicians, but in gradual absorption of the Ponapean political culture into the relations among the various members of government, over the course of several elections. I shall return to this shortly.

The second example I offer is drawn from the experience of several American attorneys who have worked on Ponape in various capacities, including service as legal aid lawyers and legislative counsels. The U.S. judicial system introduced into Micronesia depends for its efficiency upon several factors that lie beyond the immediate courtroom environs. Two of these are precedent and appellate procedures. In general, courts are guided in points of law by preceding decisions, as spelled out in opinions and catalogued in law libraries. When a particular decision is disagreed with, it can be appealed to a higher court. Inherent in the appeals system, however, is the notion that there is an ultimate decision—and that it, like all other decisions, will be based on precedent (unless it is a rare and significant case of reversing precedent, as in the U.S. civil rights decision that "separate but equal" was an impossibility).

Attorneys who represent Ponapeans in litigation report that while the judiciary is frequently employed to resolve disputes, neither precedent nor an ultimate appellate decision is generally understood. I believe that this is so for many of the same reasons that I used in explaining the communal nature of the Ponapean polity. Perceiving no specific locus for authority, but seeing it instead as existing embedded among actual relations between people, Ponapeans view decisions as being conditional and temporary, subject to change in the individuals concerned or the relations between them. While Ponapeans rely heavily upon precedent in the conduct of traditional politics, there are so very many possible precedents for every situation that they are not seen as guides to action so much as explanations and justifications *for* it, after the fact. A decision is made on pragmatic grounds, then rationalized in terms of precedent. A legal decision that accepts the precedent as the *determining* factor does not make good sense in Ponapean society. Similarly, because decisions are arrived at on pragmatic grounds that reflect the relations between the parties and between them and the adjudicator, there can really be no ultimate decision. As relations among the various parties and the conditions in which they exist shift, it is expected that the decision-making itself must vary. Thus losing a case on any given occasion does not logically imply that it might not be won on another occasion, and some Ponapeans return again and again to council, requesting that previously unsuccessful cases be taken up again. Law, like life, is expected to be flexible, to respond to immediate conditions, needs, and opportunities. A system of law and of government that asserts timeless principles is understood, but one that expects them to be lived by is not. Because authority is not alien, separate, or distinct, but lies within the fabric of community life itself, Ponapeans at some level perceive themselves as being in control of their own lives; it is, I think, a sociocultural system that confers enormous individual freedoms, yet works with great efficacy because this freedom depends upon the well-being of the community.

It is for these reasons that Ponapeans can operate within the introduced electoral/bureaucratic system with the same notions of hierarchy and autonomy that characterize the traditional system. While the dynamics of Ponapean politics frequently entail intense competition and continual jockeying for position, so thoroughly communal is the Ponapean polity that individual success is understood in terms of the community's benefit. Unlike true peasants, who have known generations of subservience to feudal powers and understood gain as ultimately benefiting someone else (a lord, a landlord, a tax collector), Ponapeans do not share in what George Foster (1967) has described as "the image of limited good," in which one man's gain necessarily implies another's loss; this is known in game theory as a zero-sum game.

In the absence of an alienated or truly differentiated locus of authority, individual success does not come at the expense of other community members but rather includes them. Ponapeans perceive their chiefs as greedy because they are the focal points for the continual presentation of feast goods. But chiefs are, in general, men whose political advancement is in large measure determined by their contributions and who are expected, ultimately, to redistribute significant portions of what they have been given. In the traditional Ponapean political economy the items that confer prestige—yams, kava, pigs, and general community service—are not in scarce supply. Authority, then, does not come about by controlling access to these things, but by producing and distributing them. Power cannot be obtained by cornering the market, as it were, because a leadership role exists only when members of the community see in it their own direct benefit. Status is accrued through skill and labor put to use for the community.

This is not meant to sound utopian. There are both important differences in status and in personal and family wealth in Ponapean communities. But the two exist in tandem in a fashion that differs fundamentally from the relation between the two in capitalist society. As Max Weber showed in *The Protestant Ethic and the Spirit of Capitalism* (1952) and as clearly demonstrated by the philosophy and policies of the U.S. government in the 1980s, there is in capitalism a notion that worldly success and wealth are in themselves manifestations of underlying virtue, that affluence in and of itself confers status. (The older the wealth and the less obvious the earning of it, the greater the status it confers, *vide* Veblen's *Theory of the Leisure Class* [1953].) On Ponape, accumulation that is unaccompanied by distribution is not understood. *"Kaidehn kowe mehn wai"* ("you're not an American") is a common retort to instances of stinginess. The notion that status implies generosity has profound effects upon the process of government on Ponape today, as does the understanding that personal relations determine principle rather than the reverse.

The Evolution of Ponapean Politics

As I have already stressed, most Ponapean social and political interaction takes place within the sections, the island's basic communities. Within the sections, the entire political process takes place on a face-to-face basis and authority is to be found within the group as a whole, represented but not controlled by the section chief. The sections are in turn bound together by the paramount chiefdoms. Prominent individuals within the chiefdoms—men with high titles—are well known not because of their titles but because of their participation in numerous feasts and other social activities. Their titles, though partly dependent upon hereditary status, are more directly the product of political acumen and activity. Ponapean leaders occupy intensely public positions, and they channel, rather than possess, the authority of the community.

Because political communities are genuine communities on Ponape, political actions are based on interpersonal relations, not abstract principles. This is possible, indeed highly effective, because members of the community are acutely aware of who benefits from any given action and how they benefit. Members can choose to participate in or refrain from the community's activities. Politicians in the electoral/bureaucratic system understand this, and their own actions are informed by and predicated upon their membership in Ponapean communities, not the principles that underlie the original formation of the system. The faceless "equality-before-the-law" character of bourgeois democracy allows the individual no control over his or her own participation in society nor the benefits accrued by others. The outrage of expatriates at what they perceive as inefficiency, irresponsibility, and misallocation of funds is certainly justified from the point of view of principle. Ponapeans concur in these judgments. But for anyone for whom politics are communal, these are not shortcomings but necessary, efficacious, and beneficial political acts. I am keenly aware of the likelihood that this will be construed as criticism; it is intended as praise. The faceless, principled quality of bourgeois democracy lends itself readily to manipulation, legalistic maneuvering and irresponsibility on a scale so vast as to threaten the existence of society itself. Because the lacework of authority in Ponapean communities cannot be accumulated and converted into power, the system is not a threat to itself. The apparent administrative failures portend, I think, a government that will be in no way as efficient as those of industrial societies, but for precisely that reason will be far more responsive to the needs of the entire community. Ponapeans, unlike Americans, perceive their existence as primarily social and behave accordingly. They do not suppose that some invisible hand shall magically make things right, and they are, consequently, an eminently more pragmatic people than we, who, living in vast and faceless societies, cast our fates to the wind.

This unwillingness to have abstract principle determines the quality of one's relations with others, even as a political system that assumes it is being implemented is paralleled by the issue of force in Ponapean society. While there have been occasional and apparently isolated incidents of violence on Ponape, there does not seem to have been organized use of force by Ponapeans since the end of the ill-fated Sokehs rebellion in 1910. The Ponapeans warred among themselves and against the Spanish as late as 1898, but the technology and discipline of the Germans seems to have intimidated them. The Japanese are invariably spoken of as harsh disciplinarians, and though I have heard tales of minor harassment, I know of no organized resistance to them. The American period has seen the use of jail sentences and the development of an armed Ponapean police force. But for the last seventy years or so there has been little or no application of legitimate force by Ponapeans against Ponapeans to implement government policy. Given the Ponapeans' emphasis on consensus and their enormous tolerance for defiance, this is not especially remarkable. One wonders, however, about the future. I am not prepared to attend fully to this issue in this context, but it is certainly relevant to the present discussion and demands some consideration.

There are a number of firearms in Ponapean hands today, despite gun-control laws. A few of these are light rifles used for deerhunting, but there are also handguns. I have no idea of their numbers or of the availability of ammunition for them. This is reminiscent of conditions early in the German administration. The Ponapeans in those days were heavily armed, and the Germans were understandably concerned. Following a devastating typhoon in 1905, the island suffered a food shortage (one of the very few noted in Ponapean traditions) and the Germans offered to trade food for guns—a striking reversal of the dominant trade patterns on Ponape in the preceding century. The people of Sokehs chiefdoms did not join the rest of the island in this exchange, and this in part explains the singularity of their revolt against the Germans five years later (Ehrlich 1978). Placed in this context, a gradual rearmament does not represent a departure from Ponapean tradition. If some Ponapean community or chiefdom or region were to object strongly to a government policy and refuse to comply, it is not at all clear how a Ponapean government would respond. In the long absence of a tradition of centrally implemented force and given the strong pulls toward autonomy of individuals and communities, one perceives the low-key operation of Ponapean government as a politically—as well as culturally—determined course.

There are at present two Ponapean polities (along with that of the United States). I have argued that they are both responsive to a Ponapean political culture, a set of cultural assumptions about the nature of the body politic and proper political conduct. While they function at present as different spheres, they are neither entirely distinct nor separate and are gradually becoming less so. The differences between the two are important, and each is partly responsible for the shape and effectiveness of the other. Though neither imposes a great deal upon the other, there is a form of symbiosis between them.

The great continuity of the traditional system of chiefly and communal politics is in some measure possible because chiefs and communities have not been responsible for modernization. They have not had to shoulder the burden of developing public health, education, and works programs, nor have they been charged with creating an export economy to produce foreign exchange. The most striking discontinuities and disruptions of life have been instigated by foreigners, and while Ponapeans and Micronesians have begun seriously to consider the roles that they themselves play in social disturbances, their communities, at least beyond the borders of the town, remain well integrated.

The electoral/bureaucratic system has functioned rather smoothly thus far because it is funded externally and has not had to make demands directly upon Ponapean communities. There has been no corvee, no conscription, no pillaging, and all but excise taxes are insignificant. The high level of wage employment has meant that young Ponapeans have had little reason to emigrate in search of work. The government has encountered little opposition not only because of its aura of colonial authority, but because it has had to do little that has been construed as offensive.

Life in Ponapean communities has been significantly affected by changes in health care, education, communications, transportation, and economics. The same could be said, of course, of nineteenth-century Ponape. Ponapeans long ago became dependent upon steel tools, machine-made cloth, kerosene lamps, and a host of other simple necessities of daily life and lost none of their Ponapeanness for it. I would argue that these newer changes will likewise see the Ponapeans retaining their own distinctive culture. As they continue to take over local government and as funding for that government continues to decrease, substantial adaptations must be expected. These changes will reflect the matrix of Ponapean culture in which they take place and will be responsive to the communal nature of Ponapean politics. Status and resources will be allocated in much the same fashion as they always have, or so I believe. But the very factors that hint at the strength and success of a Ponapean polity—that is, the face-to-face, communal quality of the island's politics—suggest problems for the federation of islands of which it is part.

Ponape and a National Government

It has not taken long for the Ponapeans to encounter problems with the Micronesian federation. When they voted against a new relationship with the United States, called free association, and called instead for independence, the national government immediately interpreted their vote as an act of defiance. There was a grain of truth to this; while the people of Ponape were not objecting to federation, they were protesting the form the national government seems to be taking.

Free association trades Micronesian sovereignty for massive U.S. financial support. Many Ponapeans believe that the national government is growing too dependent on American funding and that it will allow the United States to continue to do most of Micronesia's decision making. It seems as though some Ponapeans see their national government in the process of becoming one more foreign power seeking to control their lives. Their vote for independence in the 1983 plebiscite grew directly out of the strong Ponapean cultural bias toward local autonomy.[5]

The notion that power is essentially a cultural universal that varies only in degree may not be especially useful. It allows archaeologists, for example, to claim that the amount of labor needed to build a series of stone structures is a measure of the power of the chiefs buried in them when there is, in fact, no evidence of what motivated those who built them. And it results in mistaken assumptions about the ways in which people respond to the introduction of the state. The state is, after all, a cultural—as well as political—artifact, and it is Ponapean cultural notions of how communities should govern themselves that shape their participation in the new government evolving on their island.

Notes

1. An earlier draft of this paper was presented at the Conference on Evolving Political Cultures in the Pacific Islands, at the Institute for Polynesian Studies, Laie, Hawaii, in February 1982. I wish to acknowledge support from the National Institute of Mental Health, the City University of New York's PSC-CUNY Faculty Research Program, the National Endowment for the Humanities, and the Wenner-Gren Foundation for Anthropological Research, all of whom have helped fund this research. My fieldwork on Ponape—February 1974–August 1975, June–August 1979, 1981, and 1983—has been possible, and successful, only because of my Ponapean friends' great kindness and interest in my work. I believe all that I write is in some sense a repayment of my obligations to them, and I am always hopeful that my admiration for them shows through the scholarly detachment I try to assume.
2. A full description of Ponapean secrecy and a discussion of the role it plays in Ponapean social organization are in Petersen (1978).
3. The strains toward autonomy and humility in Ponapean culture occasionally lead chiefs to abandon their stations and take seats for themselves among those preparing the feast goods.
4. Ponape State also includes a number of smaller outlying islands, with autonomous traditions, that are also chartered as municipalities.
5. Much fuller discussion of the 1983 plebiscite can be found in Petersen (1984b; 1985).

References

Athens, Stephen J. 1983. The megalithic ruins of Nan Madol. *Natural History* 92 (12):50–61.

Bernart, Luelen. 1977. *The book of Luelen*. Pacific History Series, no. 8. Honolulu: University Press of Hawaii.

Berlin, Isaiah. 1976. *Vico and Herder*. New York: Viking.

_____. 1980. *Against the current*. New York: Viking.

Clastres, Pierre. 1977 (1974). *Society against the state*. New York: Urizen.

Ehrlich, Paul. 1978. The clothes of men. Unpublished Ph.D. dissertation, SUNY Stony Brook.

Foster, George. 1967. *Tzintzuntzan*. Boston: Little, Brown.

Haas, John. 1982. *The evolution of the prehistoric state*. New York: Columbia University Press.

McHenry, Donald F. 1975. *Micronesia: Trust betrayed*. New York: Carnegie Endowment for International Peace.

Petersen, Glenn. 1978. Full disclosure: Knowledge, secrecy, and social distance in Ponapean society. Paper presented at the meetings of the Association for Social Anthropology in Oceania, February 1978.

_____. 1982. *One Man Cannot Rule a Thousand*. Ann Arbor: University of Michigan Press.

_____. 1983. From chiefdom to state: Political evolution in contemporary Ponape. Paper presented at the New York Academy of Sciences, January 1983.

_____. 1984a. The Ponapean culture of resistance. *Radical History Review* 28–30: 347–66. (Vols. 28–30 were published in a single issue.)

_____. 1984b. A moral economy and an immoral trusteeship. *Cultural Survival*. Occasional Paper no. 12:89–96.

_____. 1985. A cultural analysis of the Ponapean vote for independence in the 1983 plebiscite. *Pacific Studies* 9:13–52.

Riesenberg, Saul. 1968. *The native Ponapean polity*. Washington, DC: Smithsonian Institution.

Veblen, Thorstein. 1953 (1899). *The theory of the leisure class*. New York: New American Library.

Weber, Max. 1952. (1920–21). *The Protestant ethic and the spirit of capitalism*. New York: Scribner's.

3

Central Borneo and Its Relations with Coastal Malay Sultanates

Jérôme Rousseau

This chapter is a preliminary consideration of the relationship between small coastal states and groups of the interior in precolonial Borneo. The sultanates wished to control the inland groups but were too weak to do so; central Borneo groups would have liked to be entirely independent of the Malay sultanates, but found this impossible to achieve. Relations between the sultanates and central Borneo were tense, sometimes violent, but the benefits of trade for both were such that a modus vivendi was found. Colonial rule eventually changed profoundly the nature of the interaction between central Borneo and the sultanates.

The Malay Sultanates of Borneo

The coastal areas of Borneo have been subject to a number of different historical influences and in particular the spread of Malay culture. It seems likely that the Malay population and Malay sultanates developed primarily through conversion to Islam of local groups rather than large-scale Malay immigration.

These Malay sultanates were not the first states to appear in Borneo. Archaeological and historical evidence indicates the presence of Hinduized states in Borneo in the first centuries A.D. Indeed, there was a Hindu kingdom in Muara Kaman that was conquered by the Malay sultanate of Kutei and converted to Islam in the early seventeenth century. There is very little evidence about these Hinduized states or their relations with inland groups.

The Borneo sultanates became vassals of Majapahit in the fourteenth

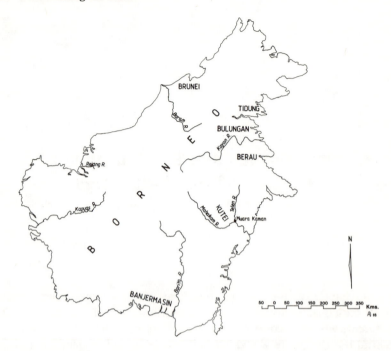

century, but this relationship ended in the first quarter of the fifteenth century (Eisenberger 1936:3). The relationship does not appear to have been close, possibly because, with the exception of Banjermasin, these states were very small indeed. We will deal here almost exclusively with the states of East Borneo, namely, Kutei, Berau, Bulungan and Tidung, for which much information is available on the relation between coastal states and inland groups.

Central Borneo

In the context of this paper, *central Borneo* refers to a group of related ethnic groups rather than to a simple geographical designation (Rousseau 1974). These groups do originate from central Borneo, but some of them have moved closer to coastal areas.

Borneo is roughly circular, with rivers that radiate from its center. The inhabitants of their upper reaches are culturally and socially related to each other and have had contacts with each other across river basins. At the same time, the rivers constitute another social axis that counteracts this centripetal tendency, and part of central Borneo's population has moved downriver when possible and advantageous.

A few of central Borneo's inhabitants were nomadic hunters-gatherers, but the large majority were shifting cultivators living in longhouses; they had hereditary leadership and social strata, and they practiced headhunting. Typically, population density was low (sometimes less than one per square kilometer) and villages were independent of each other in their daily life. There was political organization beyond the village level insofar as regional matters were dealt with by councils of chiefs and some men and villages established hegemony over other communities.

Characteristics of the Borneo Malay Sultanates

We will see in the next section that trade played a central role in the development and continued existence of the sultanates. We consider here some of their general characteristics. Given their small size and relative weakness, it becomes relevant to ask in what ways they were states. The sultanates were states most obviously at the ideological level; sultanates defined themselves as regional polities with a territory that in theory they controlled exclusively and with the right to impose taxes and carry out the rule of law. At least some sultanates had a written code of law, such as Kutei with its "Beraja nanti," which is based on the Koran (Commisie voor het adatrecht 1937:300). The sultan was a hereditary ruler surrounded by a royal family: he had the right to bestow titles and appanages. The administration of the state was carried out by officials with distinct spheres of influence. The sultanates had formal relations with each other; at various periods, Kutei was vassal to Banjermasin, Berau to Kutei, Bulungan to Berau, and Tidung to Bulungan. The model of the state clearly provided a blueprint for regional relations.

In practice, the Borneo sultanates had a coastal nucleus: the areas close to the capital were effectively controlled by the sultan and his followers and were taxed on a regular basis. The state was also in a position to control the trade that passed through this area, to tax it, and in some cases to curtail it . as a form of pressure against inland groups that it did not effectively control.

In general, there appears to have been little attempt to develop production within this nucleus; rather, the main sources of revenue derived from trade. Referring to the sultan of Kutei, Bock (1881:37) mentions: "His income is derived from three recognized sources: first, a duty of ten per cent on all articles imported or exported; second, a monopoly of the salt and opium trade; and third, the produce of the coal-mines at Pelaroeng and Batu Pangal." (The coal mines were of course a recent development linked to steamships.) Besides taxing traders, the sultans and their followers also controlled specific areas that they reserved for themselves for the gathering of jungle produce (Bock 1881:49). For this and other reasons, they needed slaves. Slaves were obtained by capture or bought. Expeditions were organized for the specific purpose of capturing slaves, often from nomadic groups. By the end of the nineteenth century, the Malays had abandoned this practice, although the groups of the interior still enslaved nomads (Spaan 1901:3). Debt-slaves could be obtained through trade (Knappert 1905:586). The sultans also received slaves as tribute: Dalton, who visited Kutei in 1827, reported that the sultan had waged war on some Dayak groups because they had failed to deliver to the sultan the children they had to give him every year. These were sold to the Buginese (Knappert 1905:581).

Trade

Trade of jungle produce was a central element in the relationship between central Borneo and Malay sultanates. Indeed, trade played an important role in the social interaction between all groups; it took place not only between Malays and Dayaks, but also between the various groups of the interior. Anybody could at some point be involved in trade, and a commodity could go through a number of intermediaries. Among central Borneo groups, the chiefs were the most important traders.

Central Borneo groups had a largely self-sufficient economy: they did not need trade for the essentials of life and produced all their own food; they also smelted their own iron—and were justly renowned for the quality of their swords. This of course significantly reduced the degree of control that the sultans might have had over them. Nevertheless, trade goods were not unimportant: people preferred to wear cloth rather than bark, they sought such valuables as jars, bronze cannons, gongs, glass beads, and shell and other ornaments, which were prestige property, especially for the ruling stratum; they also obtained tin objects and salt, which was not generally available in the interior. (There were a few salt springs.) In return, they gave birds' nests, camphor, various kinds of wild rubber, medicinal products, bezoar stones, rhinoceros horns, deer antlers, animal skins, swords, baskets, mats, gold, and rattan. The relative importance of these various items varied through time; in the late nineteenth century, rattan became the main article of trade.

Besides the fact that trade brought mostly luxury items to the interior, another factor limited Malay control over central Borneo. Because of the geographical position, the groups of central Borneo were not obliged to trade only with the coastal groups in their own river basins; they could cross watersheds and trade elsewhere. In particular, the development of Brooke rule in Sarawak was a strong attraction to the inhabitants of eastern and western Kalimantan.

The demand for jungle produce was the main reason for contacts between central Borneo groups and Malay sultanates. There were two ways of obtaining such produce, which were not mutually exclusive: direct collection of produce or trade. A Malay entrepreneur might hire a number of men whom he would lead to the jungle. The entrepreneur kept the lion's share of the profits. Malay traders either organized trading trips or settled in an upriver village. The latter approach required some form of agreement between the trader and village chief, who would accept the trader only if he found an immediate advantage in the arrangement.

The presence of Malay traders in the interior was not motivated only by the quest for profit; indeed, until the establishment of Dutch rule in the interior, residence there was not free of danger, as the Malays were potential victims of headhunting. Most Malay residents of the interior had left the coast because of some crime; they would try to enter into a marital alliance with the daughter of a chief in order to obtain some right of residence, but in general a chief did not allow them to stay long in his village. The attitude toward these Malays varied according to circumstances. Some chiefs who wished to increase the size of their groups were more willing to accept them especially if they had some specific skill, e.g., if they were curers or craftsmen. Whenever marriages took place, they did not significantly affect the local population, in the sense that the woman would remain in her village and it was up to the Malay husband to adapt to local practices. Indeed, several of these marriages were temporary, and the man left his wife when life became difficult to seek a place in another group (Nieuwenhuis 1904:276).

When it was advantageous to have some Malay traders and jungle collectors upriver, the local chiefs were in a position to control their presence: "As long as the young Bahau chief Ding Ngo controlled the area below the rapids, he managed to keep out the Buginese jungle produce collectors and traders from Kutei. Others came from the Barito . . . and they were more amenable to his wishes. The Buginese of the lower Mahakam . . . were followers of Kutei" (Nieuwenhuis 1936–37:239).

While trade was of constant importance to the coastal Malay population, this was not the case for upriver groups, for which trading was of more episodic significance. To prosper, the sultanates needed a large hinterland. Although no precise data are available, there appears to have been a significant increase in trade around the turn of the twentieth century, because of an increased demand for some products, and because of pacification and the disappearance of headhunting, which facilitated trade.

The Malays did not have a monopoly on trade, as central Borneo people also traveled downriver to the trading centers to sell jungle produce. There is no way to know what proportion of the trade was in Malay hands before the twentieth century. In the early twentieth century, Malay and Chinese traders played a predominant role.

Trade was obviously of fundamental importance to Malay principalities. Grijzen (1925:116) goes as far as to say that the heads of principalities "were originally nothing else than the first jungle-produce collectors who settled on the coast of North-east Borneo." They were then able to establish some power over the coastal Dayak, but those of the interior maintained their independence. Walchren (1907:763) says that the collection of jungle produce used to be the almost exclusive source of income for the Malays of Berau and Bulungan. The sultans did not encourage agriculture, as trade was more profitable to them: 10 percent of the value of forest produce went to the sultan (ibid.: 763). The sultan, through his slaves, also participated directly in jungle collection: as previously mentioned, he reserved for himself some areas with valuable produce, such as birds' nests caves. The sultans also found their power base in the other traders and jungle collectors. They befriended the leaders of jungle collection groups and gave them land on which to settle and titles and offices as village chiefs within the area effectively controlled by the sultan. Some of them also received from the sultan exclusive rights of exploitation over specific districts (ibid.:764).

Levies on trade were a main source of income for the sultans, but others profited from trade along the way. For instance, in the lower Kayan area, the two major chiefs Lig Pay and Anyi Lohong imposed a tax on all traders who passed through their territories. However, they did so to such an extent that it discouraged trade (Walchren 1907:789). The Dutch abolished the practice (ibid.:811).

The Relations between Borneo and Malay Sultanates

As we have seen, trade was the major motivation for interaction between central Borneo and the coastal Malay sultanates, but the sultans had other designs on the interior: they wanted to control it, in order to develop trade and to collect taxes and tribute. This necessarily brought them in conflict with central Borneo and particularly with its chiefs, who had their own position of privilege to protect. The problem was already evident at the conceptual level because the sultans claimed as their territory the whole river basin of which they occupied the mouth, as far as the watershed, while in fact they did not control the hinterland (Grijzen 1925:132).

The nature of the sultans' control varied according to circumstances. For instance, in 1849 the sultan of Tidung's power extended over 2,000 Segai households, 600 Berusu households, and 320 Muslim households. From the Segai he extracted an annual tax of 12 gantang of rice per household (1 gantang = 4,51); from the Berusu, 15 gantang; by contrast, the Muslims were to provide an indeterminate quality of *padi* at the prince's will. It seems that the Muslims were modestly taxed, their main contribution being to provide the sultan with boats (Hageman 1855:79). Hageman does not explain these differences, but they may be due to the fact that the Muslims were the sultan's natural power base and light taxes would help to guarantee their support. In addition, many Malays were traders and contributed to the state's coffer through the trade tax. The Segai may have been taxed more lightly than the Berusu because their support was more tenuous: only a proportion of the Segai were under the influence of the sultans of Tidung, Bulungan, and Berau, while most or all of the Berusu were.

The sultans controlled only the Dayak who lived a few days' travel from the capital, and such control was established through the latter's hereditary chiefs. The sultans gave them Malay titles, and several of them converted to Islam (Knappert 1905:611; Bock 1881:64–65). But the support of the chiefs was far from guaranteed. Unless they lived very close to the capital, they had good reasons to keep their independence. In some cases, the sultans took advantage of dissension to gain influence. The presence of the sultanates opened alternatives for central Borneo aristocrats who had not managed to establish a position of power in the traditional structure. For instance, Kertas, the son of the Uju Tepu chief, became Muslim and took the name of Raden Temenggong. He contributed to establishing the sultan's influence over his village (Nieuwenhuis 1907:36).

The sultans were sometimes able to determine the selection of Dayak chiefs. For instance, in Mara, the first Dayak village up the Kayan River, the sultan had installed the eighteen-year-old son of the hereditary ruler of the Melarang and Segai; however, he did not trust him and kept him in the capital, with the consequence that the other Segai chiefs refused to recognize him (Walchren 1907:760). Toward the end of the nineteenth century, the sultan of Kutei also detained several chiefs of the middle Mahakam in his capital for a few years. This backfired on him when some of them died of cholera (Nieuwenhuis 1907:37). Less adversarial methods were also used to influence upriver chiefs. For instance, the sultans of Bulungan paid their gambling debts when they were in good terms with them (Walchren 1907:770).

The sultans of Berau occasionally closed some rivers to commerce in order to put pressure on upriver groups (Spaan 1901:4); it is difficult to see how such a measure would have been really effective except as bluff, as the sultans stood to lose more by such a prohibition on trade than the interior groups did. Indeed, a common response to sultans' attempts to control groups of the interior was for the latter to move upriver. "The Sultans, and in particular the father of the incumbent, were powerless to prevent this" (Walchren 1907:761). This was of course a matter of concern to the sultans, as their prosperity depended on the presence of the inland groups. Thus the sultans of Kutei "had heard that several Dyaks had left Long Wai [in the Telen], and gone to another *negorei*, or county, beyond the limits of Koetei, and he had sent up to say that no Dyaks were to leave his territory on any pretense. He wanted his kingdom to be thickly populated, and those that had left were to come back, or be fetched back by force if necessary" (Bock 1881:69). These were brave words, but it is difficult to see how such a demand could have been acted upon. Another example of the weakness of the sultanates was the fact that the upriver chiefs had some success in preventing their neighbors from trading downriver when they were in bad relations with the sultan (e.g., Walchren 1907:759).

In addition, there were limits to the sultans' access to the interior. While the sultan of Kutei considered the upper Mahakam to belong to him, he was not allowed under any circumstances to travel beyond a particular point in the lower Mahakam (Grijzen 1921:14). The same applied to the sultan of Bulungan, who was not allowed in the "real Dayak areas." The document does not explain how this rule came about, but from the context it clearly predates Dutch rule. It is not clear whether a supernatural sanction was attached to this prohibition. We have an example of an occasion when this rule was transgressed: The sultan of Kutei accompanied Bock's 1879 expedition up the Mahakam, probably with the intention of using the strength of the expedition to travel safely upriver and establish his influence there. The sultan had sent an advance party, of which one man was killed: "The people had a strong objection to being governed by, and taxed for the benefit of, a Malay ruler; and the visit of the Sultan might be construed by them into an attempt to impose his authority upon them which they would possibly immediately resent" (Bock 1881:147).

In northern Borneo, the strength of upriver groups seems to have been even greater: "The Sultan of Brunei had for years . . . been afraid of the Kayans of the Baram, and to thwart them had been in the habit of sending envoys to intrigue and create dissention among the Baram tribes" (Hose 1927:184). "In the old days, it was not uncommon for a strong party of Kayans to descend upon a settlement of the more peaceable coastwise people, and to extort from them a large payment of brass-ware as the price of their safety" (Hose and McDougall 1912, 1:180). Indeed, the sultanate of Brunei was attacked on several occasions by Kayan expeditions (St. John 1862, 1:3; *Sarawak Gazette*, November 2, 1872, p. 4).

Colonial Transformations

At first, the Dutch had little interest in central Borneo; they were satisfied to control the coastal sultanates and use them as intermediaries in their relations with central Borneo. This had the effect of strengthening the sultans' hand against the groups of the interior. Toward the end of the nineteenth century, the Dutch reversed their attitude. The influence of Rajah Brooke of Sarawak had become such that they feared he wanted to control all the interior of Borneo, and they felt the need to show their presence there. While the sultanates continued under the form of protectorates, the interior areas were controlled directly by the colonial administration, and the sultans' influence over central Borneo dwindled. Trade of course still took place between the interior and the coast; indeed, its volume increased considerably, but the relation was now purely economic, as political control was in other hands. In abolishing headhunting and slavery, the Dutch also eliminated significant factors of the traditional system.

Conclusion

In precolonial times, there was an uneasy balance between the central Borneo groups and the coastal Malay sultanates. *Stalemate* might be a better term. The Malays derived their wealth from the interior, but were unable to control it well; the groups of the interior were self-sufficient for the necessities of life, but could obtain trade goods only through the coast. There might have been reasons for maintaining amicable relations—and this indeed did take place—but the differences of interest were such that conflicts were inevitable. In order to have sufficient revenues and given the relatively modest volume of trade, the sultans were sometimes tempted to overtax the Dayak, who would then leave for the interior. To central Borneo people, Malay traders were a source of valued goods; but they were also fair game for headhunters. All these factors tended to limit the interaction between the two areas, and this was a relatively stable situation that neither group was in a position to change: the Malays were effectively too weak and the interior groups, who had the manpower, had neither the political organization nor the desire to control coastal areas.

References

Bock, Carl A. 1881. *The headhunters of Borneo: A narrative of travel up the Mahakkam and down the Barito*. London: S. Low, Marston, Searle and Rivington.

Commissie voor het adatrecht. 1937. Beradja Nanti (Niti). Het Koetaische rechtsboek (Tijd onbekend). *Adatrechtbundel* 39:299–342.

Eisenberger, J. 1936. *Kroniek der Zuider—en Oosterafdeeling van Borneo*. Bandjermasin: Liem Hwat Sing.

Grijzen, H. J. 1921. "Memorie van overgave, Zuider—en Oosterafdeeling van Borneo." Thirty-eight page manuscript in the Archives of the Ministry of Colonies, The Hague.

_____. 1925. Onze Dajak-politiek in Noord-Oost-Borneo. *Koloniaal Tijdschrift* 14:113–42.

Hageman, J. 1855. Aantekeningen omtrent gedeelte der oostkust van Borneo. *Tijdschrift van het Bataviaasch Genootschap* 4:71–106.

Hose, Charles. 1927. *Fifty years of romance & research; or, A jungle-wallah at large.* London: Hutchinson & Co.

Hose, Charles, and William McDougall. 1912. *The pagan tribes of Borneo: A description of their physical, moral and intellectual condition with some discussion of their ethnic relations.* London: Macmillan.

Knappert, S. C. 1905. Beschrijving van de onderafdeeling Koetei. *Bijdragen tot de Taal-, Land- en Volkenkunde* 58:575–654.

Nieuwenhuis, A. W. 1904–1907. *Quer durch Borneo.* 2 vols. Leiden: E. J. Brill.

_____. 1936–37. Het dagelijksch bestaan van Dajakstammen in onafhankelijke streken. *Tropisch Nederland* 9:125–28, 143–44, 157–60, 168–73, 189–92, 205–208 221–24, 237–40, 251–56.

Rousseau, Jérôme, ed. 1974. *The peoples of central Borneo. Sarawak Museum Journal* 22 (special issue).

_____. 1979. Kayan stratification. *Man* 14:215–36.

Spaan, A. H. 1901. Extract uit de nota van overgave van der onderafdeeling Berouw. Twelve-page manuscript in the Archives of the Ministry of Colonies, The Hague.

St. John, Spenser. 1862. *Life in the forests of the Far East, or Travels in northern Borneo.* 2 vols. London: Smith, Elder & Co.

Walchren, E. W. F. van. 1907. Een reis naar de bovenstreken van Boeloengan (Midden-Borneo) 12 Nov. 1905–11 April 1906. *Tijdschrift van het Koninklijk Nederlandsch Aardrijkskundig Genootschap*, 2e ser. 24:755–844.

4

Transformations of State Power in Kelantan and Pahang, West Malaysia

William D. Wilder

Introduction

The formation of states is a nonstop process, by which I do not mean merely the creation of new states *ab origine*, a trend that has led for the past thirty years to the greatly expanded United Nations; I mean the drive to internal *trans*-formation, analogous to the perpetual socialization of persons.[1]

As ancient kingdoms extant today, the sultanates of the Malay Peninsula are a case in point. These Malay sultanates manifest a series of modern superimpositions on the traditional system that have taken place in such a manner that allowed the older, indeed quite ancient, forms of state to continue to have a viable existence. But in the process of adaptation, the ancient form has undergone major changes and has now assumed a different order of importance and significance in the contemporary Malaysian political system (Kahar 1970:2). In purely historical terms, the sultanates are straightforward instances of "constitutional monarchies," but in anthropological terms this judgment ignores a number of significant features, such as their subjects'—or peasant Malay—views of political action. Clive Kessler's recent monograph (1978) is directly concerned with this anthropological dimension; he argues that the political behavior of rural Kelantanese Malays has shown a continuous and active involvement with the traditional state system for more than a century (1838–1969) during which sound observations are recorded. Although I do not agree with all of Kessler's conclusions, I think it is worthwhile examining his proposition that observed political behavior in the 1960s in the state of

Kelantan, West Malaysia, can be understood as a transmuted form of much older, traditional behaviors.

Or the problem may be looked at in another way. What was the degree to which the traditional sultanates and other traditional states in Southeast Asia really functioned as significant units for action and policy? Does their modern persistence signify a continuity of function in political terms or merely an ossification? The problem now takes on a peculiarly Southeast Asian accentuation. Tambiah (1976) and Geertz (1980) have both commented anthropologically on the seeming paradox by which Southeast Asian states have persisted with little more than a ritual of power to lend them their political substance; thus "culture came from the top down while power welled up from the bottom" (Geertz 1980:85), a radical disjunction of the expressive and instrumental functions of power. In this distinctive manifestation of the state, existing in hundreds of named statelike entities in the course of history, the ruler was the center and focus of a *contemplative* "politics," while in the active political sense—where measurable resources were striven for in the day-to-day run of affairs—the ruler was "peripheral" (idem: 69). Winzeler (1976), in a discussion of the origins of this variety of the state, characterizes it as "incomplete" and, in a sense, "unsuccessful." In general, it is a type of state whose persistence appears to be in contradiction with the absence of effective means for ensuring the same state's survival.

Thus, we may ask how a "weak" state, with its "passive" and "peripheral" ruler, secures its continued survival, and how in the twentieth century, when such a state is, on the face of it, further weakened by the limitations of a modern constitution, it continues to wield influence in the political arena. How does the continued existence and persistence of the sultanate function as a focus of political thought and action in the countryside? Perhaps my second, more anthropological formulation, in which the sultanate acts in passive and symbolic ways, is the more accurate one for the understanding of "power." The examples below will indicate that some contemporary Malay villages show political responses of a kind we might call obstructionism and factionalism; they are responses to state-level activity and in some way express the villagers' relations to the state. I will suggest that a resistance to state control is taking place—on the evidence of these examples at any rate—on grounds of the perceived division or fragmentation of state authority and not on grounds of class antagonism, as some writings on social change in rural Malaysia have suggested. This is not an either-or argument: it holds simply that it is easier to account for local reactions, in Kelantan and Pahang states, in terms of traditional concepts of the state's unity (which includes a marked degree of local autonomy) than the imposed concepts of class formation and class conflict.

There are essentially two parts to the presentation of this argument: first, an outline of concepts of the state in Malay culture, and second, the nature of local-level political activity. After these are discussed and exemplified below, I discuss the lessons to be drawn.

Traditional Malay States

The formal structures of the traditional Malay sultanates are today preserved, along with certain constitutional powers, in nine[2] of the eleven states of West (i.e., peninsular) Malaysia. The salient features of the western Malayan states in the nineteenth century, just before colonial rule, are described anthropologically by John Gullick (1958) in an important—and perhaps still the best general—account of these sultanates; some of the key points of this monograph will serve as a background to the field reports from two states, Kelantan and Pahang.

The Malay states were modeled after the sultanate of Malacca. In the fifteenth and sixteenth centuries (1400–1511) "the Malacca sultanate was a compact and centralized political system which lived on the foreign trade of its port" (Gullick 1958:8; note: numbers in parentheses hereafter refer to page numbers in Gullick 1958). In 1511 Malacca was defeated by the Portuguese under Albuquerque and the Malacca ruling house established itself in neighboring Johore state. The other states of Pahang, Perak, Selangor, and Negri Sembilan, in different ways, also received ruling houses based on the pattern of Malacca. It should be remembered that Malacca itself was a reproduction, on a smaller scale, of the still earlier kingdoms of western Indonesia (7–8).

The northern peninsular states such as Kelantan became, after the fall of Malacca, tributaries of Siam, though at one time they had been under the control of Malacca. At the time the British arrived on the scene in the eighteenth and nineteenth centuries, each of the states of the western Malay Peninsula was established with a ruler, ordinarily called sultan, and with classes of royalty and aristocracy eddying around him. Under the Federation of Malaya Agreement of 1957, the rulers of all the nine states were made constitutional rulers of their own state within the federation and accorded the title Sultan (except for Perlis, with the title Raja, and Negri Sembilan, with title Yang di-Pertuan Besar). As Gullick rightly says, the influence of Malacca in the peninsula was "immense" (7).

The Malay word for state is *negri*. Originally the word meant "city," but in the later Malay states it came to mean an extent of territory under an independent ruler (sultan). However, the terrain in Malaya is such that premodern settlements almost invariably clung to "river-valleys and river basins with the access to the sea, and it was therefore the" river valley that was practically suited as the unit of political rule. (21)

There were three administrative units in a state—the state itself, the district, and the village. In the Malay states of the 1870s, each played different parts in the political system; they were not necessarily in a stable relation with one another.

The state itself was ruled by one member of a royal patriline who was called Sultan or, in Negri Sembilan, Yang di-Pertuan. He was surrounded by court officials drawn from royal or aristocratic patrilines. The state centered on the figure of the ruler. Moreover, "the functions of the royal ruler were to exercise the limited powers of central government, to conduct external relations, to provide leadership in foreign wars and to embody and symbolize the unity and welfare of the state" (21; cf. also 95).

The members of the royalty together formed something like a pa-trilineage (which in turn formed part of the ruling class); they derived their status from their proximity to the direct line of descent from the sultan (cf. 69). Other members of the ruling class were aristocratic because they de-pended politically on the sultan for their status, but were ranked on the basis of the arrangement of offices on the Malacca model; although in theory appointed by the sultan, they gained their offices through their successful control of a district in the state.

The ruling classes of each state intermarried among themselves. Inter-marriage across state frontiers was almost unknown (66). Each state, there-fore, maintained itself around the position of the sultan, upon which the justification of political power depended. The sultan was the "apex" of the political system.

Just as the traditional system of titles and status depended for its validity on the sultan, so the state itself was an entity rationalized by reference to the supernatural attributes of its ruler. The state thus had an existence independent of its real territorial extent. The state derived its "power" as much from its symbolism as from its powers of coercion. This power was invested in the ruler's majesty (*daulat*) (45), in the ceremonies of homage by local district chiefs, and in the state regalia of weapons and musical instruments and the various courtly splendors maintained by what funds the state could coax out of its chiefs. In these symbolic ways, the state maintained a cultural "stagecraft" not unfamiliar to Malaysian immigrants from Java and Sumatra. The state was a symbolic unity; the strength of the state's symbolism served to maintain its outward form while the actual conditions of economic and political conflict disrupted its practical life (132–34; cf. Milner 1982:51).

Observers were, and are, struck by the small scale of the Malay states relative to their "great tradition" pretensions (cf. Scott 1977). In 1607 the Dutch admiral Matelief called with his ship at Kuala Pahang, on the east coast of the Malay Peninsula facing the China Sea. He reported the Pahang capital settlement, not far away, as "of mediocre size" (Linehan 1936:39–40). "The houses are of reed and straw except the King's palace which is made of wood" (quoted in Linehan). As late as 1971 an anthropologist's impression of the Pahang royal capital shows it as "essentially rural"; Pekan, the capital, is conspicuously dominated by "Malay-style attap-roofed, wooden houses on stilts grouped into clusters of kampongs," by traditional markets, and by the persistence of many traditional crafts and means of transport (Nagata 1979:62). So much for the state's central organ, represented by its ruler and his court.

The state's territory was divided into districts, *daerah* or *jajahn*: "Like the state . . . a district was either an area lying on one or both sides of a reach of the main river of the state or it was a side valley down to the point of junction with the main stream" (21). Authority in the district rested with the chief, who was styled *Datok* or *Tuan*. This chief was drawn from the patriline that held control in the district, and in theory, his appointment was approved by the sultan of the state; the chief owed allegiance to the sultan according to his rank among the chiefs in the state. The manner in which a chief fulfilled his allegiance varied enormously.

The village (*kampung*) was the smallest political division of the state; one or more villages were grouped under a headman (*penghulu*), a commoner. The village was the social and residential unit for most Malays, and in the typical state the villages were the productive sector of the economy; they were also subject to calls by district or local chiefs for labor, tribute in goods or money, and fighting men. Unlike the districts, among whose leaders there was often fighting, the villages were not fixed units. Civil wars served rather to keep the *kampungs* mobile. Where disorder was worst, "it was said of the Malay chiefs in the 1870's that they were quite ignorant of the numbers of settled, wandering and floating population of their districts" (23). Every man before 1874 was said to go armed literally to the teeth with not only his *kris* (Malay dagger) but with many other kinds of weapons.

The traditional (precolonial) Malay state (cf. Reid and Castles 1975; Andaya 1979) lacked what we now call an infrastructure. It lacked governmental or legal structures (Milner 1982:8). In the eyes of many well-informed nineteenth-century observers, it lacked territorial definition (ibid.). Toward the twentieth century, however, the colonial regime in Malaya— from 1889 in Pahang state—made up for all these defects. As I have already stated, the colonial development resulted in an amalgam of state forms, rather than the disappearance of the old state.

Vernaculars of Power

As compared with better-known occidental kingships and oriental despotisms, the Malay states might better be thought of as quasi-states. Rome's statecraft consisted in its ability to tax the realm. After A.D. 500, this form of state power had almost disappeared in the West, though not in Byzantium and the Arab states. The early Islamic states of the Near East taxed not only trade and commerce but also (and more important) land.[3] Malay rajadoms, by contrast, did not usually have the means of taxation and particularly not land taxation. Moreover, their populations were both fluid and mobile and small in numbers, typically of the order of several thousands; this is not large as compared with the *smallest* political units of traditional Chinese, Hindu, or Arab states, which were organized into substantial "lineages," "sub-castes," or "clan-sections." The Malay state might best be thought of as an enlarged family-household. Hence the Malay state was, in effect, an extension of the ruler's household and was run on similar lines.[4] Milner argues that Malay states were "in the final analysis, commercial ventures" (1982:16). He remarks how the sultan or raja financed his activities through ad hoc means more resembling predation and plunder (*merampas*, looting) than regular taxation (1982: chapter 2).

This image of the royal coffers as consisting of plunder is still vivid in the minds of Pahang Malay villagers. When they reminisce about the old order in independent Pahang, they stress their efforts to *avoid* encounters with their raja (or *bendahara*, as the Pahang ruler was called before 1881), particularly when his men raided villages for village girls, virgins for the royal household. Such periodic royal incursions into the peaceable countryside are also called *merampas*. An analogous concern of Malay villagers was expressed even in the 1960s about the threat of—naturally unwelcome—advances by outsider-Chinese men to village wives, suggesting a transposition, to the modern day, of the primordial idea of citizens' rights.[5] Peasant villagers' attitudes toward the state may be seen as condensed very nicely in these graphic protestations.

Continuities of Kelantanese Politics

The next, and more difficult, part of the argument is to determine how this statutory personal, rather politically individual, rule by the Malay sultan, since overtaken by modern Western constitutional government and an up-to-date administration, continues to exhibit its political potential. I will present examples of this historical problem, though less for purposes of documentation than as stimulus for interpretation. Specifically, how far are frictions in the modern political arena, especially in local politics, related to the traditional state? Clive Kessler argues that Kelantan state circa 1970 was the outcome of a hardening of the lines of class inequality, for which the seeds were laid down as early as the nineteenth century, long before British colonial intervention. Kessler's study reveals, in a wealth of local and historical details, the skillful maneuvering by several different parties, of the "old" and "new" orders, within the various Kelantan administrative niches.

Kessler observes particularly the way in which at critical moments

> Kelantanese politics were deadlocked at the highest level—in the capital, between rival elites, opposed factions, contending parties, between state and federal authority, and within the Majlis Ugama [Religious Council]— ... [also in the township there was] a bitter stalemate, depriving the Local Council of its ability to function. Similarly, extending their influence from the township to the villages, as they had from the capital to the township, the parties could not resolve, but could only deadlock the underlying social conflicts that they activated and articulated in the countryside [1978:240].

He judges that Kelantanese peasants in the 1960s were engaged in a "politics of survival, replete with dead ends, false starts and blind alleys" (idem: 244). The jostling for power through modern democratic procedures in newly independent Malaya (later Malaysia) led to a division of authority in the state (Kelantan); after its victory in 1959, the PMIP (Islamic party, opposed to the Alliance party, which was all-powerful in the rest of the federation) failed to capitalize on its electoral victory in relation to other branches of the state's administrative apparatus—the Majlis Ugama (Religious Council) and the civil service, two elites rooted in the "old" order close to the sultan (1978:185–86).

Kessler describes Kelantanese state and local politics during the 1960s as a balanced opposition, but he then reduces them to "antagonistic class based interests," inviting us to assume that peasants in Kelantan constitute a distinct class and that, "contrary to the contention of many observers" of Malaysian political affairs (1978:241 n.1), social and economic class "exerts a clearly powerful influence upon Malay politics" (ibid.). He argues that modern party politics, once they intruded upon the indigenous and colonial background, both "transformed" and "perpetuated" older antagonisms. These antagonisms obtain between: town and country, nobles and peasantry, and traditional rulers and local leaders (1978:207). But if these are, as he says, "fundamental political antagonisms" (ibid.), then I do not see how they can all reduce to class interests. There seems to me to be a confusion here. (Compare Scott 1977, cited below.) Class interests require an alignment of some kind that the above list does not display in practice. Kessler's view of Kelantan is Eurocentric, in that the Malay concepts of class, ethnicity, the state, and even Islam (the last dealt with in a separate chapter) are subordinated to a strikingly conventional historical view of the supposed effects of colonialism. (See 1978:241.)

Class and Party

It would be foolish to deny that, in independent Malaysia, with its high standards of administration and its rapidly growing economy, class divisions have not formed on the usual social and economic grounds (cf. Nagata 1979:146). But I suggest that we cannot account satisfactorily for local-level Malay political behavior by means of an essentially Eurocentric model. The examples I shall give, from both Kelantan and Pahang, are salient instances of multilevel politics, in my experience; what we need, however, is a suitable sociopolitical framework to explain them. First let us briefly review the examples:

1. In the 1950s and 1960s the Kelantan peasants, as voters, showed a preference for PMIP (Islamic party) candidates who were "nonentities," persons with little education and little political experience, as against UMNO candidates who were better-educated and more experienced (Kessler 1978:169). This process resembles and may even be connected with an older tendency for village headmen to be men of minimal character and leadership abilities, as well as lacking in formal qualifications. This aspect of local leadership was of some concern to the Malaysian government in the 1960s. (See Wilder 1982:173–174.)
2. In the 1960s the PMIP ruling party in Kelantan tackled the "cardinally important matter" of land control and land development policy, in deliberate opposition to the Alliance (UNMO)-dominated central government. This rebellious position taken by PMIP entailed a loss of resources and hampered the long-term prospects of PMIP, but in Kessler's view, it nevertheless attracted decisive electoral support for PMIP from peasant voters at local and parliamentary levels. Kessler's meticulous study of the historical background to the agrarian politics of Kelantan shows that the above events are not freakish responses to new problems. The examples illustrate Kelantanese popular peasant reactions to a perceived fragmentation of state rule manifested by such tendencies as (a) elite control, and (b) various forms of landlordism. My interpretation of the peasantry's display of common cause in these two types of situations is that, in some way (as yet not clear from the evidence), they perceive the state (*negri*) to be benign when undivided (with its control rather remote from the villages) but malign and dangerous when fragmented into diverse organized groups in control. In short, the peasants are in reaction against the emergence of a state-within-a-state, the sort of development that takes place when there is a

rise of tenancies on agricultural land (or, alternatively, through competition between state and central government powers) or when the rise of party leaders and other elites threatens village consensus. Connected with such reactions is the occurrence of *factional* opposition.

3. Some parallel examples of political impasses can be given from Pahang state. I quote briefly from an account given in more detail elsewhere (Wilder 1982: chapter 9). In the 1960s in rural Pahang, the federal government undertook land development on a large scale. Certain of these schemes were implemented by Pahang state development agencies. (Pahang government was UMNO-dominated, like the federal government, and obstruction of these schemes at state level did not occur, as it had in Kelantan.) A puzzling feature of the state-implemented schemes—which on the whole were well organized and certainly well financed ventures—was the apathy or positive rejection of them by villagers, on a scale sufficiently extensive to cause or partly cause the failure of many schemes. The following lines were adapted from Wilder (1982:164–165):

An important factor in the widespread failure is almost certainly the low level of demand for new rubber land among Pahang Malay villagers. Why did the administrators overestimate land hunger in the villages?

The answer is that the information required to estimate accurately the villagers' demand for land, and therefore to regulate the supply, was distorted by the design of the programmes. In the late 1950's in newly independent Malaya, the criterion of accuracy in planning estimates was thought irrelevant. It was the conviction among policy-makers that rural development targets could be achieved by instituting 'crash programmes' which, as is well-known, are pre-set and characteristically rigid in their response patterns. In the villages, examples of this conviction are easy to find, and Malay villagers were well aware of the tendency of administrators to ignore local conditions. This knowledge may have been responsible for the many 'negative' reactions displayed by villagers to the Bukit Penak scheme.

This example describes the extension of state control over a major resource, rubber as a cash crop in Malay villages. But there is evidence to show that this extension of state control was in fact an interruption of the ongoing *local* responses, which were instrumental in the rapid opening up of new land. What had happened is that local land development had long since been stimulated directly by market forces. This can be seen from some simple statistics. During the decade 1951–60, the annual average price of rubber topped one hundred cents a pound in four years (1951, 1955, 1959, 1960) and fell below eighty cents in only two years (to sixty-seven cents in 1953–54). In the decade beginning one year later (1952–61), the increase in smallholder acreage planted with new rubber (presumably a direct response to price rises in the market) was, in percentage growth, greatest in Pahang state (30 percent). New rubber planting on Pahang smallholdings (both state-sponsored and individual new planting) increased by 44,000 acres (overall Federation of Malaya increase totaled 204,000 acres) (Jackson 1964:261–62, from Annual Report of the Rubber Research Institute 1962). The increase in new rubber planting for Pahang is probably an underestimate; Pahang was one of the difficult security areas during the emergency. Increased demand for new registrations of land titles and the security problems (slowdown in field survey reports, et cetera) resulted in a backlog of two-hundred-thousand land applications in all state land offices in the federation, and in 1960 a moratorium on further applications was imposed by the Kuala Lumpur (central government) administration. What was the effect in the villages? It seems certain that the backlog of smallholder applications and the booming rubber prices in the 1950s produced an increase in the *illegal* planting of rubber in some places. In the subdistrict of Bera, where I worked, squatting (or illicit planting of rubber) did exist, but not widely. However, at one village, Kampung Batu Papan, squatting was especially common; this was apparently the only village in the whole subdistrict with such a high rate of illicit occupation. But the fact was only discovered by the district land office when land thought to be unoccupied came to be inspected for land development. (This project was ultimately resited.) This same village was known throughout the subdistrict for severe factionalism; it even had two headmen, only one, of course, recognized by the administration. At one point the sultan of Pahang himself made a special visit to this troubled village to try to clear the air. In other villages, further signs of politically inspired factionalism appeared. (See Wilder 1982: chapter 8, especially 143–147 for examples.) Disputes over the government funding of mosque construction seem to have been common. Such are the responses of the peasantry—in terms of their agrarian understanding of external authority—in the two Malaysian states of Kelantan and Pahang. It is important to note that these two states show *similar* peasant responses despite different agrarian problems: in particular, PMIP never controlled the Pahang government (though it has a following in many villages) and the agricultural situations are entirely different. What then might this evidently common occurrence of squatting, obstructing, and disputing about mosque construction mean?

Discussion

Until 1960 or so, the majority of Malays in both Kelantan and Pahang lived on lands set aside in the early twentieth century by the British as "Malay Reservations." The Reservations Enactment meant that these Malays, as peasants depending on access to land, did not have to compete with non-Malays for their essential means of livelihood. I suggest that this historic form of land provision (cf. Kessler 1978:69) functioned as crucial

extension of the traditional Malay sultanates, in which all land theoretically belonged to the ruler; the land, in other words, insulated Malays
from their ruler as well as from non-Malays. Land is of little if any political
importance from the point of the modern complex state, which attempts to
extend state control over *all* resources. The traditional ruler symbolized the
unity of the realm, and he was the sole arbiter in the affairs of the state
(although in practice, the local chief often served this role); the ruler was
also remote from the localities. The colonial regime preserved this fiction
remarkably well, with its various measures to protect on the one hand the
rulers and on the other the traditional communities. Only with independent Malaysia did the new forms of state seriously begin to erode the
structure of traditional rule.

How might we interpret these varied yet distinctive peasant responses to
the exercise of external "power"? If factional responses paralyze the state's
maneuvers to extend its decision-making and other powers to village level,
do they serve thus to resist and weaken state instructions? It does seem as
though they ensure, if only for a period of time, the continued remoteness
of the "new" outside leadership. I am here touching on a theme that runs
constant through the history of world peasantry—that of antirepression.
As broached by James Scott and others, Malay local-level responses would
manifest themselves as the "shadow society" or as "counterpoint" to elite
politics originating in the center (Scott 1977:19, citing Wertheim). The
shadow society thus derives from the state's actions. The constant opposition that peasant communities seem to present to elite governance does *not*
always take the form of violent rebellion, but shows itself also in a variety
of local ritual, symbolic, and legal "deviations" from the pattern of the
dominant culture. It would be instructive, in the light of this argument, to
know if factions and other political obstructions are charted in the new
colonies of agriculturalists (FELDA and the like); I would guess that this
type of activity is not a great problem in such novel contexts—but I could
be wrong! Field data drawn from these new environments would be a
valuable test of the present argument.

Notes

1. At long last, this notion of a perpetual socialization or relearning as distinct from
   primary socialization has been given a name: metanoia (Burridge 1979). This
   term connotes an everyday change-of-state-of-being, "a continuing and ongoing
   series of developmental transformations . . ." (Burridge 1979:210).
2. In the nineteenth and early twentieth centuries these nine states had traditional
   rulers who were progressively "tamed" (to use Heather Sutherland's apt description) by the British through various forms of indirect rule. The remaining two
   peninsular states were (with British Singapore) only port enclaves, like Macau

and Hong Kong. Malaysia's eleven peninsular states first came together as the independent Federation of Malaya in 1957. Singapore initially gained its independence in 1959 and then again in 1965 after two years as a part of Malaysia.

3. I am indebted to the talk given by Dr. Christopher Wickham "Political Power in Early Islamic States: A Set of Propositions," delivered to a seminar in the School of Oriental Studies and Center for Middle Eastern and Islamic Studies, University of Durham, February 24, 1983.

4. The newly independent sultanate of Brunei is today and in practical terms organized in just this way. It is "a highly personalized and somewhat anachronistic system of government. The sultan rules not by the constitution introduced in 1959, but under a state of emergency, though its powers are rarely invoked. Nobody seems have much idea of what, if anything, the state officials do. The dividing line between state funds and the royal purse has not been identified. 'This is a privately owned country,' said one banker, explaining the establishment attitude to such issues. 'You're being rude. You're asking to see the sultan's private checking account and it's none of your business.'" (N. Cumming-Bruce, *The Guardian*, May 20, 1983). In a later dispatch, on the eve of independence, the same writer quotes the acting chief minister of Brunei as saying that in a system in which almost all state business, from oil policy to civil servants' leave, requires the sultan's official approval: "We do not want to be ruled by labourers and taxi drivers, but by those who know how."

5. A traditional-modern parallel is used to effect by Pramoedya Ananta Toer in his novel recently translated as *This Earth of Mankind* (Bumi Manusia). He portrays the traditionalist mother explaining to her son: "'In the bygone ages,' Mother began, just as she did when I was still small, 'countries would wage all-out wars to win a maiden like my daughter-in-law, *mbedah praja, mboyong putri*, was our ancestors' proverb, victory over kingdoms, possession of its princesses. Today things are more secure. It's not like it was when I was little, let alone when your Grandmother was little. Even though the Dutch are so very powerful they have never stolen people's wives or daughters like the kings who ruled our ancestors. Ah, Child, had you lived in those days you would have been constantly called to the battlefield to be able to keep possession of your wife, that angel.'" (Pramoedya 1982:285). Pramoedya intends ironic suspense in this passage, since almost immediately the reader discovers that Dutch colonial law, successor to traditional royal rule, does remove the son's wife.

6. It was said that the troublemakers were outsiders, mostly Kelantanese, who originally paid the headman to let them settle in the village. Kelantanese emigrate in large numbers because of the land shortage in Kelantan. North-central Pahang lies on the railway line from Kelantan and is therefore a stopping place for emigrants from Kelantan.

7. Also see, for example, Geertz 1973: 406–407 on "counteractive, subdominant themes" in cultures; Goody 1983: 183f. on the hidden hostility to imposition of Christian norms in early Europe; and Gilsenan 1982: 228–29 on oppositions within the culture of the Holy Law in the contemporary Middle East.

References

Andaya, B. W. 1979. *Perak: The abode of grace, a study of an eighteenth century Malay state.* Kuala Lumpur: Oxford University Press.

Burridge, Kenelm. 1979. *Someone, no one: An essay on individuality.* Princeton: Princeton University Press.

Geertz, Clifford. 1973. *The interpretation of cultures: Selected essays.* London: Hutchinson; New York: Basic Books.

_____. 1980. *Negara: The theater state in nineteenth-century Bali.* Princeton: Princeton University Press.

Gilsenan, M. 1982. *Recognizing Islam: An anthropologist's introduction.* London: Croom Helm.

Goody, Jack. 1983. *The development of the family and marriage in Europe.* Cambridge: Cambridge University Press.

Gullick, J.M. 1958. *Indigenous political systems of Western Malaya.* London School of Economics Monographs on Social Anthropology no. 17. London: Athlone Press.

Jackson, J. C. 1964. Smallholder cultivation of cash crops. In *Malaysia: A Survey,* ed. Wang Gung-wu. London: Pall Mall Press, pp. 246–73.

Kahar Bador, A. 1970. *Political authority and leadership in Malay society in Perak, Malaysia.* Tokyo: Institute of Developing Economies.

Kessler, C. S. 1978. *Islam and politics in a Malay state: Kelantan 1838–1969.* Ithaca: Cornell University Press.

Linehan, W. 1938. A history of Pahang. *Journal of the Malayan Branch Royal Asiatic Society* 14 (2):1–256; Malaysian Branch Royal Asiatic Society Reprints no. 2, 1973.

Milner, A. C. 1982. *Kerajaan: Malay political culture on the eve of colonial rule.* AAS Monograph 40. Tucson: University of Arizona Press.

Nagata, J. A. 1979. *Malaysian mosaic: Perspectives from a polyethnic society.* Vancouver: University of British Columbia Press.

Pramoedya Ananta Toer. 1982. *This earth of mankind* (Bumi Manusia: A novel). Harmondsworth: Penguin Books.

Reid, A., and L. Castles, eds. 1975. *Pre-colonial state systems in Southeast Asia: The Malay Peninsula, Sumatra, Bali-Lombok, South Celebes.* Monographs of the Malaysian Branch of the Royal Asiatic Society no. 6. Kuala Lumpur: MBRAS.

Scott, J. C. 1977. Protest and profanation: Agrarian revolt and the little tradition. *Theory and Society* 4:1–38, 211–46.

Tambiah, S. J. 1976. *World conqueror and world renouncer: A study of Buddhism and polity in Thailand against a historical background.* Cambridge: Cambridge University Press.

Wilder, William D. 1982. *Communication, social structure and development in rural Malaysia: A study of Kampung Kuala Bera.* London School of Economics Monographs on Social Anthropology no. 56. London: Athlone Press.

Winzeler, Robert L. 1976. Ecology, culture, social organization, and state formation in Southeast Asia. *Current Anthropology* 17(4):623–32.

5

State Formation and the Incorporation of Nomads: Local Change and Continuity among Jordanian Bedouin

Joseph M. Hiatt

The integration of nomadic populations has proved to be an especially intractable problem facing some developing nations in this century. In many cases, the nomads have enjoyed free-booting earlier existences, and characteristically they have a strong preference for their way of life, scorning central government, its agents, peasants, and other sedentary people. When central government has gained the advantage of administrative authority and superior armed forces, the nomads still have tended to resist public service programs and other administrative overtures as attempts to suppress them. Nor has this suspicion been wholly unwarranted, since nomads have been widely viewed with resentment by their governments, and they are even regarded by some development planners and administrators as social evolutionary throwbacks who must be drawn into the larger social order. What is more, the method most frequently chosen for dealing with nomads has been planned sedentarization; therefore, while the avowed aim of such schemes always is to integrate the nomads to enhance their living standard, the goal most often appears to be to deal with the social reality by trying to obliterate it.[1] Yet not all cases of nomad integration have progressed under conditions quite as harsh as hinted above; nor for that matter have all instances of sedentarization resulted from state-implemented programs.

This chapter concerns the experience of nomads who, unaccustomed to governmental control, suddenly found themselves enclosed within a new state and eventually became integrated within it. Specifically, it deals with the Khreisha hamula (i.e., approximately a maximal lineage) of the Beni

Sakhr bedouin tribe who were encapsulated within the Emirate of Trans-jordan in 1921 and became sedentarized after it was reconstituted into the Kingdom of Jordan in 1948.[2] Their integration into the state appears at first glance to have been voluntary, but in reality it was urged on by exter-nal forces. Indeed, the very formation of the state and the encapsulation of the Khreisha were important contributors to the process. Additional forces were involved, moreover, some with more immediacy and even with dire effect, and the following discussion attempts to give proper perspective to the effect of these various influences.

The first section of the chapter reconstructs the pre-emirate so-ciopolitical organization of the Khreisha as well as their pastoral economic system around 1921 and briefly discusses the corporate character of the lineage. The next section describes important events that had traceable impact on the integration of the nomadic Khreisha into the state. That discussion begins with the creation of the emirate, mentions measures that the new government undertook to develop itself and to establish its au-thority over the bedouin, and then widens in scope to include environmen-tal and international economic forces impinging on the Beni Sakhr. The primary agent in the development of the desert region and the bedouin of Jordan has been the army, and attention is given here to the role it played in changing attitudes and activity patterns of the Khreisha. The final section of the paper focuses on the political organization of those bedouin, high-lighting changes and continuities in their authority structure that contrib-uted to their integration into the state.

Pre-emirate Economy and Political Organization

The Khreisha are members of the Beni Sakhr, one of the most powerful and respected bedouin tribes of the Kingdom of Jordan. The tribe is seg-mentary in makeup, being divided into the Twaqa' and Ka'abna, which I have called clans (Hiatt 1981: 68–69), subdivided into lineages such as the Khreisha, and further subdivided down to the level of the family. In other words, the tribal organization largely conforms to the descriptions con-tained in the basic anthropological literature on such structures (e.g., Evans-Pritchard 1940, 1949), although it also exhibits inconsistencies, such as foreshortened genealogies and unbalanced segments, similar to those observed by Peters (1960) among the Sanusi bedouin of Cyrenaica, Libya. Documentary sources indicate that the tribe has been so structured at least throughout the span of its known history.

The tribe and its subsections over the centuries have relied for their leadership upon individuals distinguished for their wisdom, generosity, vigor, strength of following, and other qualities. Those leaders, or sheikhs, served as spokesmen at whatever level of the tribal structure they were recognized and embodied the honor and integrity of the part for which they stood. They also gave feasts and entertained in its name and arbitrated disputes between its members. Yet such individuals led by consent and depended upon the consensus of their followers, and if they ceased to display their honorable qualities or died, their adherents could melt away. In this sense, the tribe with its segmentary structure would appear to be incapable of establishing or maintaining permanent offices of leadership that remain when vacated by an incumbent to be filled by another.

The closest approximation to the development of such positions among the Beni Sakhr has occurred when certain lineages of the tribe grew in strength of numbers and, apparently with great consistency, produced outstanding individuals with leadership qualities, thereby fostering for themselves reputations as sheikly groups. Such was the case with the Khreisha with respect not to the entire tribe but at the subtribal level of the Ka'abna, where they have exercised leadership for at least a century and a half.

Besides their reputation as a lineage of sheikhs, the Khreisha have enjoyed long-standing esteem among Transjordanian bedouin as members of a powerful camel-herding tribe, one of the so-called noble bedouin tribes. The camel carried more value among desert bedouin and brought to its owner greater prestige as a stock animal than did the sheep. The Khreisha, of course, needed mutton and wool, which they obtained by raiding or from client tribes or sheepherding bedouin in return for protection and acts of assistance in time of hardship. The Khreisha were, in fact, multiresource exploiters, drawing their sustenance from pastoral and nonpastoral sources, yet until their encapsulation within the new state, they were primarily nomadic pastoralists whose economy centered on camel raising. And when they began herding sheep, most certainly for the first time, as a result of recent historical developments, it may be imagined to have been regarded as something of a decline in their circumstances.

For livestock raising without benefit of fodder or feed substitutes the pastoralist needs pasturage and water for his herds; he also needs land on which these resources can be found in sufficient abundance and distribution for him to move his animals during the year from grazed out areas to fresh pasture with adequate water supplies. The Beni Sakhr, over the course of several centuries, established such a tribal territory, now covering most of the northern half of the current Kingdom of Jordan and stretching from the mountainous rim of the Jordan Valley on the west into the north Arabian Desert in what is today Saudi Arabia in the east.

In broad terms, their pastoral use of that territory and its resources year after year took the following pattern: In the winter season they migrated to the eastern part of their territory where the land dips down into an extensive valley system (the Wadi Sirhan). Rain trapped on the valley floor soaks into the ground, and this usually afforded the herders excellent pasturage. Numerous deep wells dotting the upper edge of the valley and claimed by the bedouin assured them of ample water, and the valley depression sheltered them and their livestock against severe winter winds. With the arrival of spring the bedouin moved back westward out of the desert and to the edge of the populated zone, where rainfall is normally greater and agriculture is practiced. During years of good rainfall they could move leisurely across the intervening desert and steppe in an irregular path; but when rain was scarce they would need to cross their territory quickly to take advantage of any pasturage and puddles that might have appeared in the temperate zone following the winter season. Man-made pools and naturally occurring underground cavities that catch rain runoff, along with a few streams among the western hills, provided other water resources. As for pasturage when resources were poor, the bedouin resorted to supplies obtained from peasant cultivators.

Trading, another component of the economy of these multiresource exploiters, was one method of obtaining goods from settled populations. The opinion, based on recent research, spreading among scholars who care about nomads, holds that most such peoples in historical and current instances have been dependent in some way upon sedentary producers of food and other commodities (cf. Spooner 1972:126f.). This was certainly true of the Khreisha, who as bedouin pastoralists produced only part of the food and goods they used. They neither grew barley, wheat, or other crops, produced tea, worked metal, nor engaged in other activities to meet their basic needs. It was not that agriculture or other occupations tied to fixed locations were inconvenient for them to undertake as nomads; instances of cultivating nomads are known from Iran and elsewhere (e.g., Salzman 1971). Rather, with apparent similarity to many known nomadic groups, the Khreisha firmly believed in the superiority of their nomadic life and held in contempt sedentary peoples and all aspects of their existence, such as agriculture and landownership (*pace* Kazziha 1972: 18). Around the turn of this century, for example, the Ottoman government tried to bribe the Khreisha into settling down with offers of landownership, and those nomads refused on the grounds that it would make them like peasants. Traces of this contempt, in fact, are evident today among Khreisha who are now settled. To obtain items they could not, or would not, produce, the Khreisha and their fellow Beni Sakhr tribesmen traded for them, usually in well-protected markets of larger towns. When possible they extorted the goods from peasants or they raided and took them, these two practices constituting the remaining components of the Khreisha economic system.

The practice of extortion actually was a protection-for-a-price agreement. The bedouin presented a perpetual threat of raiding to settled cultivators who invested themselves in their land and crops and were disinclined to leave them. The bedouin exploited that sense of immobility by arranging not to raid the peasants' villages and fields and to protect them from other bedouin marauders in return for payment of tribute in the form of needed goods and food. In this way the Khreisha and other Beni Sakhr subgroups were able to control a number of peasant villages as virtual feudal fiefs, and they even spoke, and still do speak, of those relationships as "owning" the villages.[3]

As for actual raiding, it was carried out against other bedouin tribes, villages and farms, and even government-sponsored caravans on the pilgrimage to Mecca. However, unless the raid was part of a blood feud and an act of warfare, killing was to be avoided, the aim being to take booty. From bedouin tribes that often meant theft of livestock, and in this regard the raid served a crucial function for the Khreisha and other bedouin. In times of drought animal stock are vulnerable and can die off quickly and in large numbers. Theft of stock is another way by which herds could be depleted suddenly and sharply. Rebuilding the herd through animal reproduction would take too long, whereas raiding provided the pastoralist with a useful, if somewhat strenuous and even risky, method of quickly regaining mature animals needed to sustain a pastoral enterprise (cf. Sweet 1965).

In most instances, individual males owned the livestock and responsibility for making decisions on herd management and movement lay with them; however, use of Khreisha land was governed by a collective principle, showing that in certain matters the group subsumed the individual. Right of access to the territory and its resources was tied to membership of the Beni Sakhr, and when drought or other disaster decreased the pasturage or water supplies, their utilization was overseen by the sheikh who helped sort out disputes over priority of access. Further, non–Beni Sakhr were usually obliged to obtain approval of the tribe through the person of its sheikh in order to use the resources.

It is apparent that the Khreisha regarded themselves as a distinct section of the Beni Sakhr tribe with their own identity, and at times they functioned as a corporate entity. In its strict economic-legal sense, corporate organization serves the purpose of moving liability away from individual group members, whereas anthropological usage of the term *corporation* mostly emphasizes the element of the group members functioning as a unity, sharing rights and responsibilities. That is, liability is moved toward human partners by being spread over the whole or at least to more than just one of the members. Such was and still is true among the Khreisha, whose members are committed to a web of joint responsibilities and rights. In cases of homicide, for example, the Khreisha share the guilt for a murder committed by one of them and would be vulnerable, under certain conditions, to acts of revenge by the victim's relatives. They also feel impelled to seek revenge for murder or injury perpetrated against one of them. This sense of linkage and its obligations and prerogatives are limited in practice, if not in theory, and the intensity of feeling is weaker between Khreisha who share no ancestor within the preceding four or five generations. But generally this reduced support and sense of cohesion only become apparent in disputes within the Khreisha, especially between members of the two major alignments of families, which occasionally surface in Khreisha affairs.

The Khreisha continued as nomadic pastoralists throughout the 1940s and into the 1950s, when the first of them began to settle down at a site on the edge of the Jordanian desert-steppe. By that time they had adopted agriculture to the extent that they had peasants cultivating plots of land in their territory; they had accepted landownership in principle and practice, and they had abandoned herding camels for the less prestigious sheep. They were also serving in the national army and had adopted alien political structures for contacting the central government, whose authority they had acknowledged in other ways as well. Various fundamental features of their structure are still evident, such as remnants of the corporate character of their lineage; however, their existence has also changed in social, political, and economic aspects. The ensuing discussion describes continuities and changes that have emerged among the Khreisha following their incorporation into the newly formed state, and special attention is directed at political developments, the introduction of fixed governmental offices into the tribal setting, and the impact that had on the sheikh's authority. Before considering those effects, however, some space should be given to the events and processes which were important in bringing them about, by way of background.

Formation of the State

The Beni Sakhr and other powerful bedouin tribes dominated Transjordan under the Ottoman administration because it was on the edge of the empire, far from the center of administrative power. The government regarded the area primarily as a source of tax revenues and, being otherwise little interested in it, committed few troops there. Further, this frontier abutted the desert, where the bedouin were at home, and they could raid settlements and evade punishment by fleeing into the desert, which the governmental troops did not know.[4] This situation changed with the collapse of the Ottoman empire and withdrawal of its claim to Transjordan in 1917, followed by the establishment in 1921 of the British Mandate Commission with authority over the area and later by the creation of the Arab Emirate. Transjordan then became a political entity in itself with a government directly interested in imposing order on the area and soon possessed of an army that tried to do so.

As one step in that direction the emirate government saw the usefulness of integrating the nomads into the state, but measures it undertook toward that end were ill-conceived or ill-used and failed. For example, a structure with oversight powers, the Bedouin Control Board, was set up to give special attention to bedouin matters and with sole authority to review complaints and legal cases involving the nomads. Also, two seats in the National Assembly were reserved for the tribesmen of the desert zone to ensure that they had a voice in shaping policy that affected them. The board failed after it had been used by its first president to serve his ambitions, and it fell into disuse and was eventually abolished. The legislative opening, too, helped the bedouin little, because they shared few interests with sedentary sectors of the general citizenry and shunned coalition building. While these measures led nowhere, other events involving no specific governmental intention to integrate the nomadic tribesmen had a more effective impact: among them were the creation of international borders and the imposition of transit requirements, the establishment of a standing army with a desert police force, and government reform of the agricultural and land-tenure conditions in the country.

The new international borders exerted a relevant force because they were drawn athwart the migrational routes of the Beni Sakhr, the Huwaytat, and other Transjordanian tribes; and they led to the obstruction of bedouin movement between their summer and winter pastures. It is true that bedouin are not respecters of such artificial barriers, and the greater part of the hindrance actually arose from enforcement of the transit regulations governing the border areas. These were written when the borders were drawn and included the alien obligation that the bedouin officially clear border crossings; they also subjected the nomads to searches at the border for contraband goods and scrutinization of their livestock by head counts. Further difficulties with the border emerged because the new Saudi and Transjordanian governments tried to disrupt each other by alternately wooing and harassing the other's bedouin into changing their national affiliation.

Of all factors that figured into the bedouin integration, however, the national army was especially beneficial. Indeed, it played such a central role in the lives of the nomads that it deserves detailed attention here. Succinctly stated, the military was the medium by which the Khreisha and other bedouin became persuaded to accept the central government and by which they were encouraged to adopt agriculture and other features of modernization. This was remarkable, because bedouin such as the Khreisha had a long-standing, one might almost say congenital, suspicion of central governments and a contempt for sedentary people such as peasant agriculturalists. Yet by the 1950s the Khreisha had revised their ideas and values on these points and were themselves settling down, as well as serving in the army conspicuously and with loyalty. It was remarkable not only that the bedouin changed their attitudes and accepted agriculture, education, and the authority of the central government through the agency of the army, but that they had accepted the army as a source of innovation and help in the first place. The overriding questions needing answers are, Why did they turn to the army and What set of circumstances led them to submit to its influence?

A number of factors combined to make the bedouin alter their long-held beliefs and attitudes concerning sedentary peoples and government; particularly notable were developments in the environmental, economic, and political spheres. The environment, for one, exerted an especially negative force. The late 1920s and the decade of the 1930s—in other words, the years of the British Mandate and the early emirate after creation of the national army—brought a series of droughts to Transjordan, which at times were so unremitting as to constitute practically a permanent catastrophe. Animal stock, sheep as well as camels, suffered greatly, and herds were sorely run down. In his reports on the region for some of those years, Capt. John Glubb, the desert administrator under the Mandatory Commission, evoked pictures of the steppe land strewn with sheep carcasses. Herd owners tried to recover some of their losses resulting from mortality and diminished animal quality by selling from their remaining stock. The net effect of that tactic, however, was to reduce the animal reserves in the desert further.

There was even a third force at work constricting the bedouin's circumstances. About this same time, the worldwide depression of the 1930s struck and local and international demand for meat dropped, dragging prices down. On top of their own problems of environmental disaster and economic privation, the bedouin were unable to sell stock animals as profitably as they had been able to do previously.

Together these environmental and economic events promoted the army among the bedouin for a straightforward reason: the nomads turned to it for their survival. In response to the drought and the catastrophic economic conditions in the countryside, the army offered grants of cash as well as food and grain assistance. Further, it provided jobs on road construction projects for bedouin and others who were suffering without income. Administrative reports on the desert region written during the 1930s reveal the crucial economic role that the army was filling, because entire families who were normally pastoralist were dependent on the salaries that individual members were earning as soldiers. The fact that the army was helping them, plus the benefit of a salary ensuring a livelihood, contributed to the development of an increasingly favorable attitude toward the army among the bedouin.

Also worth mentioning here was the improvement of the ability and reputation of the army as a fighting or kind of warrior force. That surely would have made turning to it for help somewhat easier to accept, because the Khreisha and other bedouin place high value on military strength and prowess. Along with the formation of the emirate there arose internal security needs, and as one step toward meeting those needs, the new government used its new army to eliminate bedouin raiding. The army's first successes were limited mainly to protecting villages in the more densely settled areas, while the bedouin continued their marauding and were only irregularly apprehended and punished for it. In the late 1920s a new unit, the Desert Patrol, was added to the military structure: its purpose was to police only the desert, and it was to be manned entirely by bedouin, on the belief that they would know best how to deal with the desert population. This force was enormously successful in chasing down raiders, in many cases confiscating their camels, and soon raiding had virtually disappeared among Transjordanian bedouin. Also, the decisive actions and the economically inconvenient punishments did not fail to impress the bedouin. By the late 1930s considerable prestige was being attached to membership in the ranks of the army and most particularly the Desert Patrol.

The army assisted the bedouin in other ways that most certainly influenced their attitudes and behavior. Two especially significant ones were the introduction of education and the establishment of schools in the desert and the encouragement of the Khreisha and others to accept cultivation, at least to rent out their land for additional income. Schools initially were held at police posts or in tents and were movable, so that they could follow the bedouin on parts of their migrations; later they were housed in fixed structures. In this way a school was periodically convened and, in the early 1950s, was established at the place where the Khreisha eventually chose to settle. At first, attendance was sporadic and the number of students limited, mostly to the sons of sheikhs; however, by the 1970s attendance, being mandatory, had become general if not universal. And those Khreisha who had acquired educations were applying them in professional, governmental, and other occupations.

As for agriculture, the Khreisha decision to allow cultivation experimentally in their territory was timely for governmental purposes and had a marked impact on those bedouins' attitudes toward their tribal land and affected their corporate identity.

The emirate government soon after its creation promulgated a policy of land survey and title reform that had the dual aims of clearing up the confused land-tenure system remnant from the Ottoman Empire and of taking stock of the fledgling emirate's agricultural resources. The project was comprehensive and began with a survey covering the settled parts of the country, where all cultivated land was measured and boundaries delineated, and then extended to the desert-steppe, where potentially arable land was sought and recorded.[5] The government dealt with the bedouin territories by registering them in the names of tribal sheikhs.

According to earlier practice among the tribes, the territory was overseen and managed by the sheikh in trust for the group, although all members had access to it. From an outsider's perspective the act of registration might have had the appearance of a mere formality, the noting on paper of a situation that already existed. Yet significant in this development was the governmental intrusion into the relation of bedouin to the territory that they had won and occupied over a period of hundreds of years. No less noteworthy was the fact that the alien device of title registration had been applied to their land and they had obviously acceded to its use.

From this beginning the hand of the government has become more authoritative with regard to the tenure of the Khreisha and other bedouin in their traditional grazing lands. Since the first survey was conducted forty years ago, two others have been conducted in Khreisha territory, and with each one the once corporately held lands were increasingly subdivided. Plots were registered in the names of additional individuals who began using the lands for their separate livelihood. Some became landlords, continuing the practice of rental to peasants and Palestinian cultivators for income; some more recently have even sold parcels of land to raise capital for investment in trucking and other ventures.

The Khreisha, who originally scorned sedentary people and their way of life, in the 1930s had submitted their territorial control to the scrutiny and authority of the central government and had begun to rely for sustenance upon its army and upon income obtained from the occasional rental of land. Finally, in the 1950s they began to settle at one of the sites used for agricultural purposes within the desert-steppe but close to the edge of the temperate zone.

Explaining their sedentarization obviously would be made quite simple if one factor had been the sole effective or even the dominant cause, yet oral and documentary sources suggest that although the Khreisha did choose to settle, they acted so under the weight of a number of factors. The army, for example, exerted an influence by making steady incomes and highly valued vocations accessible to bedouin, who previously had relied on the unpredictable, sometimes barely supportive, livelihood of pastoralism. It also diverted young men, at least temporarily, away from pastoral responsibilities and out of the family. Education, too, siphoned off some of the labor pool, although initially in small degree. From their dealings with the government Khreisha leaders began to realize that it was there to stay and that the bedouin would have to be educated and trained in useful skills if they were to compete in the new socioeconomic order and survive. And when the school was established in a fixed location in the early 1950s attendance was made easier by sedentarization, at least seasonally, of the children with women.

The practice of pastoralism became more difficult as personnel from the family or for hire were now harder to find at the same time that revenues from salaries and other sources were decreasing dependence on livestock for sustenance. Under these conditions some Khreisha were further moved to sell their herds, adding even more to their financial resources. The disposal of herds eliminated the main reason for the bedouin to move anymore, and for these among various other reasons the Khreisha saw wisdom in becoming sedentarized and began to settle.[6]

This section has barely outlined the proceess whereby the Khreisha became incorporated into the Emirate of Transjordan and later became sedentarized in the reconstituted Kingdom of Jordan. Over the period of their encapsulation the Khreisha have endured changes of their societal organization and economic system, of their attitudes and values, and certainly a modification of their ideology of the superiority of the nomadic way of life. The following, final section focuses on a narrow range of phenomena—change in the political organization of the Kreisha, specifically their authority structure, and the way those changes fitted into the increasing administrative integration of those bedouin.

An earlier section of this paper represents the tribe as a segmentary structure seemingly incapable of developing and maintaining permanent offices of leadership. It also indicates that tribal leaders have been acknowledged and that certain tribal subgroups (such as the Khreisha) have even been able to establish reputations, as sheikhly lineages characterized by honorable and esteemed individuals with leadership qualities. The sheikh had the authority to summon a council of the heads of lineages or households for discussion of issues and the making of decisions affecting the tribe or his portion of it, yet in a sense, too, he led by following. Such gatherings enabled group members to air their views, and during the discussion the leader often served more to elicit and guide debate in order to obtain a sense of prevailing opinion. The sheikh was also the spokesman for his particular section, representing it and its position in dealings with outsiders. This, in general form, was the political structure of the Khreisha when the British Mandate was imposed on the area. The British, using lessons on indirect rule learned in Africa, found in Transjordan a social setting not incompatible with methods of administering local populations by means of indigenous leaders. The sheikh of the Khreisha at the time, for example, was a man of considerable honor and reputation, and recognizing this, the mandate administrators consulted him, as well as other sheikhs of the Beni Sakhr and other important tribes, in matters concerning the desert zone and bedouin administration. The arrangement remained thus throughout the period of the drought in the 1930s, the subsequent shift from camel to sheep pastoralism late in that decade and the 1940s, until the Khreisha began settling down in the 1950s around the time of that sheikh's death.

About that later time the political organization of the Khreisha underwent a fundamental change in that two permanent positions known as *mukhtars* were instituted with government encouragement within the Khreisha settlement. While not actually affixed to the tribal structure, those positions existed in its midst, being filled by members of the lineage. In all likelihood they were created to change the tribal authority structure by grafting onto it an alien political institution or to supplant tribal sheiks. If the latter had been the intent, there could not have been a better opportunity, with the recent death of the sheikh, to intrude some permanent office of authority. However, the *mukhtars* functioned in a clerical capacity, registering births, marriages, divorces, and other such events and helping the Khreisha to obtain government documents when needed; also they served in a general way as contacts between the bedouin and central government. With the filling of those two offices—by means of voting, no less—the Khreisha acknowledged the government's authority in yet another way, as they had done by acceding to the surveys and title registration of their land and by enlisting in the army and Desert Patrol.

The original occupants of those offices served the Khreisha for about twenty years, but eventually their positions became superfluous, and by the late 1970s they had ceased to play any useful role. One of the two incumbents no longer even resides in the Khreisha settlement. The other remains *mukhtar* in name only, although he is accorded some recognition at social gatherings on the basis of that position.

A major contributor to the decline of those offices was the introduction into the settlement of local representatives of governmental ministries and other administrative offices. During the two decades of the *mukhtars'* service, the government increased the number of services it offered to local populations, thereby creating a need for more efficient and specialized offices. In the present case, the registry function of the *mukhtars* was given to a civil servant within the Interior Ministry's department of civil affairs, while the responsibility of governmental contact was split between another civil servant in the local office (*an-nahiyya*) of the provincial administrative system and one of the Khreisha who was elected to a municipal position (*ra'is al-baladiyya*) somewhat akin to that of town manager.

The *mukhtars*, the first officeholders among the Khreisha, had by the 1970s been succeeded by more specialized officials, and by the end of the decade there were operating in the desert-steppe settlement of the Khreisha other offices staffed with civil servants, including a post office, a medical center for general medical care, and another for obstetric and pediatric care. The central government acquired an administrative link with the Khreisha settlement by means of the *mukhtars* and then multiplied its connection through numerous offices providing governmental services.

During the period that the *mukhtars* functioned and were replaced and partly because of the very rise of the state, the role of the sheikh has been diminished. He no longer possesses the authority or the power to extend his protection to all who come seeking it. As one of the Khreisha put it, "formerly he was *ad-dustour* (literally, 'the constitution') of the tribal section, but he's not so anymore." Once he would have been able—indeed, he would have been expected—to protect any murderer who fled to him for sanctuary against revenge killing by the victim's relatives; now he would be obliged to yield to the state if it wanted to prosecute the fugitive. This is a touchy issue because King Hussein has over the years depended upon bedouin support to quell attempted challenges to his reign and to keep him in power; therefore, it is likely that neither the throne nor the bedouin would want to reach a point of open conflict between their interests, between the sheikh's desire to maintain a public image of strength and generosity and the prerogatives of governing and power claimed by the state.[7]

Further, the creation of the *mukhtarships* and the addition of other offices have also taken away from the potential authority of the sheikh by sharing responsibilities among several individuals now located within the settlement. Whereas the sheikh served as the representative and contact person for outsiders dealing with his tribal section, this function then was shared with the *mukhtars*, and more recently government agents have taken a role in the contact function to the extent that they are now assigned to branch offices located in the settlement.

The sheikh does retain certain rights and authority. He can call together a sitting of the lineage men to make decisions on matters of importance to the lineage, and he is still visited in his tent by people seeking his influence or intervention in a problem or some other form of help. Also, while the town manager carries responsibility for overseeing the settlement and lobbying for government services, the sheikh has kept the role as spokesman for the lineage and exemplar of its honor and identity. Finally, his approval is a sine qua non for requests and other representations submitted to the government. In short, the sheikh has retained his structural position and his responsibility for the lineage, but his role has been narrowed and diminished in its prerogatives in the face of increasing needs and prerogatives of the state.

Summary and Conclusion

While they have been able to keep features of their tribal organization, the Khreisha have also endured extensive alterations and adjustments of their lives as they have become integrated within the emirate of Transjordan and the Kingdom of Jordan. This process in recent decades, i.e., since the emergence of the kingdom, has had the appearance of a voluntary undertaking. The government apparently had no specific program of sedentarization for the Khreisha or other Beni Sakhr, and its involvement with the Khreisha took the form mostly of grain assistance or provision of services such as education. Yet, viewed over the long term, from the moment of actual enclosure of the bedouin within the emirate, it emerges that the Khreisha became integrated and sedentarized and their society modified because of a series of intrusions by government and other external forces.

The creation of the emirate thrust obstacles in the form of international borders and the regulations attending them in front of the bedouin, restricting their customary nomadic pastoral activities, and the hindrance imposed by this political development was heightened by drought and global depression. Several changes of a basic nature occurred at this time or followed soon afterward, including the shift from camel pastoralism to the much less esteemed sheep raising and the reversal of bedouin attitudes toward the national army. At one time the Khreisha regarded with suspicion all dealings with central government and rejected its offers of assistance. Now they accept the rule of the king and the authority of his government. And the armed forces in their various branches are frequently sought as careers among bedouin men who are well represented at both the officer and enlisted levels. The Khreisha have altered their attitudes toward and their uses of their traditional territory, too. Once corporately held and exploited by all of the lineage and overseen in trust by the sheikh, it is now subdivided, dispersed to individual plot holders, and registered separately in their names and is used for personal ends. The integration of the Khreisha, in other words, has brought changes of customary practice as well as revisions of ideologies and values, and all of it occurred by degrees and was influenced by factors beyond the control of the Khreisha. In this sense their integration is to be understood as having had voluntary and involuntary elements in its occurrence.

Notes

1. In recent years confidence in sedentarization as a means of elevating the economic circumstances of nomadic populations has declined. In numerous projects aiming at sedentarization or other forms of intervention the results have not come close to those planned or desired. One major development agency (USAID) has even begun to reevaluate its commitment to such programs and is reportedly planning to cut them back in at least some geographical areas.
2. See Bailey (1969: 147–48) for a discussion of encapsulation as a technical concept.
3. The bedouin did not always have the upper hand in these situations, as indicated by one report of the townspeople of Tafila in southern Transjordan becoming resentful at their subordinate status, hiding their best goods, and paying their tribute with other goods of inferior quality (Guarmani 1938:17).
4. For a more detailed account of this historical situation, see my discussion (Hiatt 1981: chapter 2, especially pp. 51–59).
5. In its understandable concern to include the maximum limit of cultivable resources, the government reached, some feel unwisely so, into the dry areas, which receive on average only two hundred millimeters of rainfall per year. This amount of precipitation cannot support dry agriculture, and irrigation is not practiced, mainly because it would put too great a strain on the country's financial and hydrological resources. In any case, it is now possible to see the effects feared by some experts. As the hard, compacted surface of the steppe land has been broken by plows, the dirt is pulverized to such a fine consistency that it flows down car windshields and other smooth surfaces like a thick liquid and is choking in a high wind. Concomitantly, the ground surface is being eroded by wind and water action.
6. The importance of imitation should not be ignored in this respect. The death of the Khreisha sheikh in the early 1950s may well have encouraged the trend toward sedentarization, at least to the extent that his wife and children then took up residence at the steppe-land settlement, thereby providing a symbolically forceful example to other still mobile households. Several Khreisha claimed to the author that they had settled because others did so and had flourished nonetheless.
7. There are, however, situational exceptions in this relationship. For example, the presence of two murderers among the Khreisha is no contradiction of the principle involved here, because they are from Syria and had committed their crimes there. The sheikh's power had remained intact to the extent that he could offer sanctuary in these instances, and the government's authority was not called into question because the crimes had not been committed within its territory, nor were the individuals its citizens.

References

Bailey, Frederick. 1969. *Strategems and spoils: A social anthropology of politics.* New York: Schocken Books.

Evans-Pritchard, E. E. 1940. *The Nuer.* Oxford: Clarendon Press.

_____. 1949. *The Sanusi of Cyrenaica.* Oxford: Clarendon Press.

Guarmani, Carlo. 1938. *Northern Nejd: A journey from Jerusalem to Anaiza in Qasim.* London: Argonaut Press.

Hiatt, Joseph M. 1981. Between desert and town: A case study of encapsulation and sedentarization among Jordanian Bedouin. Unpublished Ph.D. dissertation, Department of Anthropology, University of Pennsylvania.

Kazziha, Walid. 1972. *The social history of Southern Syria (Transjordan) in the 19th and early 20th century.* Beirut: Arab University.

Peters, Emrys L. 1960. The proliferation of segments in the lineage of the Bedouin in Cyrenaica. *Journal of the Royal Anthropological Institute* 90(1):29–53.

Salzman, Philip C. 1971. Movement and resource extraction among pastoral nomads: The case of the Shah Naqazi Baluch. In *Comparative Studies of Nomadism and Pastoralism* (special issue), ed. Philip C. Salzman, *Anthropological Quarterly* 44: 185–97.

Spooner, Brian J. 1972. The status of nomadism as a cultural phenomenon in the Middle East. In *Perspectives on Nomadism*, eds. William Irons and Neville Dyson-Hudson, pp. 122–31. Leiden: E.J. Brill.

Sweet, Louise. 1965. Camel raiding of North Arabian bedouin. *American Anthropologist* 67(5):1132–50.

6

Ideology of Reciprocity between the James Bay Cree and the Whiteman State

Colin Scott

Introduction

This paper's aim might seem an optimistic undertaking, given the limitations of available information: to chart ideological transformations from the colonial fur trade into the present, when relations between the James Bay Crees of Quebec and Euro-Canadian society (i.e., "Whiteman") have assumed the form of a "fourth world" minority encapsulated by a modern welfare state. Much of this paper is based on extrapolation of the ideological past from contemporary Cree oral tradition. The controls of historical method that can be exerted on such interpretations are all too few. Contemporary narrated text, after all, can never be set alongside the unrecorded discourse of generations of Crees who have come and gone since the earliest events referred to in the narratives. The earliest Cree texts committed to writing for the region date only from the late nineteenth century, within the lifespan of the eldest living Crees. But contemporary oral tradition, however transformed by the successive projects of successive *bricoleurs*, bears the unmistakable mark of events both remote and proximate in time, offering an indispensable glimpse of the histories of nonliterate traditions (cf. Willis 1981). And if reconstruction to the standards of historical method is not permitted by the available texts, we can hope to be on firmer ground in delineating the bearing of history, as configured in oral tradition, on the ideological present.[1]

The phenomenon of specific concern here is the persistence of reciprocity as a paradigm for discourse about and with the Whiteman, despite exploitative colonial commerce and the sometimes coercive measures

81

of the modern state in more recent decades. Given that the exercise of domination normally requires a measure of consent on the part of a politically subordinate population, it may be observed that the ideology of reciprocity has been an important mechanism in securing the consent of Crees to Whiteman authority—but especially inasmuch as this ideology has been useful to Crees in securing a measure of material benefits and autonomy.

Hearkening back to the early evolution of stratification and centralized authority, Godelier (1978:767–68) has argued that relations of domination and exploitation must initially have arisen through general consent, with recourse to violence developing once material inequalities had been established on the basis of that consent. The ideology that secured consent would initially have been anchored in egalitarian principles of exchange: the material products rendered by subordinates to dominant individuals or groups may have seemed of lesser value than the reciprocal provision of magico-ritual services deemed essential to the reproduction of life itself. Modern ideological responses to the Whiteman state in the northern Cree region suggest that reciprocity is a very versatile principle for the legitimation of authority, even where there are long-standing and unapproved material inequalities and where the exchange is between culturally distinctive groups. This is so because ideologies of reciprocity retain some presence and force even in stratified societies with strong central authorities, as exemplified in the present case by the Canadian welfare state.

In any society, "negotiating" ideologies of particular interest are likely to coexist with "altruistic" ideologies of positive reciprocity (Parkin 1976). To be sure, altruistic exchange often conceals the development of unequally distributed interests. But as Parkin argues, it is inadequate to interpret altruistic exchange as a mere cover for the maximization of particular interests, because that tack ignores the specific force of ideology: "An altruistic ideology, including the notion of the "pure" gift, achieves conceptual and semantic distinctiveness only by standing in an opposed relationship to a negotiable/exploitative ideology. We have to understand the process by which there is a shift in emphasis in a society from one kind of ideology to the other for the legitimation of particular events and activities" (ibid.:187). While negotiating particular interests, fur companies and central governments in northern Quebec have claimed altruistic intentions. But this ideology lends legitimacy at the cost of real concessions required to substantiate claims of reciprocity.

In the discourse of Cree elders at Wemindji, my field research community, the development of relations with the modern state is presented as a continuing manifestation of a historical relationship with the Whiteman that commenced with the fur trade. While positive reciprocity persists as the dominant model of relations internal to Cree society (Scott 1982, 1983), it has had a more varied history in the interethnic arena of relations with Whiteman authorities. Here too, the paradigm of reciprocity is remarkably persistent as an abstract logic of social relations, but the semantic load of the Whiteman category in relation to that logic has been much less steady.

A key concern in discourse concerning the Whiteman is the extent to which exchanges with him conform to ideals of reciprocity as opposed to exploitation. In relation to these criteria, divergent—even contradictory— evaluations of the Whiteman are common. This ambivalence can be attributed to a number of circumstances. First, there are historical shifts in the behavior and apparent motives of the Whiteman. At certain conjunctures the Whiteman image would appear to be an unequivocal endorsement of his moral authority; at other conjunctures the image of the Whiteman is a thoroughly delegitimized one. Second, contrasting evaluations of the Whiteman relate to somewhat distinctive functions for the reproduction of Cree society. On the one hand, positive evaluations sometimes amount to putting a necessary relationship in an optimistic light— viewing the Whiteman as irredeemably exploitative would only entail demoralization in such a circumstance and would ignore altruistic features of Whiteman ideology of potential benefit to Crees. On the other hand, negative evaluations of Whiteman practice are important illustrations of what relations among Crees must not become, if Cree society is to survive. Third, given the concern of liberal state institutions to reflect social justice, both positive and negative representations of Whiteman have had significant rhetorical effect on Whiteman themselves.

Let me proceed to the specifics of the ideology in question, drawing on three sources: 1) a brief sampling of some literature pertaining to native ideology during the traditional fur trade; 2) mythical and quasi-historical formal narrative of contemporary Crees, as it relates to the "Whiteman" category; and 3) evaluations of the Whiteman that attach to the recollected events of recent decades, from the 1930s and 1940s—when economic crisis occurred and state wildlife management and welfare policies began playing a role in domestic production—to the 1970s, when the government of Quebec and Canada signed an aboriginal land claims agreement with the native people (Cree and Inuit) of northern Quebec (James Bay and Northern Quebec Agreement; Anon. 1975).

The Traditional Fur Trade

Relations between the James Bay Crees and state-level European societies span more than three centuries, having developed into articulations between Cree society and Canadian state institutions per se only in this century. The dual functions of proprietorship and governorship that were nominally vested with the Hudson Bay Company under its charter amounted in practice to little more than a license to trade, and the company's monopoly of the trade was itself frequently undermined by competing national and commercial interests. From the latter decades of the seventeenth century well into the eighteenth century, the English and French struggled for control of the trade into James and Hudson bays. Competition from French-Canadian traders continued into the first quarter of the nineteenth century.

The company policed its fur trading posts and the English state was involved in protecting the company's links with the outside world, but the native inhabitants of its vast "properties" maintained indigenous social controls and leadership patterns as the only forms of government in effect at any remove from the posts. It was the technological advantage of using certain European tools, weapons, and supplies that tied native hunters materially to the trade. Trade was advantageous from the hunter's standpoint because the secondary effect expended in providing furs, food, and transport to the traders was more than offset by increased security and efficiency in the primary subsistence effort, using European supplies. Under normal circumstances of price and credit availability, hunters found significant room for maneuvering in emphasizing more efficient subsistence production as against fur production (Salisbury 1976), since their requirements for exchange value from the latter activity were finite.

During the fur trade, forms of political articulation between the traders and the hunters exhibited innovative as well as traditionally Cree features. Morantz (1977) and Francis and Morantz (1983) have described the "trading captain" system that operated during the eighteenth century in the areas east of James Bay. The system flourished under conditions of stiff competition between rival fur companies. "Gangs" of Indians from a region would travel together to conduct summer trade at the coastal posts, under the leadership of a native "captain" who received special recognition for this status from the company. A gang would be comprised of up to thirty canoes of men with furs at the peak of development of the trading captain system. The captain received from the company a quasi-military uniform, as well as brandy and tobacco in quantities for distribution to the men in his gang. His prestige and influence in organizing gangs in future seasons increased in proportion to the gifts he could command from the trader for distribution. By 1800, Francis and Morantz (1983:125) tell us, "gifts" came to as much as half the total value of a gang's entire winter trapping.

The giving of gifts was an especially key factor in securing the limited hegemony exercised by the company during periods of competition. One trader, although largely misconstruing Indians' motivations, makes clear the importance that hunters placed on receiving these gifts:

> Now, an Indian was never satisfied with a trade which was a fair and exact exchange, at the fixed prices of the time, until he had received "something for nothing" at the top of the transaction. It did not matter if a trader raised the prices of furs and lowered the prices of goods to him on the distinct understanding that no present was to be expected or given, the Indian always expected that "something for nothing" so dear to all man- and womankind, at the end of the barter [Cowie 1911:195; quoted in Braroe 1975:144].

Whatever motivated the Indians' quest for "pure" gifts, the company's compliance served to perpetuate an indigenous ideology of reciprocity as a model for external relations. The political use of gifts was important to traders, given the limited utility of price strategies to maximize the volume of the trade. Rich (1960) cites evidence that competing fur companies in the eighteenth and nineteenth centuries experienced considerable difficulty in getting native hunters to respond to price incentives. The latter sought limited exchange value; offering them higher prices simply meant that their needs for trade goods were met by bringing in fewer furs.

Gift giving was a more versatile strategy, because it fostered a sense of loyalty to a generous exchange partner and enhanced the trader's authority. Indians for their part might reasonably expect to be rewarded for loyal service, and the potential rewards were significant given the material power of the Whiteman partner. The legitimation of authority was heavily contingent on generosity within the Cree system. Braroe (1975) points out that the Cree word for "leader" (*uuchimaau* in Wemindji Cree dialect) is a derivation of the verb "to give away": ". . . the inequality of the exchange when a gift was thrown in was symbolic of the traders' superiority in wealth and power, just as the same relation was expressed in unequal exchanges between a chief and his followers. Loyalty and submission were extended to those who could be counted upon to be generous with material goods" (ibid.:144). Hudson Bay Company local managers were given the title *uuchimaau* by an undetermined date during the traditional fur trade, a title that they retain in Cree villages today, although in recent decades their authority has been in relative decline.

The nature of ceremonial gifts helped get around the limitations imposed by the hunters' finite needs for trade items. Easily transportable tobacco and immediately consumable alcohol were not necessities of the hunt, but they were highly valued. They could serve as well as any valued item to augment the prestige and influence of company managers and native captains.

From traders' standpoint, gifts were less important when competition was low, and Cree dependence on imported goods could be counted on to ensure a more or less steady supply of furs. After 1821, with the merger of the rival Northwest and Hudson Bay Companies, the latter assumed a monopoly position. Meanwhile, the company was developing secondary posts inland from the coast, reducing the importance of large trading expeditions. The quantity of gifts to expedition leaders was reduced, and formal captaincy was discontinued.

Internal to the Cree system of domestic production, it appears, fur production remained supplementary to subsistence production right into the contemporary period (Feit 1978, 1982; Tanner 1979; Scott 1979). Control of land-based resources remained, de facto, a jurisdiction of the traditional institutions of tenure and hunting group leadership (cf. Feit 1985 for a description of this system as it functions today).

In 1870 Hudson Bay Company lands, as defined by its charter, were transferred to the new state of Canada. Federal medical personnel and police occasionally visited the posts, and limited relief rations for widows and invalids were being provided by the turn of the twentieth century, according to Wemindji informants. These rations were administered by company managers. Beginning in the late 1800s, Anglican missionaries taught literacy to eastern Crees in syllabic orthography and eventually achieved almost universal adherence to the church among Crees, although the aboriginal cosmology of life in the bush remained substantially intact. The company, in lending its moral and administrative support to these incipient manifestations of the Canadian state, generally maintained its position as the leading Whiteman authority well into the present century.

Initially by charter and later due to the weak development of state bureaucracy in the north, Hudson Bay Company was left to the pursuit of its interest in the trade. Those interests rarely transcended the economic, and their political defense depended largely on accommodating indigenous notions of reciprocity and leadership when purely economic incentives were insufficient. If the deployment of company wealth within this political framework sometimes resulted in new opportunities for individual aggrandizement or in altered organizational strategies on-the-ground, these still hinged upon and tended to reproduce a pervasively egalitarian ideology. It was possible in some periods for Cree leaders to be more generous and to attract larger followings than they might have in routine subsistence pursuits, but generosity remained the central criterion.

Reciprocity and the Mythical Whiteman

Let me now turn to the Cree texts. The formal narrative shortly to be sampled was delivered by men who are presently elders of the community of Wemindji. They were young men just beginning to raise families in the difficult period of the 1930s, as recollected by some of these same narrators in the next section. Most of the remaining discussion concerns the relationship between their mythical discourse and their secular accounts of history.

In Cree, narrative is broadly classified into two genres: "myth" (*aatiyuuhkaan*), in which narrated events transcend secular time (a predominately figurative expressive mode), and "tidings" (*tipaachimuun*), in which reported events are understood literally to have occurred in the experience of living people or their human ancestors (cf. Hallowell 1964, Preston 1975a, Savard 1979a and 1979b, Scott 1983).

Much Cree mythology presents a glowing picture of relations with the Whiteman. If the material imbalance of exchange is contemplated, it is logically handled as a function of generosity rather than exploitation. An elderly Wemindji hunter concluded a cycle of myths about Chakaapaash, the eastern Cree hero-transformer, with this episode:

> As Chakaapaash was out walking along the coast, he saw a ship floating in the ocean. So he went over to see the ship, and when he got on board he was given Whiteman's food by the people who were on the ship. It was something which he had never eaten before. So he took some home to his sister. In return, the people in the ship had told him to give them something to eat. So he went home, and when he got there, he gave it to his sister. She showed how grateful she was for what he brought back for her. The people were able to hear her all the way out on the ship when she thanked them for the food.

> "They want some food, so I'll take it back to them," he said to her. So he took meat to them. He took one whole leg of squirrel to them. When he got there, he brought aboard the leg of squirrel. When he put it down, its weight was so great that the vessel began to list sharply. And he returned home. That ends the story about the ship.

Here both partners behave correctly and respectfully by standards of "generalized" reciprocity (Sahlins 1965). Crees state that the ideal for exchange is to recognize what a partner might need and, if one can, provide it without expectation of something in return.

The myth nonetheless portrays reciprocal generosity verging on competition. Ambiguity and humor are signaled by the fact that a haunch of squirrel would seem a ludicrously minute quantity. In ordinary life, the squirrel is the least important game, normally left to small boys. But those familiar with the Chakaapaash cycle of myths know that squirrels are the hero's favorite game and, accordingly, a substantial gift. There is room here, initially at least, to judge the Whiteman as the more generous. Perhaps it appeared as a dilemma to Crees to attempt to reciprocate Whiteman gifts of great magnitude. The reply in the myth is an unusual demonstration of gratitude and readiness to reciprocate, culminating in the overbalancing of the Whiteman's gift by that of Chakaapaash.

Myth, then, while expressing fundamental concern and some ambiguity over the balance of exchange, authorizes the original relationship to the Whiteman as one of generalized reciprocity.

"Tidings" are concerned with the same issue addressed by the Chakaapaash myth: what is the place of the Whiteman, and more specifically, the English in the Cree world? In one historical narrative (Scott 1983:229–34), the problem of the very earliest perceptual ambiguity, as experienced by a Cree shaman is presented in absorbing detail. A Cree shaman would frequently seek the assistance of a *misstaapaau* (spirit helper) through the medium of the conjuring lodge (*kubsaapihchikan*). A Cree interpreter commented that the verb "he conjures" (*kuhsaapihtik*) sounds like "being able to see from up there while being down here." He was reminded of a periscope when he heard of the conjuring lodge as a boy. The explanation given by another interpreter was similar—the conjurer is "able to see far. When you're down here, you can't see very far. But from up high you can see a lot." And so it is that the first indication that the Cree people have of a Whiteman's ship still far out to sea is through the use of the conjuring lodge.

The ship, however, is a problematic percept. It seems at first to be just standing in the water, its mast evoking a tall spruce, with the sails completing the image of a white animate "person." Further reconnaissance enables the *mistaapaau* to ascertain that the "tall spruce white person" is really something called a ship, that it is approaching and might find the people, and that it is safe to approach the ship.

More conservative forces, the others in the group, refuse to approach the ship, so the shaman goes only with his wife. In a second version, ambivalence toward the strangers is expressed in social structural terms. The man's father-in-law attempts to restrain his daughter from going with her husband, but relents. (The younger man would reside with his father-in-law for an extended period following marriage, so the latter represents an elder authority.) Finally, evidence that the man and his wife are treated generously induces others to follow suit.

It is interesting, parenthetically, to compare this Cree account with a firsthand report of the first encounter by a European. Where Wemindji Cree tradition places the first contact at Old Factory, a summer gathering place, European history locates it near the mouth of the Rupert River, some sixty or seventy miles south of Old Factory, in 1611. Cree tradition has the French making earliest contact; in European records it was Henry Hudson's English ship *Discovery*. The time was early spring, with the ship still icebound. A local Indian finally visited the ship. A *Discovery* crew member recorded:

> To this savage our master gave a knife, a looking-glass, and buttons, who received them thankfully, and made signes that after he had slept he would come again, which he did. When he came he brought with him a sled, which he drew after him, and upon it two deeres skinnes and two beaver skinnes. He had a scrip under his arme, out of which he drew those things which the master had given him. He took the knife and laid it upon one of the beaver skinnes, and his glasses and buttons upon the other, and so gave them to the master, who received them; and the savage took those things which the master had given him, and put them up into his scrip again. Then the master shewed him a hatchet, for which he would have given the master one of his deere skinnes, but our master would have them both, and so he had, although not willingly. After many signes of people to the north and to the south, and that after so many sleepes he would come again, he went his way, but never came more [Asher 1860:114, quoted in Francis and Morantz 1983:16].

Hudson establishes the relationship with gifts, in keeping with generalized reciprocity. But the attempt to equate values suggested by the Indian's behavior on the second visit indicates barter. Hudson clearly deviates from generalized reciprocity in insisting on getting more than he is offered for the hatchet. Trade quickly followed the preliminaries of gift giving, but the one depended on the other.

The Cree account emphasizes a more open-ended reciprocity at the first exchange and goes on to relate two noneconomic features as the relationship develops. Sexual reciprocity is alluded to. We are told that the first Englishman in those parts, given the respectful name Chishaawaamstikushiiyuu (*chishaa* meaning "old" and connoting "wise" and "powerful," *waamstikushiiyuu* meaning "Whiteman of English origin") married an Indian woman from Maatuskaau, a short distance north of Old Factory. In time they have an Indian son-in-law, who eventually accompanies Elder Englishman to his home and jokes before departing about how he will "fool around" with white women. To be sure, this visit to England represents one of the rare opportunities in which sexual reciprocity could have occurred. The Hudson Bay Company Whitemen typically arrived without women and took Indian wives if they did not live as bachelors. Nevertheless, the youth is warned by other Cree to be careful how he jokes with the Whiteman.

A second noneconomic feature of reciprocity is military assistance from the English, to which the voyage home of Elder Englishman gives rise. Perhaps it is not accidental that the greater generosity of Crees in terms of women is juxtaposed with the greater capability of the English to be of military assistance. The French had cheated the Indians, so Elder Englishman goes home to enlist English support. The company "stands for the people."

The importance of this ideology to the commercial interests of the company is evident. The company Whitemen are portrayed as genuine leaders, more concerned than their national and commercial rivals with defending Cree interests. As Salisbury (1966:325) suggests, the best myth may not be created by those who benefit most from them: "the people who are likely to benefit by a myth . . . are likely to have historical knowledge, but their interest may be to keep quiet, and to let myths be created by those who know less."

What "historical" knowledge did Crees have about the fur trade, and what did they lack? Clearly, the Whiteman was perceived as materially more powerful and wealthy. Still, capital accumulation from the trade itself was an invisible phenomenon, especially inasmuch as the value-in-exchange of furs accumulated materially only in Britain and southern Canada. Acknowledgment of the Whiteman's material power did not per se lead to the judgment that he was exploitative; indeed, to the extent he appeared responsive to altruistic ideology, Crees might well have hoped to benefit, "cargo-"like, from the exchange. The Whiteman's wealth conferred authority, but entailed a moral duty toward his Indian partners as well.

A myth narrated to Turner (1894:338) by an Ungava Naskapi illustrates this:

Creation of people by the wolverene [sic] and the muskrat.

As a wolverene was wandering along the bank of a river he saw a muskrat swimming in the edge of the water. He accosted the latter animal with the inquiry: "Who are you? Are you a man or a woman?" The muskrat answered: "I am a woman." The wolverene informed her that he would take her for a wife. The muskrat replied: "I live in the water; how can I be your wife?" The wolverene told her that she could live on the land as well as in the water. The muskrat went up on the bank to where the wolverene was standing. They selected a place and she began to prepare a home for them. They ate their suppers and retired. Soon after a child was born. The wolverene informed his wife that it would be a white man and father of all the white people. When this child was born it made a natural exit. In due time a second child was born which wolverene decreed should be an Indian and the father of their kind. This child was born from its mother's mouth. After a time a third child was born, and the wolverene announced it to be an Eskimo and father of its kind. This child was born *ab ano*. In the natural course of events a fourth child was born, and the wolverene decided it to be an Iroquois and father of its kind. This child was born from its mother's nose. After a time a fifth child was born and the wolverene decreed it should be a Negro and father of its kind. This child was born from its mother's ears. These children remained with their parents until they grew up. Their mother then called them together and announced to them that they must separate. She sent them to different places of the land, and, in parting, directed them to go to the white men whenever they were in need of anything, as the whites would have everything ready for them.

Wolverine, a trickster character in eastern Cree-Montagnais-Naskapi myth, precedes humans as the possessor of culture, including knowledge of weapons, fire making, cooking, architecture, and shamanism. Muskrat's mediation of water and land foreshadows a later mediation of these elements by a trading partner who comes by sea. Ethnic seniority among the offspring of the marriage corresponds to the Cree ideology of leadership and responsibility of the eldest for younger siblings. The ethnic hierarchy is reinforced, additionally, by mode of birth. The Whiteman, born vaginally, is eldest. The second born Indian has a prestigious oral exit. By contrast, the traditional enemies of the Cree-Naskapi—Iroquois and Inuit—are born nasally and anally. The Negro, historically associated with the Whiteman, is more happily born, albeit as baby of the family. Muskrat instructs her children to expect assistance from the eldest.

It is true that Cree hunters benefited in their own eyes from exchange with the Whiteman, in goods that enhanced their labor efficiency and security. It can be argued that such values are incommensurable with the surplus value obtained by the company through exchange and that adequate criteria for determining who was "most generous" are elusive. But it is an issue of continuing concern to Crees, and its resolution is not as easy as the foregoing texts suggest. Images of an exploitative Whiteman are also found at and just below the surface of discourse.

Positive endorsements of the Whiteman did not preclude the gravest crises of legitimacy in times of Cree hardship, as the Hannah Bay massacre (Preston 1975b) and other occasional raids on trading posts suggest. More recently, the generation of Crees who narrate the stories presented here have borne personal witness to the fact that the company could be fatally ungenerous. Mythical counterparts of these less charitable interpretations of the Whiteman are found in *pwaatich* stories. *Pwaatich* are a category of pseudo-humans, typically of pale complexion and bearded countenance, who lurk in the bush and prey on the margins of human society. Where *pwaatich* are concerned, negative reciprocity is the order of the day.

In one of the myths I collected, several dimensions of negative reciprocity are modeled, sexual exploitation being central. The story opens on an authentically human household that includes a son and a daughter who are full-grown. Neither, significantly, is yet married. The moment is appropriate for a marriage exchange. This situation is brought into relation with an all-male group of *pwaatich*. Marital reciprocity is not possible, and they abduct the girl, ignoring customary bride service—a double hardship for the mother, apparently a widow. When the girl's brother comes to rescue her, the death by scalding of the offspring of the illegitimate "marriage" is a stark rejection, notwithstanding belated attempts by *pwaatich* to hail the visitor as their brother-in-law. The *pwaatich*'s offer to "pass the pipe" is made with treachery in mind. The brother responds in kind. His superior spiritual power allows him to turn the trick back on the *pwaatich*, killing them and reuniting the family.

The exploitation of labor power is featured in another myth, where a male Cree is enslaved by *pwaatich*. Here the *pwaatich* are linked to the category of *atuush* (cannibal), cannibals in Cree myth representing the very antithesis of human society. The structure and consequences of exploitation are parallel in the myths discussed just previously and the present one. The protagonists are drawn into a relationship with exploitative aliens who overpower them. Kituunaa, the hero of the second myth is kidnapped and enslaved, forced to hunt for his captors, but kept like a dog outside, without clothing. When hunting is poor, it occurs to the *pwaatich* to butcher and cook the hero. But again the spiritual superiority of true human beings is demonstrated. The force of Kituunaa's hope and concentration brings about a situation that permits his escape. He grossly insults his captors in the process. His group stages a punitive raid on the *pwaatich*, and with Kituunaa now reunited with his community, his sorcery is overwhelming to the enemy. *Pwaatich* women, as cannibals, are not taken captive but killed along with their men.

The association of Whitemen with the category of *pwaatich* is reflected in anecdotes about encounters with Whitemen in the bush, who are often suspected of being *pwaatich*. *Pwaatich* steal from Indians' fishnets and traps and take equipment that has been cached. In one recent encounter, some Crees near Moose Factory actually apprehended a pair of *pwaatich* stealing fish from their nets. These ones turned out to be a relatively benign variety—a father-and-son team, tourists who had grown impatient with fishing for their dinner.

In myth and in tidings of long ago, then, the Whiteman and relations with him are represented by highly contrastive images. On the one hand, he is a legitimate, even senior partner in reciprocity—an elder, a big brother and military ally. His authority is directly connected to his obligation of continuing generosity toward Crees. On the other hand, the Whiteman is closely associated with *pwaatich*, who exploit the productive and reproductive power of Cree men and women. Crees, however, preserve authentically human society rooted in positive reciprocity, which, along with spiritual superiority, enables them to resist incorporation in the exploitative designs of *pwaatich*.

Even in positive visions of the Whiteman, his authority is closely circumscribed. He is found aboard ship and along the coast at trading posts. The narrator of the traditional tidings about the first contact emphasizes several times that it is Indian land to which the Whiteman came and that it continues to be Indian land. Negative images of the Whiteman place him in the bush, in Cree domain, where his presence is inimical to human community. The formally contradictory ideologies of the Whiteman are, to an extent, functionally complementary, the first endorsing a valued exchange upon which Crees soon became dependent and the second insulating Cree domestic relations from exploitative premises that were particularly salient in the trade with whites. The dual ideology defends a boundary in cultural and material terms, while specifying the conditions for valid interethnic exchange.

Economic Crisis and the Intervention of the State

Having sketched the abstract coordinates for the figurative evaluation of the Whiteman, we may turn to the ethnohistorical interpretations of recent decades, as reconstructed from informants' recollections. Our starting point is the 1930s, which mark a breakdown in normal economic relations with the company and the first in a series of direct interventions by the state, which would increase in complexity over the next four decades. Autobiographical "tidings" details the dynamic between literal experience of Whitemen and the figurative means for modeling it.

Again, we encounter somewhat contradictory evaluations, which vary by individual, by event, and by rhetorical intention. One elder considers doubts as to whether hunters received fair exchange for their furs in the following long-term perspective: "The people who thought that the Company wasn't giving them fair exchange—that it was cheating them—didn't realize what the Company was planning to do for them. People didn't realize that the Company was taking most of that money from furs to bring in groceries, to pay for the transportation."

Another elder developed this line of thought:

> I used to get only ten dollars for a hundred muskrat. There was this Russian who told me that the money the Company had—there's a lot that they didn't give us—he didn't think that they really stole that money, because they knew that some day they would be bringing things in with barges. Because we were an isolated post. The Russian told me that some day we would be using airplanes to go trapping. There was no employment—the only employment we would get was when the barges would come in. The Company didn't really cheat us of anything. Like suppose you go to the store tomorrow to buy something. We've already paid for it, although you're [still] going to pay for it.

The foregoing is an intriguing commentary on the process and benefits of capitalist accumulation—one that is largely consistent with ideologies justifying capitalist accumulation in wider arenas. In immediate transactions between trappers and traders, the trappers were not paid the full value of their furs. But accumulation by the company on this basis permitted it to offer a broader range of goods to modern Crees and to offer employment income, which could be put to such useful purposes as purchasing air charter transportation to hunting territories.

Specific periods, however, are unmistakably associated with less charitable evaluations. Positive reciprocity with the Whiteman was not a convincing model in the 1930s, the years of scarce game, restricted credit availability, and depressed fur prices. Caribou had moved north out of the band's range, and now the beaver—the principal source of both food and furs for winter hunters at Wemindji—nearly disappeared. Salisbury's (1976) explanation of events is that Hudson's Bay Company began to reduce its credit accounts with trappers in the 1920s in the Canadian north, partly in response to competition from the French Révillon Frères Company, which became active after the turn of the century. Under earlier monopoly conditions, a policy of relatively large credit accounts had been permitted, and recovering debts was now risky if hunters could sell to the competition. Salisbury suggests that even before the price drops of the depression, trappers had to resort to more intensive trapping of beaver to maintain equipment inventories. Feit (personal communication) cites evidence that "rationalizing" trappers' charge accounts to conform with modern credit practices became policy elsewhere in the Canadian north earlier than it did east of James Bay. But the policy reached the eastern Crees after 1930, more or less coinciding with declining prices. To explain declining beaver stocks, which were normally carefully managed, Feit (1978, 1982) stresses the consequences of competition for the resource by white trappers in the southern James Bay region. Crees temporarily abandoned routine management practices in order to trap out beaver, since their competitors would only have done so, anyway. White trappers were using aircraft to get as far north as present-day Wemindji territory.

To worsen matters, small game grouse and hare went into low points in their population cycles. The response of an exchange partner motivated by altruistic ideology would have been to extend additional assistance to hunters until the famine had passed. Instead, in view of dropping fur prices and diminishing fur catches, the company reduced the supplies advanced on credit to hunting families going to the bush. In some instances, the value advanced at the beginning of the season fell from previous levels of fifteen hundred dollars to as little as one hundred dollars. Individuals and whole families starved to death. Commented one elderly hunter of the company's behavior during that period, "It was like they owned the people." Ki-tuunaa's slavery suggests itself as an apt metaphor.

Some rehabilitation of the Whiteman's image came with two interces-sions by the state—the establishment of beaver preserves and the extension to Crees of social welfare transfers. The first was a provincial government response, which came, according to informants, at the time small game populations had turned upward in their cycles, easing the famine some-what. At this time, late in the 1930s, a former company manager at Rupert House named James Watt arrived to offer Wemindji-area hunters (then trading at Old Factory) a beaver recovery program. Watt and his wife had been instrumental in convincing the Quebec government to support beaver preserves, to register Indian territories as traplines, and to put them off-limits to outsiders. The program had already commenced farther south in the region. Watt was now extending it northward. It involved mapping hunting territories and obtaining hunters' agreement to kill no beaver until the population was securely on the way to recovery. For four to ten years, varying by individual territory, beaver were not killed. As the beaver were again opened to trapping, "quotas" were granted by the provincial govern-ment and administered by Watt to the hunters of each territory, based on reports by each Cree hunting group leaders of the number of active beaver lodges on each territory. In effect, the system depended on the voluntary cooperation of these leaders as well as of other hunters.

Winter hunting group leaders, each normally the spiritual custodian of his group's territory, are called *amisk uuchimaauch*, or "beaver bosses."[2] Watt and later a son who inherited his duties as conservation agent were designated by the diminutive *amisk uuchimaash*, or "little beaver boss." The linguistic clue suggests that native bosses retained primary authority. However, Cree hunters went to considerable lengths to respect the instruc-tions of the non-Cree agent. The government allotment of quotas to indi-viduals to hunt on specific territories promoted the ideology that people were less free to come and go than they had been previously. Traditionally, it was standard procedure to share territories, and the wisdom of this flexibility was apparent in the current situation. The beaver came back first on territories farther inland, and inland beaver bosses therefore invited hunters from coastal territories to come with them to hunt. To effect such invitations, however, it was now necessary to obtain permission from the "little beaver boss." With that permission went an official quota that made it legal, from the government point of view, for the guest to trap. In their accounts, Crees make mention of the "little beaver boss" allowing coasters to go inland and even to him "sending" coasters inland.

Much of this suggests that Watt exercised genuine authority, despite the government program being operable only through the traditional beaver bosses' leadership. Several reasons for Cree consent in this regard can be given. Watt's efforts were perceived to promote Cree interest. As Feit (1982) points out, hunters' cooperation was consistent with their own policy of game management, while securing the additional benefit of government recognition of Cree territories and protection from intruders, which restored the viability of the traditional management system. The government was seen to be upholding the Crees' legitimate rights in the land, and Watt's personal integrity lent credibility to this perception. Preston (personal communication) indicates that Watt had been well liked and respected as a company manager at Rupert House. He had expended substantial personal resources to ease the effects of famine there.

A third reason for Cree cooperation is that traditional leaders appreciated the endorsement locally of their authority. The beaver bosses, or "tallymen," as they were known in English, were deputized and given badges as well as small annual stipends by the government administration. A similar symbiosis between government and local authorities developed in the management of migratory waterfowl, a jurisdiction claimed by the federal government in Canada. The Cree leaders for fall and spring goose hunting are designated *paaschichaau uuchimaauch* ("shooting bosses"), and winter beaver bosses whose territories adjoin the waterfowl-rich coast of James Bay are usually also shooting bosses for their territories. One such leader comments:

> The game warden used to be in charge. Like he used to meet with people and talk to them. We used to refer to him as a hunting boss. But he had more authority than us [the Indian bosses] . . . He used to talk to the hunters . . . Like he used to talk to people who went out hunting without asking permission of the shooting bosses . . . He used to come on the boat. The guy that first used to come in, he was a medical doctor . . . He must have had a lot of work to do. He was working as the Indian agent [also a federal jurisdiction in Canada] and as the game warden, too. Then there was another guy who came in, and he had just the one job as a game warden . . . He was pretty strict. He got through to the other hunters by telling them to listen to whoever was the beaver boss and whoever was the goose boss. And he made sure they were aware of what he was saying.

What regulations did the game warden want people to obey? "He didn't want people to do any shooting when it was getting dark [a cardinal sin in Cree methods of goose hunting]. We always tried to keep up the traditions of our grandfathers, and we would tell him what we had learned, and he would tell the people not to do any hunting after dark." Notwithstanding the statement that the federal warden had more authority than the native bosses, his only effective participation seems to have been to endorse the Cree bosses' system of management and attendant rules for hunting (a sophisticated and detailed system; cf. Scott 1983). His support evidently enhanced the authority of Cree bosses locally, while enabling him to exert authority in the only practical way.

A fourth factor is involved in cooperation with external authorities. As G____'s comments illustrate, the various areas of Whiteman authority were still perceived as closely linked and were, in fact, often vested in a single individual. Lack of cooperation in one area could risk retribution in another. The Whiteman's power had been demonstrated, if not by direct recourse to violence, at least by his ability to ignore positive reciprocity with violent consequences for the Crees. The uniforms and sidearms sometimes worn by wardens were symbolic of a senior authority with the ability to make forced arrests, although no recollections were offered of such arrests actually having been made. Even when the legitimacy of the company and of central governments had been at a low point, direct challenges would have been counter-productive. It was more politic to seek re-establishment of reciprocating arrangements, which for the weaker partner meant keeping its own image above reproach.

During most of the period that the beaver were "closed" to trapping, hunters were not yet receiving social welfare transfers. Widows and the elderly were exceptions. They had been receiving "helping rations" (*wiichihiiwaaun*—also meaning "something given to someone without expectation of return") since the late 1800s. The rations were alloted by federal medical doctors and issued at regular intervals by the company managers. They were of some assistance to families who lived with recipients.

It was the year before some beaver trapping was opened again that the federal government through its Indian agents acted to alleviate economic hardship with relief goods and emergency credit for all hunting families, according to local informants. This was a second important measure toward the recovery of Whiteman legitimacy. A direct connection is made between the profits the Whiteman had taken from furs and the transfer payments he was now offering. One elder comments: "The government got a lot of money from the Indian's garden. How much did the government get from all the beaver it took to use from the Indian's garden? It was thought to be their wallet. The government showed that it had compassion for its children as a result of this. The money [from fur] was saved for them [as welfare]."

This is the same speaker who earlier argued that the Crees are ultimately being reciprocated for their contributions to company accumulation with consumer goods and jobs. Here past profits are also the source of social welfare benefits. Again, it is a model that sustains a certain vision of reciprocity, while being reminiscent of an important ideological mechanism in the "mainstream" ideological reproduction of welfare capitalism. To the extent that inequities are reduced via transfers, opposition to the system is reduced. Unlike the more alienated members of the urban working class and unemployed, however, Crees have not accepted stigma as attaching to the receipt of transfer payments. Transfers are not "handouts." Traditional Crees tend to view them as "help," which they appreciate, and express pride at the same time in "helping out their (transfer) cheques" through their independent efforts. Others today state more militantly that the government is obligated to maintain social security benefits, in view of what has been "stolen" from Indian people in the past. This tone is more common among younger, southern-schooled Crees who tend to aspire to employment rather than subsistence production as a principal economic orientation. A logic of reciprocity continues to inform these opinions, but the implication is that state institutions have not adequately reciprocated Crees.[3]

Following World War II, social security programs of general application in the rest of Canada were extended to northern native communities, including welfare, pensions for the elderly, and family allowances. The federal Indian Affairs Department also increased the delivery of permanent housing, schooling, and health services at the posts. From the government standpoint, these measures would facilitate the transition from a moribund hunting-trapping economy to a modern, sedentary cash economy. Local adaptations to government measures, however, bore little resemblance to this assimilative vision.

With new welfare income, recovering beaver populations, improved fur prices, and seasonal summer employment in settlement construction projects, hunters from the late 1940s into the early 1960s had unprecedented cash incomes. As they had done with fur income in an earlier era, they used new income to improve the comfort and technological efficiency of hunting, by purchasing air charter service to hunting territories, motorized equipment, and security food supplies.

This flourescence was at the cost of increased dependence on imported consumer items. The price of dependency again began to emerge in the late 1960s and early 1970s, when income from furs, transfer payments, and seasonal employment failed to keep pace with increases in the cost of the new technology. Although hunting and trapping remained the principal economic orientation for the majority of households, certain territories more remote from the posts became underutilized, as hunters attempted to hunt nearer the settlements and make up their loss in subsistence productivity through seasonal migratory wage employment. Since wage employment was scarce regionally, underproduction in the subsistence sector exacerbated underemployment in the cash sector.

Official recognition of Cree hunting territories and government transfers, then, reaffirmed confidence in the altruistic motivations of Whiteman
authority in the wake of the crisis of the Depression. For a time, the
viability of subsistence production was restored, with an improved standard of material security. But deepened consumer dependency, combined
with long-term fur market trends, underemployment, and population
growth, seemed to point to growing difficulties in the domestic economy.
At this point, the invasion of state-sponsored and internationally financed
industry in the Cree region erupted in another crisis of state legitimacy.

Cree Responses to the James Bay Hydroelectric Project

Plans were announced in 1971 by the province of Quebec to dam or
divert all of the major rivers of the east coast James and Hudson Bay
drainage. No previous intrusion had posed so fundamental a challenge to
Cree tenure. Interference with subsistence activities by mines, forestry operations, white towns, and overzealous game wardens on the southern
margin of Cree territory had been of growing concern in the 1950s and
1960s, but the James Bay hydro project was the first to have a massive
regionwide impact on all eastern Cree communities. As Feit (1985) describes in detail, it was the occasion for the development of regionwide
consensus to oppose the project until Cree rights and interests had been
recognized and settled.

Crees had never surrendered their lands. The Quebec government took
the position that the native people had no valid claim, notwithstanding the
fact that the project would be on lands previously transferred from federal
domain on the express condition that Quebec would settle native title.
Quebec now expressed the view that the territory was crown land and the
interests of few thousand natives could not be permitted to hinder a development of alleged benefit to the people of Quebec as a whole. Over Cree
protest, government corporations proceeded with construction.

Crees responded to the project in the public media as an instance of
Whiteman greed resulting in gross negligence, socially and ecologically.
Rhetorical intentions aside, it should be stressed that the emotional and
intellectual commitment to the land of Crees who had made their lives in
the bush was profound. In Cree hunting ideology, respect for human life
and respect for other living things are mutually dependent aspects of reciprocity (Tanner 1979; Scott 1983). A journalist from a Montreal daily
newspaper was told by his Cree host during a visit to a Fort George hunting
camp: "The Whiteman has no feeling of love for all life on the earth. That's
the way we understand it. The way the Indian sees him, the Whiteman is

like a spoiled child, grabbing everything for himself, never sharing, a destructive child who never matures . . ." (Richardson 1975:151).

The themes of Whiteman as "boss" and "elder" are fully overturned here. In the course of a publicly narrated myth for which he was present, Richardson (ibid.:183) heard the Whiteman likened to an ancient monster who destroyed the earth in a flood before finding precarious accommodation on a raft with a human being and the animals who would repopulate the world. Other statements by Richardson's hosts challenge the Whiteman to recognize the incompatibility of his present selfish objectives with the Creator's purpose:

> "[The Whiteman]'s made the same way we are," said Job . . . "he has the same soul as we have. Everybody was given the same. But he is not using his soul properly, he's using it only for his own gain. He is trying to destroy lots of men. The Creator did not intend that this land should be destroyed."

> "I have read the Bible many times," said Mary, "and I have never seen anywhere that the Creator says the land should be destroyed before he is ready."

The government's current behavior contradicted the intentions it had expressed through its earlier involvement in beaver management. As one Wemindji elder, a band councillor[4] during the period of opposition, commented to me in 1980:

> When we were first told that we weren't allowed to kill the beaver, we were told it was an order from the government, so we called the beaver the "government beaver", because it seemed as though the government owned them. So we, the Indian people, tried to respect this order, and the beaver. When we were allowed to kill it again, we only killed as many as we were suppose to, not more. We always looked at it this way. But today you can see what has happened inland. The land is flooded, where the beaver used to be plentiful. The beaver is being drowned; this is not the doing of the Indian people. They still tried to respect the wishes of the government. The time has come when the beaver is being killed in another way, not the Indian people's way; where it doesn't help them in the way of food or money. It is the doing of the government, not the Indian people. When the people weren't allowed to kill the beaver so that it could increase, they tried to respect this because they knew that this would help them in the future, their children and their children's children. This is the reason the Indian people were against the James Bay Project.

The speaker counterposes the destructive aspects of present government action with earlier action that seemed consistent with Cree patrimony.[5]

Although younger, southern-schooled Cree leaders were responsible for conducting the opposition in wider arenas,[6] the perspective of community elders played a central role in the formulation of political objectives. Feit (1985) has reviewed records of early consultations between regional leaders and elders. The latter stressed the unacceptability of development without government consultation with Crees, as well as concern about the ecological consequences, the social and economic autonomy and continuity of their communities, and the abrogation of traditional rights. Elders viewed the project, in the historical context of Indian-white relations, as an important instance of a continuing conflict over control of the region's development. They saw the resolution of the current crisis as requiring restructured relations between Cree communities and Whiteman authorities, including a modified hydro project and enhanced Cree control of development. The elders' long-term goal was reconciliation, according to Feit, although they were convinced of the strategic necessity to oppose the project to achieve meaningful negotiations.

Crees were skeptical from the state about the possibility of actually preventing the project. Construction continued unabated, and physical action to bar it from Cree lands would undoubtedly have been defined as criminal interference and dealt with accordingly. The objective of a negotiated restructuring of Cree-state relations reflected a measure of Cree consent, bearing in mind an implicit factor of violence on the part of state authorities, most of whom were prepared to see the project forced ahead in the absence of consent.

There was reason to believe that negotiations could achieve significant benefits. Several factors incline state authorities to be more responsive to native protests in the 1970s than in the past. Commonly acknowledged factors are the maturation of social welfare ideology, in combination with the momentum of minority rights and environmental issues. Also, by the early 1970s it was clear that the assimilative, paternalistic policies of central governments had been socioeconomically disastrous for native people. The federal government was financing provincial and national native organizations and financed research and legal costs of the Cree claim. The Crees had access to native allies, via organizations that were growing in political effectiveness. Their response to the hydro project in state arenas was enabled first by the organizational structure of the Indians of Quebec Association and later by the Crees' own regional organization, the Grand Council of the Crees of Quebec.[7] The Cree cause found support in intellectual circles and gained considerable prominence in the mass media.

The event that convinced the Quebec government to negotiate was a Quebec Superior Court hearing in 1972. Legal counsel for the Crees, supported by the testimony of leading hunters, younger bilingual leaders, and scientific witnesses, argued for an interlocutory injunction to halt work on the project until a legal clarification of Cree interest was complete. The injunction was granted by Justice Malouf in November of 1973—in what stands as a landmark judgment on aboriginal rights in Canada. The Crees suffered setbacks, however, in the Quebec Court of Appeals, which almost immediately allowed project construction to continue and eventually ruled that aboriginal rights in the territory had been extinguished by the Hudson Bay Company charter three hundred years previous. It could be years before an appeal went through the Supreme Court of Canada. Although their legal argument was strong, the Crees were faced with the project becoming a fait accompli. The Quebec government, meanwhile, came under pressure from its investors, who were anxious about the legal uncertainties. The Crees and the government negotiated, reached an agreement-in-principle in November of 1974, and completed the final agreement a year later—the James Bay and Northern Quebec Agreement (JBNQA, Anon. 1975).

JBNQA benefits to the subsistence sector include exclusive or preferred access by natives to subsistence and fur resources in areas not required for development, environmental review procedures for future development, and the Income Security Program for hunters. The latter program substantially increased the cash incomes, through transfer payments, of subsistence-oriented households (Scott 1979, 1984; Feit and Scott 1988). In addition, the roughly sixty-five hundred Crees of eight bands received $225 million cash compensation in lieu of royalties, powers of local and regional self-government that generally exceed those of municipal administrations, and guarantees of accelerated state-funded community infrastructure development.

An adequate account of ideological elaboration in the 1970s will require further study, but preliminary reflections are possible in relation to the theme of reciprocity. For the first time, Crees took overtly adversarial action against a central government. The Quebec government and its allies in hydro development, fortunately without full cooperation from the courts or the interested public, forced a project that denied the Indians' primary rights in the land. From the Cree standpoint, recognition of those rights had been implicit in the government's registration of Indian traplines. Now the government was making it explicit that its sovereign authority extended to the disposition of the land, a position that it never relinquished in negotiations. It reserved the prerogative, in the JBNQA, to "develop" on Cree land, subject to replacement or compensation for losses to Crees. The government recognized specific Cree rights to traditional lands and resources that otherwise would have been very difficult for Crees to defend into the future. This advantage, together with other concessions, led Crees to conclude that the best agreement they could negotiate was an agreement worth having.

But Whiteman inroads on Cree patrimony, as embodied in the land, have not been accorded full legitimacy. An elder who had been able to reconcile Whiteman accumulation in the fur trade with a model of positive reciprocity over the long term, expresses greater difficulty with appropriation of Cree lands for state-sponsored projects:

> Now the Whiteman is moving the Indian aside and he doesn't even listen to him; he is doing what he has decided. He wants to own the land, this land where we are . . . he is forcing it, the flooding of our lands. It was not like that before; it was not about flooding the Indians' garden. Now, where fur was taken from, the Whiteman has flooded it . . . He is trying to take the land to own for himself. . . "Do not let the Whiteman beat you," it has been said. It is evident that the Whiteman is winning by flooding the lands of the Indian and destroying the lands where they made their living.

At the same time, the relative liberality of the JBNQA as a settlement of native claims has contributed to optimism about the responsiveness of state-level authorities to altruistic reasoning. The rights and benefits specified in the JBNQA went beyond any so far conceded to other natives in Canada. A significant increase in the material standard of living and enhanced Cree control of economic development and social service administration are valued improvements.

Provisional Cree consent to the hydro project and to future Whiteman development was secured by the JBNQA, in exchange for the benefits mentioned. Following the signing of the agreement-in-principle in 1974, Chief Billy Diamond, regional chief for the eight Cree bands, announced a "big victory" for a population of six thousand Crees in a province of 6 million Quebecers. In the aftermath of acute confrontation and hard-nosed negotiation, Diamond reinstated the theme of reciprocity: "It has been a tough fight, and our people are still very much opposed to the project, but they realize that they must share the resources" (1974:9).

Conclusion

Among Crees, the ideology of reciprocity has been elaborated in a series of historical contexts, including domestic social relations as well as their external articulations, first to commercial capitalism and later to the modern state. As a viable model "of" and "for" social reality (Geertz 1973), positive reciprocity has not ceased to dominate Cree domestic relations. But the ideology of reciprocity has also been perpetuated in the context of nonegalitarian relations with capital and the state. In this context, the legitimacy of Whiteman authority depends on the credibility of positive reciprocity as a model "of" interethnic relations. This credibility evaporated when Whiteman actions resulted in extreme prejudice to Cree welfare and patrimony—during the starvation period of the 1930s, and during the early 1970s when hydroelectric infrastructure was being built on Cree lands without Cree consent. The exploitation perceived by Crees is expressed through metaphors linking mythical monsters and pseudo-humans to Whitemen in narrated experience—achieving a dislocation of the "Whiteman" category to an inferior position in "quality space" (Fernandez 1974).

Where reciprocity failed as a credible model "of" interethnic relations, it continued to be advanced rhetorically as a model "for" a restructured relationship of legitimacy. Positive reciprocity was the implicit remedy for the uncomplimentary metaphors of the Whiteman to which the Whiteman public was exposed, via the media, during the crisis of the 1970s.

Oral tradition perpetuates the historical significance of interethnic experience for the interpretation and construction of the present. Cree elders concluded that Crees had much to lose if exploitative trends in Cree-white relations were not converted into terms of reciprocity. We need not regard their appeals to altruistic ideology as naive ones. Given the material limitations of their situation and given certain opportunities in the structure of the liberal democratic state, the appeal to altruism is an important resource for indigenous minorities. It is true that concessions by the state in response to altruistic appeals permit it to recover an aura of legitimacy short of recognizing native people as sovereign partners and short of redressing material inequality. But this is not to say that native people have mistaken the aura for something more substantial. Consent involves the informed recognition of the balance of material and ideological forces aligned against one's position, and it is continually open to renegotiation as circumstances alter.

For a group to make claims against a partner through an ideology of altruistic exchange, it must be perceived to be more yielding than that partner. Where the exchange can be defined as occurring between culturally distinctive groups, actors have the opportunity and the dilemma of establishing equivalencies among elements exchanged that have intercultural suasion. This codification of "exchange values" is an essentially metaphoric practice. If reciprocity is a structure of common significance, the relative weighting of elements entered in exchange must still be negotiated. How to evaluate the advantage to Crees of imported commodities, as against the advantage to trading companies of the surplus value embodied in furs? One conclusion was given in metaphors of furs as "stolen" and trappers as "enslaved," another in the metaphor of economic growth as "positive reciprocity," with quite different demands on the Whiteman partner who would maintain or regain legitimacy. Or again, how to evaluate the absolute sovereignty claimed by the state, versus the custodianship of life and land claimed as sacred Indian patrimony? The political discourse of natives seeks the metaphors that establish the equivalence in exchange of statehood and patrimony, with debt found owing by a Whiteman state that takes where it will not yield. Ultimately, the ethnic personae of the partners are the "exchange values" under determination, their location in "quality space" marked by the extremes of consent and violence, gift and theft.

Notes

1. This paper is drawn from doctoral research conducted at the eastern Cree community of Wemindji, located on the coast of James Bay in northern Quebec, between 1978 and 1982. I gratefully acknowledge the participation of Wemindji residents, as well as support received from the following agencies: the Québec Ministère de l'Education (Direction Générale de l'Enseignement supérieur), the Social Sciences and Humanities Research Council of Canada, the J. W. McConnell Foundation, the McGill University Programme in the Anthropology of Development, the McGill Centre for Northern Studies and Research, and the Ethnology Service of the National Museum of Man, Ottawa. I would also express appreciation for commentary received at various stages in the development of the ideas expressed in this paper from Professor Salisbury and other members of my doctoral committee at McGill University; from fellow participants in the Eleventh ICAES symposiums, "The Political Responses of Indigenous People to State Development Policies" and "Responses of Indigenous Local Systems of Authority to Imported Patterns of State Power"; from Professors Harvey Feit, Richard Preston, and Matt Cooper at McMaster University; and from graduate students at McMaster, with whom I have had the pleasure to interact in seminars.
2. Feit (1985) includes a detailed description of this system of tenure and leadership.
3. Larsen (1983:124) has reported similar ideology about transfer payments among reserve Micmac in Nova Scotia, who have reconceptualized the Indian/white relationship as one of delayed exchange, in which welfare payments are partial compensation for stolen land.
4. I have not incorporated in the discussion the development of local band councils. The institution of the band chief and council is described in detail elsewhere (Kupferer 1966; Preston 1971; Feit 1985). It had developed at the James Bay posts by the 1930s and 1940s, at the behest of company managers, local missionaries, and/or federal Indian Affairs agents. Cree chiefs and councils were needed for coordinating community participation in programs and employment initiated by these external authorities and in the early years were sometimes simply appointed by them. Chiefs and councillors were usually territory bosses (hence respected traditional leaders) as well as leaders in the church. Their new role was precarious. Bitter recriminations from other band members resulted during the famine when chiefs were unable to influence external authorities to help. Even when band councils were elected by the community and administered increasing resources from the government during the 1950s and 1960s, their power to influence policy was very restricted. Their local leadership role remained notori-

ously difficult, if sometimes masterfully executed. Preston (1971) and Feit (1985) show significant continuity of traditional principles of leadership in the practice of chiefs and councils and in the process of their legitimation locally. However restrictive, their role as broker was recognized by other Crees as necessary. In the early 1970s, their support was critical to the local legitimation of the self-selected regional Cree leaders who opposed the hydroelectric project, as Feit (ibid.) describes. In the 1970s the increasing importance of bilingual skills in dealing with state agencies led to the replacement in local elections of most traditional elders by younger chiefs and councillors.

5. Of twenty hunting territories that comprise the Wemindji community area, eight have been affected by marginal to severe flooding by reservoirs and diversions.

6. My present focus on the ideology of people who are now elders postpones for later study the question of variations of interest and ideology within the contemporary Cree population. Many younger Crees today would emphasize the importance of economic development to provide regular jobs as a priority. These interests obviously helped shape the goals that Cree people envisioned beyond resistance to the project. Although southern-schooled Cree leaders negotiated with the government and now administered the settlement that resulted, the perspective of Cree elders remained central in the formulation of political objectives, for several reasons. They were authorities in the subsistence sector, to which the majority of Crees remained primarily oriented. The interests of hunting Crees were those perceived locally to be most directly threatened by the project. The integrity of the hunting way of life, moreover, was one of the Crees' strongest arguments in the courts and in mass media accounts that generated support among the wider public. Even for Cree regional representatives, most of whom were not personally committed to hunting as an occupation, its defence was of major symbolic importance, as well as a matter of family loyalty, given primary kin links between young leaders, elders, and others in the traditional sector.

7. LaRusic et al. (1979), Feit (1979, 1980, 1985), and Salisbury (1983, 1986) offer a variety of perspectives on the development and composition of regional-level representation during early opposition, negotiations, and implementation of the settlement reached.

References

Anonymous. 1975. James Bay and Northern Quebec Agreement/Convention de la Baie James et du Nord québécois. Québec: Editeur officiel du Québec.

Asher, G. M., ed. 1860. *Henry Hudson the Navigator*. London: Hakluyt Society.

Braroe, Niels W. 1975. *Indian & white: Self-image and interaction in a Canadian plains community*. Stanford: Stanford University Press.

Cowie, Isaac. 1911. *The company of adventurers*. Toronto: William Briggs.

Diamond, Billy. 1974. *A time of great decision has come for the Cree people*. Mimeo.

Feit, Harvey. 1978. Waswanipi realities and adaptations: Resource management and cognitive structure. Ph.D. dissertation, McGill University, Montreal.

———. 1979. Political articulations of hunters to the state: Means of resisting threats to subsistence production in the James Bay and Northern Quebec Agreement. *Etudes/Inuit/Studies* 3(2):37–52.

_____. 1980. Negotiating recognition of aboriginal rights: History, strategies and reactions to the James Bay and Northern Quebec Agreement. *Canadian Journal of Anthropology* 1(2):159–72.

_____. 1982. The future and hunters within nation-states: Anthropology and the James Bay Cree. In *Politics and history in band societies*, eds. Eleanor Leacock and Richard Lee. Cambridge: Cambridge University Press, pp. 373–411.

_____. 1985. Legitimation and autonomy in James Bay Cree responses to hydroelectric development. In *Indigenous peoples and the nation state: Fourth World politics in Canada, Australia and Norway*, ed. Noel Dyck. St. John's, Newfoundland: Memorial University Institute for Social and Economic Research, pp. 27–66.

Feit, Harvey, and Colin Scott. 1988. Income security for Cree hunters: Initial socioeconomic impacts and long term considerations. Montreal: Programme in the Anthropology of Development, McGill University.

Fernandez, James W. 1974. The mission of metaphor in expressive culture. *Current Anthropology* 15:119–45.

Francis, Daniel, and Toby Morantz. 1983. *Partners in furs: A history of the fur trade Eastern James Bay, 1600–1870*. Montreal: McGill-Queen's University Press.

Geertz, Clifford. 1973 (1966). Religion as a cultural system. In *The interpretation of cultures*. New York: Basic Books.

Godelier, Maurice. 1978. Infrastructures, societies and history. *Current Anthropology* 19(4):763–71.

Hallowell, A. Irving. 1964 (1960). Ojibwa ontology, behavior, and world view. In *Primitive views of the world: Essays from 'Culture in History,'* ed. Stanley Diamond. New York: Columbia University Press, pp. 49–82.

Kupferer, Harriet J. 1966. Impotency and power: A cross-cultural comparison of the effect of alien rule. In *Political anthropology*, eds. Marc J. Swartz, Victor W. Turner, and Arthur Tuden. Chicago: Aldine, pp. 66–71.

Larsen, Tord. 1983. Negotiating identity: The Micmac of Nova Scotia. In *The politics of Indianness: Case studies of native ethnopolitics in Canada*, ed. Adrian Tanner. Social and Economic Papers no. 12, pp. 37–136. St. John's: Institute of Social and Economic Research.

LaRusic, Ignatius, Serge Bouchard, Alan Penn, Taylor Brelsford, and Jean-Guy Deschênes. 1979. *Negotiating a way of life: Initial Cree experience with the administrative structure arising from the James Bay Agreement*. Montreal: SSDCC for Department of Indian and Northern Affairs, Policy Research and Evaluation Group.

Morantz, Toby. 1977. James Bay trading captains of the eighteenth century: New perspectives on Algonquian social organization. In *Actes du Huitième Congrès des Algonquinistes*, ed. William Cowan. Ottawa: Carleton University, pp. 224–36.

Parkin, David. 1976. Exchanging words. In *Transaction and meaning: Directions in the anthropology of exchange and symbolic behavior*, ed. Bruce Kapferer. Philadelphia: Institute for the Study of Human Issues.

Preston, Richard. 1971. Functional politics in a Northern Indian community. *Proceedings of the 38th International Congress of Americanists*. Vol. 3, pp. 169–78.

_____. 1975a. *Cree narrative: Expressing the personal meaning of events*. Mercury Series no. 30. Ottawa: National Museum of Man.

_____. 1975b. Eastern Cree community in relation to the fur trade post in the 1830's: The background of the "posting" process. *Proceedings of the Sixth Al-*

gonquian Conference. Mercury Series no. 23, pp. 324–35. Ottawa: National Museum of Man.

Rich. E. E. 1960. Trade habits and economic motivations of the Indians of North America. *Canadian Journal of Economics and Political Science* 26:35–53.

Richardson, Boyce. 1975. *Strangers devour the land: The Cree hunters of the James Bay area versus Premier Bourassa and the James Bay Development Corporation.* Toronto: The Macmillan Company of Canada Limited.

Sahlins, Marshall, D. 1965. On the sociology of primitive exchange. In M. Banton, ed. *The relevance of models for anthropology.* ASA monograph No. 1. London: Tavistock.

Salisbury, Richard. 1966. Structuring ignorance: The genesis of a myth in New Guinea. *Anthropologica* N.S. 8(2):315–28

_____. 1976. Transactions of transactors? An economic anthropologist's view. In *Transactions and meaning: Directions in the anthropology of exchange and symbolic behavior,* ed. Bruce Kapferer. Philadelphia: Institute for the Study of Human Issues, pp. 41–59.

_____. 1983. Les Cris et leur consultants. *Recherches Amérindiennes au Québec* 13(1):67–69.

_____. 1986. *A homeland for the Cree: Regional development in James Bay 1971–1981.* Montreal: McGill-Queen's University Press.

Savard, Rémi. 1979a. La faim et la mort. In *Destins d'Amérique: Les autochtones et nous.* Montréal: L'Hexagone, pp. 15–26.

_____. 1979b. Chasseurs-philosophes. In *Destins d'Amerique: Les autochtones et nous.* Montreal: L'Hexagone.

Scott, Colin. 1979. Modes of production and guaranteed annual income in James Bay Cree Society. M.A. thesis, McGill University, Montreal. Programme in the Anthropology of Development Monograph Series no. 13.

_____. 1982. Production and exchange among Wemindji Cree: Egalitarian ideology and economic base. *Culture* 2(3):51–64.

_____. 1983. The semiotics of material life among Wemindji Cree Hunters. Ph.D. dissertation, McGill University, Montreal.

_____. 1984. Between original affluence and consumer affluence: Domestic production and guaranteed annual income for James Bay Cree hunters. In *Affluence and cultural survival: Proceedings of the spring meeting of the American Ethnological Society,* ed. Richard Salisbury. Washington, D.C., March 20–21, 1981.

Tanner, Adrian. 1979. *Bringing home animals: Religious ideology and mode of production of the Mistassini Cree hunters.* St. John's: Institute of Social and Economic Research, Memorial University.

Turner, Lucien. 1894. Ethnology of the Ungava District, Hudson Bay Territory. *Eleventh annual report of the Bureau of American Ethnology,* 1889–90. Washington, D.C., pp. 150–350.

Willis, Roy. 1981. *A state in the making: Myth, history and social transformation in pre-colonial Ufipa.* Bloomington: Indiana University Press.

7

"There Is Always Somewhere to Go . . .": Russian Old Believers and the State

David Z. Scheffel

Introduction

One of the more interesting chapters in Russian political history consists of the relationship between the Old Believers and the state. It begins in the second half of the seventeenth century with a political crisis known as the *raskol* (schism), which triggered the most significant dissident movement of pre–nineteenth century Russia. The spark that ignited the *raskol* was the imposition of a religious reform that eroded the autonomy of the Russian Orthodox Church and compelled its members to adopt innovations associated with the hated Latin West. In the course of two years, between 1666 and 1667, a council of Russian and Greek prelates legislated an end to the ideology of "holy Russia" and prepared the way for the program of Westernization adopted soon afterward by Peter the Great. The defenders of national traditions, the Old Believers, were excommunicated as *raskol'niki* (schismatics) and classified as enemies of the state.

There is ample historical evidence to indicate that the relationship between the Old Believers and the Russian state has at times been rather stormy. Some of its more dramatic episodes include the protracted siege of the Solovetski monastery, whose monks engaged the czar's army for eight long years (Smirnov 1898). There is the insurrection of the *strel'tsy*, the life-guard of the royal family, who revolted in 1682 with the demand for the czars "to be crowned in the true Orthodox faith, and not in their Latin Roman faith" (Macarius 1873:436). Animosities created by the schism fueled Stenka Razin's uprising of 1669–71 (Eliasov 1963:302), and Bulavin's army, which fought against Peter the Great, consisted largely of Old Believers (Call 1979:144). The program of Pugachev's large-scale insurrection of 1772–75 contained plans for the restoration of the old faith (Siegelbaum 1979:230). Hence Michael Cherniavsky is probably correct in his claim (1966:20) that "every popular uprising in Russia . . . was fought under the banner of the Old Belief; the restoration of old ritual, icons, and books was inextricably connected with the program of massacring the aristocracy and abolishing serfdom."

All these facts are relatively well known, as the link between religious and political protest has been discussed in the *raskol* literature for over a century (Kel'siev 1860; Cherniavsky 1961, 1966; Klibanov 1965; Katunskii 1972). The attention to spectacular forms of political dissent has, however, overshadowed the need for a thorough assessment of other strategies adopted by the Old Believers in their interaction with the state. What follows here is an attempt at sketching some of these strategies in their historical and contemporary context.

In Antichrist's Shadow

The immediate result of the *raskol* was a polarization of Russian society. Prevented from openly following the traditional Muscovite way of life, the Old Believers withdrew from public life and retreated to thinly inhabited regions where contact with the state was minimal (Zenkovsky 1970). The flight to the periphery, a motif entrenched in Russian history as the most prevalent form of protest (Gorky 1922), led the fugitives to virtually all frontier areas of the expanding empire and beyond. By the early eighteenth century, some Old Believers had crossed the Russian border and settled in Polish and Turkish territories (Iwaniec 1977; Call 1979).

What propelled this exodus was the combined effect of draconian laws aimed at eradicating the Old Belief and the fear its defenders held of falling prey to the antichrist. The ominous year 1666 seemed to open an era of chaos and confusion. Not unlike the Jews faced with the destruction of the Temple, the Old Believers found themselves "at the end of an old and long-established order and at the beginning of an age lacking all precedent, all points of reference and orientation" (Neusner 1983:xi). In an attempt to re-create meaning, the traditionalists adopted the best explanation that traditional Christianity seemed to offer: the antichrist doctrine.

At first, many Old Believers expected the antichrist to arrive in the form of the apocalyptic beast, announced by the archangel's trumpet and accompanied by the more dramatic signs promised in the Bible (Miliukov 1942). When fire and brimstone failed to materialize, the opinion that the antichrist had already infiltrated Russian society unnoticed came to prevail. Out of a variety of beliefs held by different sects at different times it is possible to abstract a core agreed on by the majority of the dissidents. This core was anchored in the assumption that the schism had been instigated by the antichrist and that its human perpetrators, represented by the official church and the state, acted as his agents (Smirnov 1898). This led to the erection of boundaries that guarded the Old Believers from the dangerous contact with "reformed" Russians. The rules adopted in most congregations proscribed intermarriage, common worship, and the sharing of food and other intimacies (Vasilev 1694; Zhuravlev 1831).

The secession from public life must be regarded as the main source of conflict between the Old Believers and the Russian state. As Michael Cherniavsky astutely observed (1966:36): "As religious eccentrics the Old Believers could be tolerated as long as they ... belonged. But their real and ultimate crime was exactly their refusal to ... participate, and hence to accept the society of Antichrist." Faced with a situation where a "heretical" movement seemed to diminish the country's political harmony, the government adopted a two-pronged strategy. Its ultimate goal remained the reintegration of the Old Believers into mainstream society. Failing that, the state was willing to tolerate a degree of autonomy as long as it did not pose a threat to political and cultural homogeneity.

The definition of "threat" depended very much on the government in power and the extent to which the numerous denominations of the dissenters suppressed their distaste for the worldly society. Thus, on the surface, Peter the Great's "Ecclesiastical Regulation" of 1721 lumped all "schismatics" together as "inveterate enemies, who are always devising mischief against our Sovereign and his government" (in Cracraft 1982:99). Yet underneath this surface, many Old Believer communities were making a valuable contribution to Russia's economy and enjoyed the czar's protection (Crummey 1970).

By the early nineteenth century, the state had devised an easy method for differentiating between more and less threatening Old Believers. Those who registered their deviance, paid a special punitive tax, and prayed for the czar could, under normal circumstances, feel relatively secure. Their coreligionists who did not belong to a registered congregation but who professed to pray for the czar belonged to a more stigmatized category. Finally, those who refused to recite the czar's prayer were classified as "harmful sectarians" and were at most times actively persecuted (Sobranie 1858:66).

The centrality of the czar's prayer in separating friendly from hostile Old Believers deserves a few moments of attention. Both sides attached immense importance to this symbol. From the perspective of the state, the prayer constituted an oath of allegiance, and its omission could change the fate of a community virtually overnight (Sobranie 1858 passim; Crummey

1970). For the Old Believers, the prayer afforded an opportunity for negotiating with the state and for redrawing sectarian boundaries within the amorphous "schismatic" movement. For example, when a powerful branch of the Old Belief announced the intention in 1862 of peaceful coexistence with the state, its leadership appealed to the members to pray for the czar (Subbotin 1881; Chrysostomus 1970). This action led to a schism with a previously related branch (Chrysostomus 1970), but the government responded favorably and legislated several concessions (Ammann 1950:550,575).

The refusal in some congregations to pray for the czar may have been prompted occasionally by a more or less explicit merger between the ruler and the antichrist. This phenomenon has been identified by some scholars as an important indicator of the alienation of the Old Believers from the Russian state (Cherniavsky 1961, 1966). Although there is empirical evidence supporting such view—especially with respect to Peter the Great (Livanov 1873)—the czar/antichrist motif does not appear to be a dominant one in the *raskol*. On the contrary, one is struck by the tenacity with which many Old Believers continued to cling to the myth of the "just czar" even in the face of utmost adversity.

This myth is expressed at its best in the contrast drawn by early Old Believers between the two authorities most directly responsible for the schism, czar Alexis and patriarch Nikon. The patriarch, who instigated the reform but eventually became one of its victims, is portrayed as a "wolf and apostate," a "heretic" (Avvakum 1974:434–35) and an agent of the forces of darkness (Tetzner 1909:59–60; Akademiia nauk 1948:328). The czar, by contrast, who was ultimately responsible for allowing the conflict to escalate the way it did, is depicted as an unwitting bystander who was prevented by political machinations from interceding on behalf of the "true faith." The influential leader of the first wave of dissenters, the archpriest Avvakum, firmly subscribed to this tenet even after he had been sent into banishment, which ended in martyrdom (Avvakum 1974:434–35). To Avvakum, the czar—"set over us by God"—deserved absolute obedience. For this reason he disagreed with the omission of the royal prayer practiced in some congregations (Smirnov 1898:103; Hauptman 1963:73).

A few years after the merciless conquest of the Solovetski monastery, an account of the siege written by an Old Believer exonerated the czar of all responsibility. The bloodshed was blamed on Nikon's followers, who allegedly prevented the delivery of a message signed by the czar and renewing the old faith (Akademiia nauk 1948:334). A similar tale was spread by Stenka Razin during his campaign against Alexis. The rebel claimed, apparently quite persuasively, that the "true czar" was waiting in his camp, ready to assume the throne (Siegelbaum 1979:228). Thus, while some Old

Believers did indeed associate the "false czar" or pretender with the anti-christ, many also seem to have followed the example of other dissatisfied peasants who "deceived themselves into believing that the czar was being deceived" (Siegelbaum 1979:226). In this manner, at least a flicker of hope in a better future could be maintained.

The unwillingness of the Old Believers to challenge the legitimacy of the Russian state can be illustrated with an example drawn from the history of the militant Cossacks who fought under Bulavin's command. In order to avoid surrendering to Peter the Great, the remnant of his rebel army crossed the border with the Ottoman Empire and settled down in Dobrudja. In exchange for autonomy over internal affairs, the militant Cossacks undertook to maintain an army to guard the border region with Russia (Call 1979).

A Russian government spy dispatched to the Balkans in early 1840s singled out the Cossacks as genuine political enemies (Nadezhdin 1846:134). It was perhaps the attention given to the situation in Moscow (Kel'siev 1860) that prompted members of the *Kolokol* group on London—centred around Herzen, Bakunin, and Ogarev—to assess the revolutionary potential of the Cossack–Old Believers of Dobrudja (Livanov 1873; Call 1979).

This investigation, conducted by the brothers Ivan and Vasilii Kel'siev in the early 1860s, revealed that the fierce Cossacks were in fact docile fishermen with a high regard for traditional authority. "They all fall to their knees before their superiors," reported Vasilii Kel'siev, "the layman before the priest, the priest before the monk, the monk before the bishop, the wife before her husband, the children before their parents" (in Call 1979:160). While the envoy was trying to recruit revolutionary converts, the political leader of the Cossacks had already sent a letter to the czar assuring him of his loyalty (Call 1979:151). A message of similar content was drafted by the local bishop, in which the London-based rebels were damned for their "godless agitation" (S-N 1865).

This experience shattered Kel'siev's ideals and inspired him to seek pardon in Russia. In a letter to the czar, he maintained that the Old Believers

> constituted no political threat to the government . . . and only a dreamer . . .
> would entertain the notion that they were a potential revolutionary force.
> The Russian masses in general and the Raskolniks in particular, he claimed,
> were so tradition-bound that many of them still adhered to the notion of
> Moscow's being the Third Rome. . . . As for the Raskolniks living in
> Dobrudja, Kel'siev thought that both their loyalty to the tsar and the harsh
> conditions of that region made Dobrudja a suitable place for purging young
> idealists . . . of their revolutionary illusions [Call 1979:191–92].

The picture that emerges after this short historical overview suggests considerable richness and complexity in the relationship between the Old Believers and the Russian state. There can be little doubt that the vast majority of the guardians of the old faith regarded the state as hostile and dangerous. Some were willing to join other disgruntled factions and use arms to settle their grievances. But for the most part, the Old Believers appeared unwilling to adopt an openly hostile stance that would have forced them to attack the state head-on. Instead, they negotiated, through deeds rather than words, a position of semiavoidance, which allowed them to maintain distance from institutions thought to be harmful, without being compelled to give up contact with the outside world altogether. The strategy of "semiavoidance" also characterizes, as I show further on, contemporary relations between the Old Believers and the state.

"There Is Always Somewhere to Go . . ."

My first encounter with the Old Believers took place in the summer of 1981 in the unlikely location of northern Alberta. I had heard about the establishment of a new settlement in this area and was on my way to lay the foundation for research that still continues (Scheffel 1988). From the nearest Canadian village I dialed the telephone number of a man identified as the "mayor" of the Russian community. A girl's voice answered in heavily accented English and informed me that the mayor could only meet with visitors who spoke Russian. Unwittingly, I had stumbled upon an important component of the relationship between local Old Believers and the Canadian state.

Several years later, I realize that none of Berezovka's mayors elected since my first visit has been able to communicate in English. The office is always occupied by a worthy and respected man who happens to be unilingual. This seems odd in the context of local politics. The people of Berezovka are recent immigrants who covet Canadian citizenship and bear no historical grudge against the state that confers it. As a matter of fact, the office of the mayor (*starosta*) is claimed to be an institution designed by the residents to facilitate communication with the state. At first glance, the inability of the official to carry on a conversation in the language of the state would appear to undermine this very goal.

In order to illuminate the local attitude to the state, it is necessary to discuss the concept of *vol'nost'* or freedom, which the Old Believers value very highly. Countries, epochs, and national characters are all associated with *vol'nost'*. Unlike the Chinese, the Germans, and other allegedly regimented nations, the Russians are believed to require a great deal of freedom in order to thrive. However, according to the local definition, *vol'nost'* pertains to freedom of *action* rather than freedom of *thought*. The former applies to unhampered hunting and fishing, lack of interference in domestic affairs, freedom to move around. The latter is associated with *vol'nodumstvo* (freethinking) and abhorred. An Old Believer is not allowed to think as he pleases; the mind belongs to God and must remain receptive to the Holy Spirit. The body, on the other hand, is under direct personal control, and it is through this medium that one measures liberty.

Older informants who remember life in Russia stress the curtailment of freedom of action following the October Revolution as the main impetus for leaving their homeland. While they disagree with an ideology hostile to God, life would have been bearable had it not been for the threat of collectivization and the myriad of rules imposed by the Soviets on the Far Eastern frontier inhabited by the ancestors of Berezovka's residents. As China was nearby, many crossed the border between the 1920s and 1930s. The new home in northern China proved satisfactory until the 1950s. The refugees could tolerate Manchurian warlords, Japanese generals, and Chinese communists without feeling unduly threatened. What triggered their exodus, at least as it is seen today, was the imposition of tight controls on the traditionally anarchic northern frontier. The Old Believers could no longer hunt as they pleased; even their freedom to make fires in the wilderness had been limited. This made normal life impossible.

When Berezovka was established in the mid-1970s, the settlers expected to enjoy the type of *vol'nost'* celebrated in their Manchurian folklore. On the surface, northern Alberta offered unlimited supply of land, game, fish, lumber, and personal space. After several encounters with the Royal Canadian Mounted Police, game wardens, and other state officials, the Old Believers realized the extent to which their new frontier had been domesticated. They encountered a web of institutions interfering directly with their lives. Contrary to traditional practice, they were expected to register births, deaths, and marriages. Children had to attend public schools; adults could not drink in public; owners of cattle grazing along riverbanks faced hefty fines. The culture shock was profound.

The newcomers were expected to follow in the footsteps of other immigrants and to make peace with the Canadian state under the protection of the policy of "multiculturalism." In a nutshell, the policy encourages political integration in the new country while allowing the retention of ancestral folklore. Officially Canada's alternative to the radical "melting pot" solution associated with the United States, the policy of multiculturalism aims at creating homogenous values under the guise of political slogans celebrating pluralism.

The political integration of a new ethnic group proceeds essentially along the same path as that opened up by Russian czars for cooperative Old Believers. The group registers with the government and thus expresses its desire to *belong* to the state. The group is legally incorporated as an "ethno-cultural organization" (Alberta alone has over one thousand such entities) and becomes part of a dense network of provincial and federal councils, committees, and directorates, all somehow responsible for the implementation of multicultural goals. It is through this network that the state disburses grants for the upkeep of one's "heritage" and simultaneously compels the "ethnics" to absorb Canadian culture by adhering to long-established rules of organizational conduct. Whether one considers the actual incorporation procedure, the process of applying and lobbying for grants, or the keeping of legally valid protocols, these are powerful acculturative forces that play an essential role in the politics of multi-culturalism.

It is perfectly clear that this policy aims at preventing the isolation of ethnic groups. By expressing the "deviance" of strange customs in the jargon of the state, the host society gains a degree of control over it. While the legal incorporation now amounts to the registration of religious dissenters in the past, the ongoing contact between the ethnics and the multi-cultural network is comparable to the daily prayer for the czar. The absence of either arouses suspicion.

The suspicion of the Canadian goverment was aroused as early as 1964 when it was confronted with the desire of a group of Old Believers to immigrate. The request was flatly rejected (Isbister 1964). The reasons for the rejection were repeated word for word in 1974 when several Old Believers were already living in Canada. While the country was buzzing with the just-announced slogans of multiculturalism, the acting director general of the Home Services Branch in the department of immigration delivered this verdict:

> Their case was studied in 1964 and a decision was reached that their mass migration was contrary to departmental policy. . . . It was the department's opinion that the establishment of ethnic and cultural enclaves or communities separate and distinct from the community at large was undesirable. The department notified . . . that we could only justify the migration of people whom we had reason to believe would attempt to identify themselves with the larger interests of the country. The "Old Believers" history over the last 200 years spoke against this. The department pointed out that wherever these people settled they would encounter the same difficulties stemming from their determination to continue as an anachronistic element in the general population of the host countries [Gordon 1974].

This important and in some respects shocking qualification of the multi-cultural policy defines the context in which the people of Berezovka found themselves upon finally gaining entry—under somewhat nebulous circumstances—into Canada. The *vol'nost'* which they expected did not materialize. Instead, the immigrants received a conditional welcome, which promised tolerance in exchange for the Canadian equivalent of the csar's prayer.

The Old Believers have not fulfilled this expectation. They go on living "as an anachronistic element," separated from the general population by the same traditional boundaries as those employed by their ancestors in Russia. Outsiders are not allowed to live in Berezovka, they may not share food with its inhabitants, intermarriage is unheard of. The surrounding society is still believed to be in the antichrist's tentacles, and local residents try hard to prevent the extension of his grip to Berezovka.

The steadfastness with which the Old Believers hold on to their own values has thus far thwarted their full integration into Canadian society. They have retained the ability to continue the "semi-avoidance" characteristic of their traditional relationship with the state. The unilingual mayor is a symbol of that type of accommodation. His very existence is a response to the demand of the host society for access to a bridge that would link Berezovka with Canada, as it were. Yet the Old Believers retain control over the traffic moving along the bridge. The *starosta* does not refuse attendance at the various meetings organized by the local municipal bodies. His presence is, however, purely symbolic, and his constituents can be certain that he will not attempt to speak on their behalf. By giving and yet denying the state a channel for reaching the people of Berezovka, they continue to outwit it.

The professed inability to communicate in the language of the state has made it possible to abstain from the community building process encountered everywhere else in rural Canada. Despite its considerable size, Berezovka remains unincorporated, it boasts no civic organizations, and its residents do not demand a post office or other municipal services. The fewer formal links there are between the Old Believers and the state, the easier it seems to be to preserve a semblance of the cherished *vol'nost'*.

The limits to *vol'nost'* are more readily discernible in the economic than the strictly political realm. Unlike the genuine frontier of northern China, the heavily regulated pseudo-frontier of northern Alberta makes it impossible to live relatively comfortably and avoid direct confrontation with a state agency. Once this realization was made, the people of Berezovka learned very quickly the rules of economic survival. Within a few years, they carved a niche for themselves in the forest industry, which combines considerable freedom of movement with good remuneration. Isolated from the influence of urban culture, groups of related men and adolescents spend much of the year in remote camps, planting and felling trees.

Paradoxically, it is the work in the bush that confronts the Old Believers most directly with the might of the state. The entire industry is regulated by a provincial ministry that awards contracts and monitors compliance with its standards. The Russian newcomers have had to learn how to bid for contracts, how to handle relatively complex financial transactions, and how to reconcile domestic responsibilities with the tight schedule of government contracts.

Although most of the forest workers consider the adaptation to the new economic realities a necessity they had no choice over, many realize and resent the heavy dependence on the very state that they try to outwit in the political realm. The response is at times rather interesting, as I was able to witness one summer during the planting season. Trying to engage an older planter in conversation, I began by asking how much time the average seedling requires to reach maturity. The man glanced at me sharply and asserted that the trees they were planting would not grow much at all because of the impending arrival of the antichrist. Puzzled, I inquired about his reasons for engaging in an apparently meaningless activity. My companion grinned and retorted, "As long as there is a government silly enough to pay for useless work, I will be happy to take the money!"

This anecdote demonstrates a new function of the antichrist doctrine. While it continues to justify the decision to secede from the dominant society, it also helps overcome feelings of dependence on the state by providing secret knowledge that transforms weakness into strength. The value of this weapon is not limited to the situation sketched above. Whenever a young, reform-minded resident suggests that the community should perhaps cooperate with the state in order to gain control over education, zoning regulations, and other decisions affecting Berezovka, some elder is bound to remark that such action would appear futile in view of the short time left in people's lives.

It is difficult to determine at which point the antichrist believers change from a strategy for outwitting the state into an expression of genuine fatalism. Faced with increasingly complex methods adopted by the state in penetrating their existence, the Old Believers appear less and less able to maintain the degree of *vol'nost'* that they seem to require for cultural survival.

As more and more residents apply for old age pensions and other types of social security used by the modern state to muzzle rumblings of discontent, there is talk of another exodus. Asked about the direction of the next migration, one of my informants explained vaguely and yet strangely persuasively, "There is always somewhere to go. . . ."

References

Akademiia Nauk SSSR. 1948. *Istoriia russkoi literatury*, vol. 2, pt. 1. Moscow-Leningrad.

Avvakum, Archpriest. 1974. Life of Archpriest Avvakum by himself. In *Medieval Russia's epics, chronicles, and tales*, ed. Serge A. Zenkovsky. New York: Dutton.

Ammann, Albert. 1950. *Abriss der ostslawischen Kirchengeschichte*. Vienna: Herder.

Call, Paul. 1979. *Vasily I. Kelsiev: An encounter between the Russian Revolutionaries and the Old Believers*. Belmont: Nordland.

Cherniavsky, Michael. 1961. *Tsar and people: Studies in Russian myths*. New Haven: Yale University Press.

_____. 1966. The Old Believers and the new religion. *Slavic Review*, 26/1.

Chrysostomus, Johannes. 1970. Der Streit um das Rundschreiben (okruzhnoe poslanie) vom 24.Februar 1892. *Ostkirchliche Studien* 19:135-66.

Cracraft, James, ed. 1982. *For God and Peter the Great: The works of Thomas Consett*. New York: Columbia University Press.

Crummey, Robert. 1979. *The Old Believers and the world of Antichrist*. Madison: University of Wisconsin Press.

Eliasov, L. E. 1963. *Fol'klor semeiskikh*. Ulan-Ude.

Gordon, J. R. 1974. Old Believers. Memorandum from acting director general, Home Branch, Canada Immigration Division, Ottawa, April 5, 1974.

Gorky, Maxim. 1922. *The Russian peasantry*. Reprinted in *Journal of Peasant Studies* (1976), 11–27.

Hauptmann, Peter. 1963. *Altrussische Glaube*. Göttingen.

Isbister, C. M. 1964. Tolstoy Foundation representations on behalf of the Old Believers and similar refugee migrants. Memorandum to the Minister of Citizenship and Immigration, Ottawa, August 19, 1964.

Iwaniec, Eugeniusz. 1972. *Z dziejów staroobrzedowców na zemiach polskich XVII-XX w*. Warsaw:PWN.

Katunskii, A. E. 1972. *Staroobriadchestvo*. Moscow.

Kel'siev, Vasilii, ed. 1890. *Sbornik pravitel'stvennykh sviedenii o raskol'nikakh*. Vol. 12. London:Trübner.

Klibanov, A. I. 1965. *Istoriia religioznogo sektanstva v Rossii*. Moscow: Nauka.

Livanov, Fedor. 1873. *Raskol'niki i ostrozhniki. Ocherki i rasskazy*. Vol. 4. St. Petersburg.

Macarius. 1873. History of the Russian Schismatics, Trans. and ed. William Palmer in *The Patriarch and the Tsar*. Vol. 2. London.

Miliukov, Paul. 1942. *Outlines of Russian culture*. Part 1: Religion and the church. Philadelphia: University of Pennsylvania Press.

Nadezhdin. 1846. O zagranichnykh raskol'nikakh. *Sbornik pravitel'stvennykh sviedenii o raskol'nikakh*, ed. V. Kel'siev.

Neusner, Jacob. 1983. *Ancient Israel after catastrophe*. Charlotteville: University Press.

S-N. 1865. Sovremennyia dvizheniia v raskole. *Russkii vestnik* 55 (January).

Scheffel, David. 1988. The Old Believers of Berezovka. Unpublished Ph.D. dissertation in anthropology, McMaster University, Hamilton, Ontario.

Siegelbaum, Lewis. 1979. Peasant disorders and the myth of the tsar: Russian variations on a millenarian theme. *Journal of Religious History* 10/3.

Smirnov, P.S. 1898. *Vnutrennie voprosy v raskole v XVII veke*. St. Petersburg.

Sobranie. 1858. *Sobranie postanovlenii po chasti raskola*. Ministry of the Interior, St. Petersburg.

Subbotin, N. I., ed. 1881. *Materialy dlia istorii raskola za pervoe vremia ego sushchestvovania*. Vol. 6. Moscow.

Tetzner, Franz. 1909. Die Philipponen. *Zeitschrift der Altertumgesellschaft* [Insterburg] 11:44–84.

Vasilev. 1694. Prigovor ili ulozhenie novgorodskogo sobora 1694 goda. In *Vnutren-nie voprosy v raskole*, by Smirnov, 1898.

Zenkovsky, Serge. 1970. *Russkoe staroobriadchestvo*. Munich: Fink.

Zhuravlev, A. I. 1831. *Polnoe istoricheskoe izvestie o drevnikh strigol'nikakh, i novykh raskol'nikakh, tak nazyvaemykh staroobriadtsakh*. St. Petersburg.

8

Responses of the Hausa Society to Participatory Development Policies of the Republic of Niger[1]

Lucien R. Bäck

Introduction

The Republic of Niger emerged in 1960 from the breakup of French West Africa. The territory covers a vast surface, the northern part of which is situated in the Sahara Desert. The south belongs to the Sudano-Sahelian zone. Edging the desert lies a landscape making cattle- and camel-breeding possible. The southern part of the country allows for mainly extensive agriculture.

The pastureland is inhabited by pastoral peoples, especially Fulani and Tuareg, who are small in number. The comparatively fertile region along the border with the Federal Republic of Nigeria is inhabited by the Hausa. Their number accounts for about half the population of Niger. Other important ethnic groups are the Djerma-Songhai in the southwest and west and the Kanuri in the east.

At independence the government of the Republic of Niger faced the enormous task of giving itself legitimacy from within and of consolidating it despite various centrifugal forces and eventual foreign interference. As in other parts of Africa, the national boundaries had been drawn rather by colonial accident than with due account to regional history. Unlike other emerging nations, Niger had not experienced an overall anticolonial movement preceding independence, which could have contributed to the nation-building process.

As power had been inherited from French colonial rule, the administration had to rely on a certain degree of repression and exploitation of the peasant population. This was particularly true during the first decade after independence, when tax payments and even compulsory labor continued to be extracted from the population.

After the great drought that devastated the Sahel in the early seventies, political power on the national level was seized by the armed forces in 1974. Ever since, the strengthening of the government's legitimacy has been expected mainly from a gradual modernization of the economy and more specifically of agriculture, in which more than three-quarters of the population are engaged. Self-sufficiency in the satisfaction of food needs has been declared a national priority.

Whereas modernization attempts in agriculture started by French colonial rule had been limited to the introduction of cash crops such as groundnuts, cowpeas, and cotton, the new government concentrated on crops for the subsistence of the population, especially millet, sorghum, and rice. A surplus production was required, not only to raise the standard of living of the farmers themselves, but also to gain more control over economic exchanges with libertarian pastoral nomads and to keep the cost of living acceptable to the modern elite employed in nonagricultural activities such as administration, business, and the army. Moreover, the development of the internal economy was to allow for decreasing dependence on external powers, especially the former metropolis.

In political terms, the decolonization process was to be based on an increase of popular participation in political and economic decision making. One of the keynotes in this attempt was to be cooperative institution building. The latter was initially limited to the main agricultural regions, but afterward even introduced in other parts of the country. Cooperative societies were initially meant to integrate communal aspects of traditional village life and at the same time to present a modern alternative to the power of traditional chiefs and village elders.

The present contribution attempts to analyze why this aim has not fully been achieved. The strength of the traditional society and its ability to adapt to the modern state has "perverted" the initial cooperative ideology based on Western democratic principles. Thereby traditional society itself has not remained what it was, but paradoxically, the outcome is quite different from "Western democracy."

This contribution is based on firsthand experience in development work carried out in the region of Maradi between 1979 and 1984. This work was directly concerned with cooperative institution building among the Hausa. However, no attempt has been made in this contribution to describe project activities in detail (cf. Bäck 1983 and 1984). The purpose is rather to present a more general analysis of a development process going beyond the scope of a limited project experience. It should be noted that the present contribution is mainly concerned with Hausa society of the region of Maradi and more specifically with the area covered by the former dynasties of Katsina and Gobir. Extensive literature on the Hausa in Northern Nigeria has not been taken into consideration.

Cooperative Institution Building

One of the most outstanding features of cooperative societies in Niger is the fact that its members are not individuals but village communities. Several villages, called *groupements mutualistes* (GM) in this context, are united to constitute a cooperative society. The whole adult population of a GM meets to elect board members who are considered "delegates," who meet at the cooperative level. The delegates from the various GMs constitute the general assembly of the cooperative society electing another board among their midst. All these elections should theoretically be held "democratically," that is, in accordance with the principle "one man—one vote."

The structure was conceived in the early sixties. The main purpose of the cooperative societies used to be at that time the marketing of cash crops, especially groundnuts and a little cotton. Another function of the cooperative society was to be to serve as an outlet of farm inputs such as seeds, fertilizers, and farm equipment. Agricultural credit was to be granted to the farmers on a collective basis, as part of the net benefit from marketing was to be kept on behalf of the cooperative societies as a guarantee.

The system has remained formally intact down to the present day. However, the great drought of the early seventies brought agriculture to a virtual standstill. Especially groundnut production has never since attained outputs known during the sixties. This was partly due to the shift in agricultural policies by the government, which henceforth tended to concentrate on food production rather than on cash crops.

Existing cooperative societies were thus stimulated to add cereal marketing to their activities, and many new cooperative societies were created in millet- and sorghum-producing areas. In 1984 all villages of the agricultural region could be considered formal members of the cooperative movement. This development has also been fostered by increasing attempts of the government to promote the use of modern farm inputs all over the agricultural region.

Cooperative societies were thereby not to have economic functions only. Cooperative legislation of 1978 and 1979 (République du Niger 1978 and 1979) declared the whole rural population of Niger to be part of the cooperative movement, which should allow for self-determination and autonomy of the rural areas. Cooperative unions were to be established at different administrative levels. The final outcome of this structure was achieved in 1984. Unions were established at the levels of *cantons, arrondissements, départements* and at the national level. In 1984 the national union of cooperatives comprised approximately six hundred cooperative societies, more than half of which were situated in the agricultural regions of Maradi and Zinder. In mid-1984 the regional union of Maradi was composed of seven subregional unions, twenty-eight local unions, 188 cooperative societies, and 2273 *groupements mutualistes* (Bäck 1984:9).

One important purpose of this cooperative movement was to free the villagers from their subnational and parochial identity and let them eventually become full-fledged citizens of the new nation. They were to participate actively in decision-making processes concerning their own environment and more global national issues in order to identify themselves with the nation and the policies of the government.

As this process did not spring up spontaneously, the government aimed at "induced participation" at the grass-root level and more specifically chose theories and methods of French *animation rurale* as an approach to realize the aims mentioned above (for a full theoretical discussion of these concepts cf. Charlick 1974:2–60). The approach was initially transposed and adapted to the African context during the 1960s with the help of the "Institut de Recherches et d'Applications de Méthodes de Développement" (IRAM).

The core of the doctrine was to convince the farmers of the necessity of change and progress through discussions and group processes. Farmers were to share in the responsibilities for development initiatives. This applied to agricultural innovations, use of collective revenues, reinvestment, functional literacy, primary health care, et cetera. The approach also implied material participation by the farmers despite the relative poverty of their economy. Farm inputs such as improved seeds and fertilizers, as well as plows, carts, et cetera, were to be bought for cash or on loan. The necessary infrastructures, such as buildings, markets, and secondary roads, were to be created under human investment or with wage labor paid by the farmers themselves.

It should be stressed that cooperative societies were not the only venue for *animation* activities. As in GM and cooperative meetings participants used to be almost exclusively men, it was found appropriate to create a women's association (Association des Femmes du Niger (AFN)), which would deal with specific problems faced by women. Youngsters were grouped in youth associations (*samarya*) that would take care of social tasks not involving commercial dealings. Cooperative societies and unions, AFN committees, *samaryas*, as well as other "socio-professional associations" would constitute "development committees (*conseils de Développement*)" at the various administrative levels, which would be endowed with important political responsibilities. Representatives of these committees would at the national level be members of the Société de Développement, which would exercise functions comparable to those of parliaments in Western democracies. The political process leading to the accomplishment of the Société de Développement was not yet completed in 1984.

Among all modern political institutions, the cooperative movement clearly is the most important one. It is directly concerned with input supplies, which are considered to be indispensable for the modernization of agriculture. It is furthermore involved in food production and distribution, which is the most essential part of the government's search for legitimacy. It could finally be a concrete example of a rural institution in which farmers themselves are capable of managing their own business.

Cooperative legislation of 1978 and 1979 declared that within two years' time all cooperative societies were to be run exclusively by their members.This was a very ambitious aim in a country where more than 80 percent of the population was illiterate. But ever since, there has been a clear political will to transfer responsibilities from government employed cooperative promoters (staff of the Union Nigérienne de Crédit et de Coopération [UNCC]) to cooperative societies themselves. The *encadreurs* of the UNCC used to keep the money pertaining to marketing and credit operations, whereas under the new arrangement the treasures of the cooperative societies were to assume this task. Although all cooperatives had appointed secretaries, who were mostly literate youngsters, a good deal of the bookkeeping had usually been done by the UNCC promoters. Serious efforts were henceforth undertaken to transfer these responsibilities to the literate farmers appointed by the cooperative societies. To increase the number of literate people, literacy courses were reactivated. Since 1983, many UNCC promoters at the grass-roots level employed by the government on a mere contract basis have been dismissed. Moreover, the UNCC as a promoting body has in the meantime been dissolved.

The high political hopes attached to the cooperative movement could, however, never be implemented in economic terms. Cooperative marketing activities never regained the momentum they used to have in the sixties when groundnut sales flourished in the few cooperative societies existing at that time. The comparatively small quantities of groundnuts and cowpeas produced after the drought fetched considerably higher prices with private tradesmen (*alhazai*, sing. *alhaji*) than through cooperative societies that were bound to keep to official buying rates. Although millet and sorghum, which had been mere subsistence crops before the drought, did enter commercial circuits and started to constitute an important source of monetary income for the farmers, the grain markets, too, have essentially been controlled by private tradesmen who occasionally attempted to speculate on these commodities.

Notwithstanding the decline of marketing activities, cooperative societies have been pushed to accept important agricultural loans, especially under the impulsion of ambitious rural development projects in the regions of Maradi and Zinder since 1977. The cooperative societies and their member GMs were to designate young farmers who would be trained in modern production techniques in rural training centers financed by institutions such as the World Bank, the European Development Fund and the French Caisse de Crédit et de Coopération Economique (CCCE). Upon termination of his course, each trainee was to accept a loan for a complete set of farm equipment (especially plows, cattle, carts, et cetera). The loan was granted to the cooperative society of the trainee in question, and in principle the society was to be held responsible if the debt was not paid off according to schedule. This arrangement did not always work out as foreseen: if a beneficiary of an agricultural loan was unable or unwilling to pay, the cooperative society could do little to make up for this deficiency. On the other hand, cooperative assets from marketing activities proved in most cases too meager to serve as a guarantee for agricultural loans.

With marketing activities ever decreasing and external debts steadily on the increase, the balance sheets of most cooperative societies turned red. The lack of resources put into serious jeopardy the ambitious program of self-management of these rural institutions and did not allow them to perform emancipatory functions, as had originally been expected from them.

Government policies have been characterized by a certain ambiguity. On the one hand, farmers were to take over responsibilities of managing their surpluses and means to reinvest under cooperative organization. On the other hand, they were deprived of the power to do so in real terms by hard decisions taken by the government concerning core issues such as to whom produce was to be sold, which were the buying rates, which was the marketing season, and which was an acceptable level of agricultural debts.

The reason for this ambiguity is to be found in the fact that the cooperative development model was based on imperfect assumptions about Hausa society right from the beginning. The postcolonial governments underestimated the dynamics of traditional society and had to reconcile themselves with a certain number of facts. How this reconciliation produced a new political situation is to be examined in greater detail.

Assumptions on Traditional Hausa Society

As a first step, it may be useful to compare assumptions about traditional Hausa society lying at the base of the introduction of the cooperative development model with more thorough ethnographic accounts.

G. Belloncle, who was among those of the IRAM team who proposed a cooperative model based on collective village membership to the Nigerian government in the sixties, wrote in 1968 that Hausa villages were characterized by two essential features: a weak economic and social differentiation and "extremely democratic" decision-making processes. Technology being at a low level, outputs essentially depend on simply human labor and revenues remain with the producers. The only factor that may eventually provoke inequality is trade. The latter is, however, limited to a handful of large and centrally located villages. He stresses that the village chief is no more than a *primus inter pares*, a *talakka* (simple peasant) like the others. Important decisions are collectively made by all family heads (*masugida,* sing. *maigida*) of a village and can by no means be imposed on others even by the village chief. Belloncle does admit that in a village assembly not all *masugida* speak in public, but he interprets this behavior as silent consent that in no way disqualifies village democracy (Belloncle 1968, in 1978:266–68). In a more recent publication relating to rural development in Cameroon, Belloncle advocates the same principles based on the Nigerian experience (Belloncle 1979).

A very similar argument is presented by D. Gentil, another member of the IRAM team, who claims that collective membership in cooperative societies has freed the system from Western bias: no more financial shares required from individual members, village assemblies deciding matters of interest and designating delegates who will confer on a higher level (cooperative societies and their buying points). Management by UNCC promoters is gradually to be replaced by that of elected board members and peasant personnel designated and paid by the farmers. Training is to be provided to "demystify" the system for a whole population and to have simple bookkeeping done even by illiterates. This implies the development of simple pedagogical devices in conjunction with literacy programs in the national language. Useful devices can be pictograms, fake money, and role-playing arrangements (Gentil 1979).

Gentil considers the greatest obstacle to be government promoters' reluctance to really transfer responsibilities to the farmers. Moreover, he does admit that although village assemblies may have been common in the past, they are held nowadays only when stimulated by external promoters. Traditional patterns of communication influence participants' behavior in such meetings: the young and less important will not speak before the elders and women will not even participate. The village chief will make a decision on behalf of the others, eventually after lengthy debate, but without enforcing his personal views. However, it could be expected that there would be slow evolution and that the youngsters' views would in the future not be systematically rejected (Gentil 1984, 2:4–70).

Belloncle's and Gentil's rejection of Eurocentric models of cooperative organization (individual membership, financial shares, et cetera) is most interesting, and their search for genuinely African ways of organizing trade and commerce should be fruitful. They may, however, have gained their insights in the communication structure of villages rather from their own projections than from a critical appraisal of peasant behavior. Despite extensive firsthand experience in village meetings they attended, their various descriptions of "village democracies" are all very similar and stereotyped and present a somewhat "romantic" picture of what they expect villages to be. Especially Belloncle tends to generalize from Hausa villages to "African villages" with ease. It should, however, be stressed that Gentil, in more recent publications, has attempted to present a more critical appraisal of the failure of many African cooperative movements, making reference to inadequate political and economic conditions surrounding them (Gentil 1979, 1984).

Both authors make strikingly little reference to the extensive ethnographic work among the Hausa of the Maradi region that has been carried out, especially by G. Nicolas and C. Raynaut, since the early sixties. Nicolas, who has given the most detailed account of the region, doubts if Hausa village "communities" are sufficiently coherent to be at the base of collective interest and asserts that *groupements mutualistes* created by the government may remain fictions servicing bookkeeping purposes only (1969:34–35). Raynaut points to changes that affect social organization and agricultural production and strong inequality-producing mechanisms in Hausa society.

Nicolas refers to the historical situation of Hausa society preceding and coinciding with the impact of colonial and postcolonial rule. He presents Hausa society as being characterized by complex and hierarchical social institutions. The traditional Hausa state was governed by a "chief" (*sarki*) and his court composed of *sarauta*, both hereditary functions. The court was clearly distinguished from the *talakawa*, common people, who lived in extensive agglomerations or villages with collective rights in land (*garuruwa*). The chief of such a village (*mai gari*) was chosen within the kin group of its founders. A village was divided into domestic units (*gidaje*, sing. *gida*) inhabited by a man (*maigida*), the nearest members of his clan (*dangi*), their wives, and their children. The clans had been the most important sociopolitical institution before the creation of villages and cities and have preserved importance especially among those who still believe in ancestral norms (*anna*). This clan organization cross-cutting villages coincided to a certain extent with hereditary professional groups, the heads of which belonged to the court according to their status in the hierarchy. Islam was introduced by the Fulani especially during the nineteenth century, when the latter succeeded in penetrating and conquering some Hausa states. Religious specialists in matters of Islam, *marabouts* or *malamai*, tended to assume part of the economic and political power (Nicolas 1969:21–23).

Nicolas observes that in traditional society individuals already had a considerable freedom in allocating their resources. This even applied to women who used to have their own income. Economic behavior could not adequately be described in mere Western terms of consumption and reinvestment.

With a single harvest in a year, it may have happened that farmers sold most of their produce immediately and lived on trade and speculation for the rest of the year. Women often sold fully prepared dishes. The market, *kasuwa*, is a very old tradition. Relatively important sums were spent not only on taxes, but especially on expenses for ostentation and social obligation. Wearing expensive clothing, riding on a horseback, living in a house made of bricks, and being well decorated have been some of the outward signs by which social status is to be acquired and maintained. For a man it is prestigious to have several wives, especially if they do not work but have their tasks performed by hired laborers. Apart from this, parties are offered on behalf of one's clan, provided that one possesses a certain amount of wealth.

Pilgrimages to the sacred places of Mecca confer the prestigious title of *alhaji*. Acquiring the title of *malam* or any other function in the traditional hierarchy also necessitates important expenses. Furthermore, gifts are due to *griots* (*makada*, sing. *makadi*), who will publicly give their judgment on anyone and thus exercise a considerable influence in the ascription of social status. Presents are customary among groups of individuals at occasions such as baptism and marriage (*biki*). The many obligations often promote imbalances in the budgets (Nicolas 1969:23–31). The Hausa also know an elaborate system of credit in kind and cash with interest rates attaining up to 100 percent (Nicolas 1974).

Examining collective enterprises that were created under governmental "animation" in the 1960s, Nicolas stresses that these collectivities had to be united by more than purely economic ties if they were to succeed. In most cases, cooperative societies remained collectivities in the minds of their state promoters only. The population did show signs of reluctance, as *human investment* could have meant forced labor, *mutual group* coercion, and *system of representation* division and domination (Nicolas 1969).

In a survey of the various types of collective organization existing in the late 1960s he realizes that only associations characterized by clear objectives and transparent arrangements as to organization and individual members' gains were viable. He particularly mentions the spontaneous association of vegetable growers who united their labor and collectively invested in wells and fences (*hadakai*) (Nicolas 1971).

Recent changes in the social organization of agricultural production in the region of Maradi have been examined by C. Raynaut, who has also done extensive empirical research in a village (cf. Raynaut 1972). He observes that the *gida* as the basic unit in the labor force tends to include fewer persons, i.e., a man, his wife or wives, and children. Moreover, collective labor gradually declines. Along with the breakup of traditional family estimates goes an increasing individualization in economic activities. Especially in more densely populated areas and around the city of Maradi, there are more and more commercial dealings with the land, a completely new phenomenon, as traditionally land had no value by its own, but served only the labour force to produce economic goods. A third element Raynaut points to is the generalization of hired farm labor. For a good deal of commercial operations the farmers now require cash money, which they can often only obtain by selling their labor force, their produce, and even their land. The system allows an urban bourgeoisie (rich traders, government employees) to accumulate, whereas the peasant producers and especially the poorer strata among them became increasingly vulnerable. These inequality-producing mechanisms are also linked to the low development of production forces in agriculture as well as to the gradual decline of the quality of the soil (cf. Raynaut 1976).

Another author, R. B. Charlick, presents a full analysis of governmental efforts for "induced participation" based on an empirical study carried out in Matameye, a subregion inhabited by the Hausa. In the first place, he considers that the Nigerian government had underestimated the inegalitarian and individualistic character of the society and miscalculated the centralized power required to modify the existing structures. As schemes had been based rather on what planners assumed the society to be than on a realistic appraisal, promoting agencies employed a heavy apparatus setting itself tasks that were unnecessarily difficult for the assignment of its modernization objectives. At the same time, the difficulties of making local structures an ally in the modernization attempts had been underestimated. The result was an irreconcilable "dilemma of development" in power terms. Charlick concludes that development programs did not lead to egalitarian modernization in rural Niger, but created new types of economic differentiation in an unpredicted and antidevelopmental way. Agricultural innovations acquired by wealthy farmers did not improve their productivity but rather reinforced their traditional social power through the development of new clients (Charlick 1974:428–29).

In conclusion, Nicolas, Raynaut, and Charlick agree on one point—that government policy as to a cooperative structuring of the society has been based on an inadequate appraisal of social institutions of Hausa society both as far as traditional custom as well as emerging social organization under colonial and postcolonial rule have been concerned.

The Making of Hausa Society

Present-day Hausa society is the outcome of a historical process of several centuries, largely preceding colonial rule. The immediate impact of colonial and postcolonial state organization on traditional institutions has been fairly recent. Nicolas describes Hausa society that he encountered during his extensive fieldwork carried out during the sixties and early seventies as still characterized by a dichotomy between a pre-Islamic clan-based society abiding by ancestral norms (*anna*) and an Islamic dynastic society around citylike agglomerations (*birni*). Both had largely developed independently from colonial rule.

The social framework of *anna* society is the clan (*dangi*, plur. *danguna*), defined by patrilinear descent from a common ancestor and united by a shared heritage and cultural practices. Membership in the *dangi* is determined by birth and confirmed by ritual practices by which supernatural forces may eliminate "bastards." Each *dangi* is characterized by a set of prescriptions as to behavior between members of different generations. Moreover, clans are subdivided into patrilineages and residential groups (*gidaje*, sing. *gida*). Each clan is headed by a *magaji*, its oldest man, who is in charge of preserving the heritage (*gado*) related mainly to productive activities such as hunting, ironwork, well digging, land tending, et cetera. The heritage comprises a specific relation to the supernatural, manifesting itself in a characteristic tune expressed in words and music. Each clan is a specific ritual community with its own taboos and obligations dictated by supernatural forces and relating to certain plants, animals, and objects. Sacrifices and purifications are performed at sacred places, which may be an altar in the house of the *magaji*, his grain store or a collective field under a chosen tree. Rituals are performed according to a calendar that is specific to each clan. Use is made of the clan's own sacred objects, which may be musical instruments, arms, and jewelry. Clans claim possession of land under actual or potential cultivation and over constructions realized by their members, such as wells and buildings. Several clans usually entertain firm alliances, especially for matrimonial purposes. A woman keeps close ties with her own clan and may return to it if the marriage proves to be unsuccessful. Respect is due to members of the clan of one's mother, and it is not uncustomary that part of the matri-clan's heritage remains important in an individual's life cycle (Nicolas 1975:66–135).

The region currently inhabited by the Hausa of Niger has for centuries been a meeting place of local inhabitants and invaders from other areas, some of whom had already established or maintained contacts with North African and other more developed cultures. Oral traditions affirm that Hausa dynastic society originated from a union between "a queen of Daura" and a hero who had come from the East. Their seven sons founded the dynasties commonly called the "Seven Hausa" (*Hausa Bakwai*). There is no agreement among present-day dynasties which were the original states belonging to the "Seven Hausa," but it is commonly acknowledged that these constitute a common frame of reference (Nicolas 1975:26).

During the eighteenth century, Hausa cities were already characterized by flourishing trade, which extended not only all over the region, but as far as Mediterranean ports to the north and Bornu to the east. Foreign life-styles were imported, but the invaders also adopted the cultures of the original population. A common Hausa culture and language was forged, uniting millions of people. Various foreign states were searching to establish their influence over the region, and more integrated rulers were considered by the local population as protectors who were in the right of enrolling their subjects into armies and to receive tribute (Nicolas 1975:24–29).

In the early nineteenth century a conquest movement started by Fulani immigrants was led by a fervent Muslim, Ousman dan Fodio, who along with his followers succeeded in infiltrating Hausa dynasties. This initially peaceful movement of Islamic reform turned into a holy war (*jihad*) when the Hausa nobility refused to comply with all the religious exigencies. Ousman dan Fodio succeeded in conquering the states of Gobir and Katsina, partly with the help of the local population. Fulani hegemony was established, but soon proved to be extremely harsh and cruel. The population made an appeal to the chief of Katsina, who had been granted refuge by the sovereign of the neighboring region of Zinder. Troops of Katsina, Zinder, and Kano fought a number of battles and succeeded in breaking Fulani hegemony. The chief of Gobir had to take refuge with his counterpart of Katsina for another few years, but could finally also return to his land (Nicolas 1975:29–30).

The result of this process was that many locals had been forced to migrate and to participate in an overall Hausa culture. Dynastic rule was strengthened, initially by members of the courts only, but gradually also by the commoners. Marabouts (*malamai*) who taught Islam and its code of conduct were assigned an ever growing importance in the hierarchy.

Each dynasty was centered on a city (*birni*) extending its influence over the land around it (*kasa*). Even in precolonial times each city could easily comprise a population of several thousands, subject to the season, since many would engage in agriculture or cattle breeding during the short period of rain. A chief (*sarki*) would employ a considerable number of dignitaries amounting to whole bureaucratic administration. Armies were entertained, not only with recruits from the local population, but also with mercenaries and slaves, i.e., captives from previous wars. There used to be a market attached to each city, where foreign and local products were exchanged, such as slaves, ivory, gold, leatherware, arms, tissues, and animals. The rulers deployed considerable efforts to guarantee market peace and safe roads to promote those activities. Foreigners were authorized to sojourn in the country, however, mostly outside city boundaries (Nicolas 1975:137–42).

Inhabitants of the land belonging to a specific dynasty were to pay taxes to the chief, obey his orders, and respond favorably to any appeal to enroll in any army. Outward signs of being a subject of a specific dynasty were patterns cut into the faces of newborn babies at their Islamic baptism, which left scars in adults' faces. Each dynasty was characterized by "national" rituals in which only its subjects participated (Nicolas 1975:142-44).

The chief of a dynasty was responsible for the "health" (*lafiya*) of his land and was considered the land's "husband" (*mijin kasa*). He claimed his descent both from the eastern hero and the queen of Daura and of the ancestor who founded his chiefdom. The latter affiliation suggests that public power was linked to the heritage of the sovereign's clan (*dangi*). However, the *sarki* was not necessarily the oldest man of his clan. An electoral college composed of dignitaries, most of whom did not belong to the royal clan, chose a new *sarki* among several people who were to draw lots whereby supernatural forces could intervene. The luckiest one was likely to bring the utmost fortune to his people. Several chiefs are said to have had exceptional divine powers. The latter "pagan" aspect of dynastic rule coexisted with the fact that the quality of a reign was often measured by the number of marabouts and pilgrims to Mecca it has brought forward (Nicolas 1975:144-51).

At the time of his fieldwork in the 1960s, Nicolas observed that the chiefs still commanded considerable respect. However, colonial and postcolonial administration had cut down a certain number of their privileges. Taxes had to be handed over to the modern state, and warfare was forbidden. Trade links were put under control and sometimes made more difficult. On the other hand, traditional chiefdoms were integrated in the modern administration as provinces and cantons, and their chiefs were to receive salaries for the performance of their administrative duties (Nicolas 1975:36).

Everyday life in the Hausa society of the 1960s was nevertheless only scarcely influenced by the modern government. It was essentially determined by the two cultural traditions, *anna* practices on the one hand and Islamic life-styles on the other. Although useful for analytical purposes, this dichotomy did not exist to an extent that two traditions could be separated from one another. Most people tended to integrate elements of both cultures according to the context. Conversion to Islam often implied a change in outward behavior only: the sacrifice of goats or cocks was replaced by the ritual killing of sheep; instead of leather clothing, cloth garments were preferred, and beer drinking was abandoned. *Anna* ceremonies and veneration of supernatural forces were replaced by prayers to Allah, whereas the heritage made room for Koranic instruction. Certain illnesses could, however, stimulate a thus converted individual to fall back on ancestral norms that were not compatible with a strict interpretation of the Koran. Many individuals relied on different practices according to the advantages they could expect from one behavior or another in a given social context. Urban life-styles practiced in markets and in contacts with foreigners not only by city dwellers, but also by virtually all villagers, thereby tended to offer greater advantages in terms of material well-being and individual social mobility. This should not conceal the fact that even Islamic dignitaries continued to respect norms pertaining to the original social order, if that was for matrimonial arrangements, for the assignment of social status, or for the improvement of any individual's well-being (Nicolas 1975:429–577).

It should be stressed that whereas Nicolas could still observe *anna* practices directly in the sixties and seventies, outward manifestations of this cultural tradition have almost disappeared in present-day Hausa society. Beer drinking is practiced mostly in secret nowadays and by no means in all villages. Leather garments have almost generally been replaced by shirts and *boubou* made of cloth. Rituals to venerate supernatural forces are not performed openly anymore. Instead most people pray five times a day and fast during the month of Ramadan. Many villages have deployed great efforts to build a mosque, which generally is the most beautiful building of the neighborhood. Beer drinkers and those who eat meat of animals not killed according to Islamic law are spoken of with contempt, especially in the cities and by officials of the modern administration who defend a more "purist" interpretation of the Koran. It would, nevertheless, be interesting to compare actual social practices in present-day society with *anna* norms on the one hand and "pure" Islamic tradition on the other.

The Dynamics of "Traditional" Society in Relation with the Modern State

The colonial state had been essentially based on a relation of force, and even after independence the government continued to present itself to a certain extent as an alien power keen to collect taxes, to extract labor and produce from the population, and to enroll children in modern schools (cf. Spittler 1978). Even the current government owes its relative stability ultimately to the armed forces and its control over public order.

But the governments also made serious attempts to be recognized by the population as capable of increasing its material and social well-being. The first government after independence based its concept of modernization on a rather "unhistorical" assessment of traditional society. The power of traditional chiefs was curtailed, and they were to assume limited bureaucratic functions only such as tax collection on behalf of the government. Moreover, *animation rurale* was essentially based on a stereotyped image of village communities, which neglected a number of important social relations. The government that took over after the great drought of the early seventies has been especially concerned with food production and distribution, which are core issues in this Sahelian economy. Though pursuing the strategy of *animation rurale*, it has increasingly come to reconcile itself with the complex set of "traditional" institutions. The interplay of "modern" and "traditional" elements in the development process are to be examined more closely with special reference to what happened in and around the cooperative movement.

A cooperative society comprises an average of ten villages, which may be situated at short distances from one another if the density of population is high or at greater distances in areas with less agriculture. Each village at one time constituted itself in a *groupement mutualiste* with all the *masugida* present in a general assembly that was organized by state promoters. On this occasion, a board was elected with a president, a secretary, and a treasurer and seven other members. The meetings were partly led by the state promoters, but villages tended to let the *maigari* (village chief) speak on behalf of the population. The president of the GM was usually chosen among the relatives of the village chief or other important personalities. The secretary mostly was a young farmer who had attended school for a few years or taken literacy courses in Hausa. The treasurer often was a local tradesman, sufficiently rich to be solvent in cases of disputes over collective funds. But in practice, at GM level there was little to keep or manage. The most important function of board members was to "represent" the GM at the cooperative society and to "inform" the population of decisions taken at the higher level. State promoters often complain that attendance of general meetings of cooperative societies is low, especially when few concrete benefits may be expected from them, and that almost no "messages" are retransmitted to the villages, especially when the news is important to the state promoters' minds only.

Cooperative law prescribes that each GM should have an equal number of votes in the cooperative general assembly, which may range between three and ten for each GM. This theoretical arrangement is difficult to respect. Attendance is highly variable among villages. The most closely situated ones are likely to send many delegates, but those located at greater distances tend to send too few or none at all. The village situated at the center of the cooperative society had usually been chosen with reference to the marketing system, although several cooperatives usually shared a grain or groundnut market. But the cooperative society mostly holds its meetings in its most important village. More doubtful is the coherence of villages united in a cooperative society. The government only recently reorganized the structure of cooperative societies comprising villages belonging to different cantons. This move can be interpreted firstly as an acknowledgment of the fact that in earlier days cooperative structuring had not taken into account traditional institutions such as chiefdoms or cantons and secondly that the *sarki* was to play a more important role in cooperative matters.

The latter aspect was also confirmed by yet another recent decision of the government. Whereas the law of 1978 had invited all cooperative societies to be represented in a subregional union of cooperatives at *arrondissement* level, the real process of structuring provided for the setting up of "local" unions of cooperatives at the canton level. The subregional union is thus constituted of representatives of these local unions and not directly from the cooperatives. This development obviously is to strengthen the chief's influence on cooperative matters.

What is clear already at the level of a cooperative society becomes even more obvious at higher levels of representation. Those who are elected to be part of the system and eventually perform more or less important functions are usually close to those who hold significant "traditional" offices, especially the *maigari* and the *sarki*. They usually also belong to the better-off strata of society, as they would otherwise be unable to bear financial responsibilities. The cooperative movement may thereby be considered a framework allowing for individual promotion in society.

To an individual farmer, a cooperative society gives access to modern farm inputs at subsidized prices. Fertilizers and selected seeds are usually sold for cash by state promoters. Farm equipment with animal traction can be obtained through the cooperatives, which therefore accept a loan to be repaid over four years.

So far, demand for these inputs has greatly exceeded supply. The state experiences some difficulty in raising money to prefinance production of these tools and to subsidize the inputs. The volume of agricultural credit has only increased to a considerable extent wherever rural development projects with foreign funding have come under way. This has, however, been the case especially in the agricultural parts of the regions of Maradi and Zinder since 1978. The projects linked farmers' equipment with tools to extension programs in training centers, where during a period of approximately nine months these farmers were to be taught modern production techniques. In recent times, the farmers in question have been nominated by their villages and sponsored for their equipment by the general assembly of their cooperative society.

In an initial phase, it did happen that individuals who had been trained and equipped soon sold their tools and disappeared for a time to neighboring Nigeria without ever reimbursing their debts. The cooperative society thus proved to be incapable of exercising social control and also of paying off the debts, as solidarity was low. Only when "traditional" village chiefs were reintegrated in the process, as they were to "nominate" the beneficiaries of training and agricultural loans, things tended to improve. This experience also accelerated the process of favoring the presence of those attached to "traditional" dignitaries in cooperative general assemblies. Under the present arrangement of a "local union" covering several cooperatives, credit facilities are placed under the *sarki*'s authority more or less directly.

It should not be surprising that "traditional" dignitaries would tend to sponsor those young farmers they trust most and that the latter are found most often among their next kin. On the other hand, cooperative promoters in charge of collecting repayments of agricultural loans complain that unpaid installments often are to be explained by local dignitaries' not paying off their debts. It would be interesting to examine if for cooperative societies a correlation exists between high debts and important numbers of dignitaries among credit beneficiaries.

The extension programs of the rural development projects have not been an overall success. Despite the high cost of these projects, agricultural production has not been substantially increased in their regions. This may be due to many factors, but it has also been realized that farmers never attained outputs comparable to those of research stations that tested the use of farm inputs in situations that were as realistic as possible. Doubts exist among promoting agencies if an individual farmer who has received the agricultural equipment can produce enough to pay his installments and still preserve a surplus. In practical terms, farmers have found some solutions.

Part of the equipment is rented out and thereby sometimes used for nonagricultural purposes, for example, carts, which may be useful for any form of transport. Furthermore, the modern tools may be used on a limited plot only by a farmer, who gains important revenues from other plots cultivated with wage labor. As a farmer rarely shows all his fields to state-employed promoters unless specifically asked to do so, the latter may also obtain an incomplete picture of his economic possibilities in real terms. Farmers usually engage in more activities than state promoters care to know, and a more thorough inquiry into individual farmers' budgets would require a careful examination of all their social relations likely to involve economic dealings.

The initial idea underlying "collective" credits was that marketing activities would serve as a guarantee. Cooperative law specifies that part of the net benefit of grain and groundnut sales had to be deposited as funds in the agricultural bank (*Caisse Nigérienne de Crédit Agricole*, CNCA), which also played a key role in funding agricultural inputs (but which recently closed down). This idea had long been abandoned almost completely. The amount of money spent on agricultural credit went far beyond sums available in the funds. This was partly due to inadequate bookkeeping of the funds by the state agencies in the past, but more importantly to the decline of marketing activities in cooperative societies.

As groundnut and cowpea production has steadily decreased in recent years, millet and sorghum tended to enter market circuits and provide for a part of the farmers' cash income. Markets were essentially controlled by private tradesmen. The latter, along with cooperative societies, were officially supposed to act as intermediaries only between the farmers and state organizations created for the handling of these commodities: the SONARA (*Société Nigérienne de l'Arachide*) for groundnuts and cowpeas and the OPVN (*Office des Produits Vivriers du Niger*) for millet and sorghum. These organizations bought and sold the crops at rates fixed by the government and according to certain rules and regulations, for example as to the marketing periods and buying and selling points. The traders soon discovered that business was better on the unofficial market, which has thereby become much more important than the one controlled by SONARA and OPVN. Especially for groundnuts and cowpeas, private trade offered farmers rates at least twice official rates, and cooperative societies were in practice the only institutions bound to sell to SONARA only at rates fixed by the government. This development naturally reduced cooperative marketing of groundnuts and cowpeas to a very considerable extent.

The private tradesmen, generally called *alhazai* because of their pilgrimages to Mecca, constitute a rapidly emerging new class in urban and rural Hausa society that may increasingly be considered to dominate the whole economy (cf. Grégoire 1983). Although in most cases illiterate, they have succeeded in a short time in accumulating considerable wealth, especially with trade across the border with Nigeria. Trade and speculation are highly developed in the Hausa-speaking north of this country, which produces an exceptional range of manufactured and industrial goods. The *alhazai* of Maradi have profited from the relative strength of the CFA franc linked to the French franc by a fixed parity (fifty CFA francs equal one French franc) and the weakness of the nonconvertible Nigerian naira. A very dynamic black market developed. Recent measures taken by the government of Nigeria to curtail it by officially closing the border for several months in 1984 proved unsuccessful. Nigeria also changed all banknotes and coins in 1984, but the new means of payment was available on the black market of Maradi at the old rate within hours.

Imports through the *alhazai* are generally favored by the government of Niger, as their low cost is a stimulus to the economy. Except for groundnuts and cowpeas, there is little the local market could export to Nigeria. Millet and sorghum tend to fetch much higher prices in Niger than in Nigeria.

This does not mean that the *alhazai's* activities are not a source of concern for the government of Niger, especially when they engage in speculation with grain. The *alhazai*, being still very much integrated in the traditional society, dispose of an extraordinary network of influence in the rural areas. They not only efficiently supply the farmers with consumer goods from Nigeria, but also buy farmland in certain areas and engage in wage labor to a growing extent. A practice that is even more generalized is money lending at high interest rates. Farmers in need of cash in the dry season or at the beginning of the rainy season can borrow money from an *alhaji* and reimburse in kind or money after the harvest. The produce is thus already mortgaged before official (cooperative) markets open.

An interesting development took place between 1980 and 1984 when an attempt by the government to weaken the *alhazai's* grip on the grain market resulted in the strengthening of the position of traditional chiefs.

Between June 1980 and the same month of 1981 the price of millet on the free market of Maradi rose from 90 F CFA/kg to 200 F CFA/kg. This was considered unacceptable by the government. Attempts were made to increase the buffer stock under state control held by the OPVN. Official buying rates were considerably increased in October 1981 (from 40 F CFA/kg of millet to 70 F CFA/kg). This should normally have stimulated the cooperative societies created especially for the economic purpose of grain marketing to do a good deal of business. Paradoxically, this was not the case. Being under pressure to build up a buffer stock as quickly as possible, the government did not consider cooperative societies efficient enough to buy adequate quantities of grain. Instead, traditional chiefs at the canton and village level received cash advances from OPVN that allowed them to purchase grain directly from the producers in the villages.

In the short run, this policy proved to be successful—speculation on the grain markets was halted in 1982. However, it left the majority of cooperative societies without any economic activity of importance between 1981 and 1982. OPVN, too, ran into financial trouble. Having bought grain at fairly high prices from the producers, OPVN had to increase its selling rate to 100 F CFA/kg of millet in 1982 and to 120 F CFA/kg in 1983. These prices proved to be higher than those offered by the *alhazai*, and OPVN was unable to sell its stocks. As OPVN was politically obliged to keep buying at least limited quantities of grain from producers after each harvest, stocks piled up in an unprecedented manner. Storage costs and bank overdrafts thus constituted for OPVN a very heavy financial burden.

As OPVN was now less keen on grain purchases, cooperative societies were reactivated in 1982/83 to perform this job, but this could not consolidate their economic base. They were now to "cooperate" with traditional chiefs who would receive part of the collective benefit as a reward for their "trouble" in stimulating the farmers to sell their produce to the cooperative societies. The remainder of the collective benefit would hardly suffice to finance the various costs to be borne by the cooperative societies, such as salaries for the marketing personnel (farmers employed by the cooperatives) and expenses for small equipment (balances, lamps, bookkeeping documents, et cetera).

Cooperative societies have thus clearly lost their battle whenever they were in competition with traditional chiefs or modern tradesmen. More interestingly, the latter two institutions have been able to insert themselves into the cooperative movement and to bend it to their own advantage. This process has already been shown, as far as agricultural loans and the marketing process are concerned. But even *alhazai* have succeeded in being elected to key functions in the cooperative movement. The most striking example is that an *alhaji* has also been elected president of the regional union of cooperatives of Maradi. Though not a farmer anymore, he does employ wage labor in his fields to a very considerable extent and may be considered the most important agricultural producer of the region. But his main interest does not lie in agriculture. It should also be mentioned that this *alhaji* has recently been elected treasurer of the national union of cooperatives. As this body is to perform important functions in the management of agricultural inputs in the future, it is likely that he will pursue some of his own interests in this capacity.

Despite their poor showing in marketing activities and in agricultural loans, cooperative societies are still to perform key functions in the future from the government's point of view. The role of the cooperative societies in the *Société de Développement* is still to be defined in detail. Faced with an increasing lack of resources in times of international economic crisis, the government is searching for ways and means to transfer at least part of the burden of investments and recurrent costs in agricultural development to the beneficiaries. Among ideas being examined and tested on a limited scale are cooperative revolving funds for seeds and fertilizers, which should replace actual cash sales by government promoters, and cooperative banks for saving and credit, which should take over part of the tasks actually performed by the CNCA. More social activities likely to generate surpluses are, for example, cooperative cereal banks and supply shops, which would directly decrease farmers' dependence on *alhazai*. All these initiatives should be managed by "the farmers" themselves. It remains to be seen if they will eventually achieve their aims in the present context of the cooperative movement.

Conclusions

1. Modern states, having emerged from the breakup of former colonies without an anticolonial movement preceding independence, have often found themselves in the need of overcoming the pure relation of force on which colonial governments had been based and searching for legitimacy from within. Like other new nations, the Republic of Niger has expected legitimacy mainly from modernization of the economy and of the social order. The present contribution has examined how the imported pattern of "popular participation" and more specifically of "cooperative institution-building" has evolved in the context of Hausa society.

2. Although essentially based on Western principles such as democratic decision making and equitable shares in benefits, the cooperative pattern had been adapted to what the state considered to be the institutional framework for the modernization process: villages, not individuals, were to be members of cooperative societies. The communal aspects of "traditional" village life were to be preserved, and at the same time villagers were to gradually participate in institutions freeing them from their parochial identity. The first government after independence thereby showed a remarkable lack of understanding of the historical process in which Hausa society had been engaged for centuries. The second government increasingly adopted a more realistic view and reconciled itself with the dynamics of "traditional" society.

3. Hausa farmers are part of a complex set of social institutions within and outside villages. Ancestral norms (*anna*) assigning each individual a specific place defined by his clan, his occupation, his age, and his sex have been integrated in the generalization of Islamic life-styles—allowing for a considerable extent of social mobility. Markets have been of growing importance, and trade and speculation are practiced by virtually everyone. Rich tradesmen, *alhazai*, have in a short time succeeded in accumulating enough wealth to be in a dominant position on the markets. Traditional chiefs and their courts, descendants of important dynasties of precolonial times, have regained key functions in the political and economic spheres under the second government of Niger.

4. In the political sphere, the whole population of the rural areas are to be of the cooperative movement, which at various administrative levels is to represent the farmers among other socio-professional associations as well as women's and youth associations in the Société de Développement. The latter is to take over the political decision making from the administration. Although initially conceived rather as an alternative to the power of traditional chiefs and *alhazai*, the cooperative movement in its present outcome is very much controlled by these agents. At the village level, this development has been favored by the farmers spontaneously electing traditionally important people to represent them at higher levels. The state has played on this practice by creating "local unions of cooperatives" at the level of the cantons, thus giving the *sarki* an important say in the decision making. A tendency may be observed that even *alhazai* are elected to important functions of the cooperative movement on the regional and national levels.

5. In the economic sphere, cooperative societies were to perform marketing activities in grain since the great drought of the early seventies. Considerable speculation in grain by the *alhazai* in 1981 forced the government to quickly build up buffer stocks for a stabilization of markets. Traditional chiefs were thereby considered more capable of buying important quantities from the producers than the cooperative societies. After having been deprived of grain marketing in 1981/1982, cooperative societies have recently been obliged to share their benefits with traditional chiefs. On the other hand, the chiefs are also expected to improve the process of agricultural loans. It may, however, not be excluded that they at least partially divert these inputs to their own interests. The same holds true for new initiatives to let cooperative societies dispose of "self-managed" revolving funds in seeds and fertilizers as well as of cereal banks and supply shops (cf. Bäck 1984).

6. It remains to be seen how the newly conceived Société de Développement will cope with problems resulting from the modernization process. It may not be excluded that especially in times of low agricultural production due to unfavorable climatic conditions speculative practices may again spring up. Moreover, increasing numbers of farmers are at present obliged to sell their produce and even their land at unfavorable conditions and agricultural wage labor is on the increase. It may be assumed that the cooperative movement as it is conceived at present will hardly be in a position of counter-balancing these trends.

Note

1. The present contribution was written in 1985 and takes into account developments until 1984. Since that time, emphasis in government policies has shifted away from cooperative development to a growing acknowledgement of the importance of "traditional chiefs." The central thesis of this contribution has therefore been validated.

References

Bäck, Lucien R. 1983. La banque céréalière. Etude de cas. Modules de formation. Manuel de procédure. Three working papers for the ILO/ACOPAM project Maradi (Niger).
_____. 1984. Rapport de mission 1979–1984. Working paper for the ILO/ACOPAM project Maradi (Niger).
Belloncle, Guy. 1978. Coopératives et développement en Afrique noire sahélienne. CEDEC Université de Sherbrooke, no. 10.
_____. 1979. Quel développement rural pour l'Afrique noire? Dakar-Abidjan: Les Nouvelles Editions Africaines.
Charlick, R. B. 1974. Power and participation in the modernization of rural Hausa communities. Ph.D. thesis, University Microfilms International, Ann Arbor, Michigan.
Gentil, Dominique. 1979. Les pratiques coopératives en milieu rural africain. CEDEC Université de Sherbrooke, no. 11. Republished in 1984. Paris: Harmattan.
_____. 1984. Les mouvements coopératifs dans l'Afrique de l'Ouest "Francophone". Interventions de l'Etat ou organisations paysannes. Thèse pour le Doctorat de l'Etat, books 1 and 2, Paris.
Grégoire, Emmanuel. 1983. Développement urbain et accumulation marchande: les Alhazai de Maradi. Thèse pour le Doctorat de troisième cycle (Géographie tropicale), Université de Bordeaux III.
Nicolas, Guy. 1969. Développement rural et comportement économique traditionnel au sein d'une société africaine. Genève-Afrique 8(2):18–35.
_____. 1971. Processus mutualistes contemporains au sein d'une société africaine (Vallée de Maradi, Niger). Rapport multicop., FLSH Bordeaux.
_____. 1974. "La pratique traditionnelle du crédit au sein d'une société subsaharienne (Vallée de Maradi)". Culture et Développement 6(4):737–73.
_____. 1975. Dynamique sociale et appréhension du monde au sein d'une société Hausa. Paris.
Raynaut, Claude. 1972. Structures normatives et relations électives. Etude d'une communauté villageoise haoussa. Paris, La Haye: Mouton.
_____. 1976. Transformation du système de production et inégalité économique— le cas d'une village haoussa (Niger). Revue canadienne des études africaines/ Canadian Journal of African Studies 10(2):279–306.
République du Niger. 1978. Ordonnance No. 78–19 du 12 octobre 1978 portant statut des organismes ruraux à caractère coopératif et mutualiste.
_____. 1979. Décret no. 79–05/PCMS/MDR du 18 janvier 1979 portant application de l'Ordonnance no. 78–19 du 12 octobre 1978.
Spittler, Gerd. 1978. Herrschaft über Bauern: die Ausbreitung staatlicher Herrschaft und einer islamisch-urbanen Kultur in Gobir (Niger). Frankfurt/M/, New York.

9

Outwitting Ghana: Pluralism of Political Culture in Nanun[1]

Peter Skalník

The present paper analyzes the apparent failure of the modern postcolonial state of Ghana to mediate in the conflict between three different types of political culture[2] in one relatively small area of Nanun in northern Ghana, West Africa. The Ghanaian state, which is an over-centralized postcolonial offspring of the imported European-derived colonial state, is shown to have indirectly caused, misinterpreted, and mishandled a years-long confrontation between the neo-traditional *naam* or chieftaincy of the Nanumba and the "regulated anarchy" of the Konkomba, settlers in Nanun, whose social organization is based on kinship solidarity combined with local and "tribal" associations.

Nanun, as a traditional area or Nanumba District (the two largely overlap), as it is called in Ghanaian administrative terminology, has until recently been considerably isolated and suffered from general underdevelopment even in the context of the less developed Ghanaian North. Traditionally, Nanun has been under the authority of Nanumba chiefs (*nanima*, sing. *naa*) led by their paramount chief, the Bimbilla Naa, who resides at Bimbilla, the capital. Nanumba District in terms of territorial division of Ghana is under the administration of the Nanumba District Council, which at the time of my research was led by the district chief executive and his office. Basing my research on the historical background to the three different principles of political culture, I shall endeavor to describe and explain developments since the late 1970s when the Nanumba chieftaincy came into conflict with the Ghanaian state and the Konkomba settlers in Nanun. My argument is that the chieftaincy in Nanun is far from dead. On the contrary, it has shown a surprising capacity for accommoda-

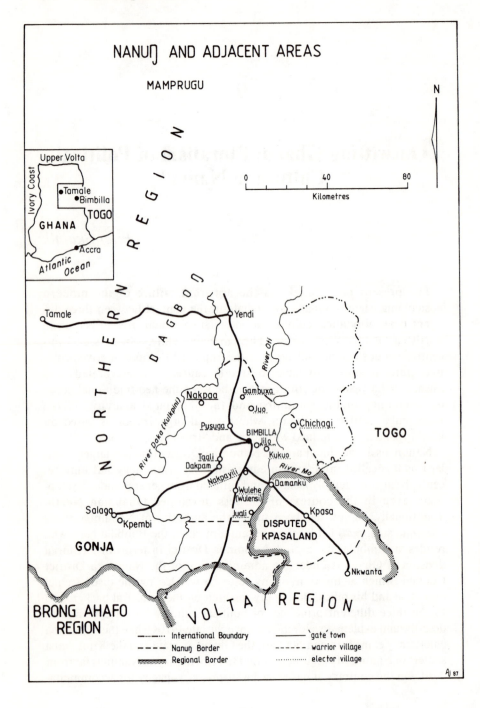

NANUŋ AND ADJACENT AREAS

MAMPRUGU

N

Upper Volta

Ivory Coast

Tamale
Bimbilla

TOGO

GHANA

Accra

Atlantic Ocean

0   40   80

Kilometres

NORTHERN   REGION

DAGBOŋ

Tamale   Yendi

River Oti

Nakpaa   Gambuxa

Juo.

Pusuga   Chichagi

BIMBILLA
Jilo.

Kukuo.   TOGO

Taali
Dakpam

Nakpayili   River Mo

Wulehe   Damanku
(Wulensi)

Salaga   Juali   Kpasa

Kpembi   DISPUTED
KPASALAND

GONJA

Nkwanta

BRONG AHAFO
REGION   VOLTA   REGION

········· International Boundary   ——— ‘gate’ town
- - - - Nanuŋ Border   - - - - - warrior village
▧▧▧ Regional Border   ·········· elector village

AJ 87

tion to social and political change and will most probably play a decisive role in future attempts at planned socioeconomic transformation of Nanun. Similar trends are seen all over the country. With the recent economic disintegration in Ghana (1976–1985), chieftaincy, together with other elements of local leadership, seemed the only guarantee of the integrity and identity of the people.

The German and later the British colonial administrators reluctantly realized that even though *naam* displayed different logic compared with the political system they brought with them (cf. Skalník 1983, 1987a), they had to use it in their administration of the territory. On the contrary, the postcolonial state of Ghana was at first hostile toward chieftaincy, in Nanun and elsewhere in Ghana. Specific conditions in the north of Ghana, however, and particularly in Nanun, where a vast majority of the population remains illiterate, have eventually compelled the successive Ghanaian regimes to admit that chieftaincy plays an indispensable role as a bridge in the relationship between the state and the popular masses. Lately, following a tragic conflict between the Nanumba and Konkomba (1981), a new assault on chieftaincy was launched by the populist regime of Flt. Lt. J. J. Rawlings, which has ruled Ghana since December 1981 (cf. Skalník 1986a,b). Again, however, the new regime soon realized the importance of chieftaincy and from 1983 started to incorporate it within a model of popular democracy, which it has since tried to design (cf. Skalník 1986c).

The Nanumba are a society whose ethnicity is expressed through allegiance to a chieftaincy called *naam* in the Nanuni language. A "reconstruction" of the actual working of the *naam* in Nanun during several centuries when Nanun was de facto an independent polity[3] will be attempted elsewhere. Indeed, such a reconstruction is necessary if we wish to understand the articulation[4] of the Nanumba *naam* and the whole social system around it, with the political and social phenomena that came to Nanun as a consequence of the European conquest. Prior to the German conquest, the historical development of Nanun revealed contact with external forces, either statelike or "acephalous" units. The influence of Asante and Gonja politics from the southwest must have particularly affected the character of the Nanumba *naam*, but only the encounter with European state civilization has been adequately documented. One of the most efficient methods of looking for a dynamic explanation of *naam* seems to be the examination of confrontations between the *naam* and the colonial state.

Colonial Conquest: Juxtaposition of the Modern State with Indigenous Political Institutions

The colonial conquest instantly revealed irreconcilable contradictions between the two systems. In the 1890s, the German colonial regime enlarged its Togo domain by penetrating as far north as possible. One path of access led from Krachi to Sansanne Mango via Bimbilla and Yendi. These latter two towns, a mere seventy kilometers from each other, are capitals of two neighboring indigenous polities, Nanun and Dagbon respectively. Nanun is several times smaller than Dagbon and, with the Mamprugu polity situated farther to the north, the two polities shared a myth of common origin. The myth or mythical charter as Malinowski would define it, stipulated solidarity and the renunciation of violence between these polities, even though Dagbon was more powerful and larger than Nanun and Mamprugu.

As part of the German northward expansion, Dr. Gruner, who was in the service of the German colonial administration of Togo, was sent to the north in 1895. He was called "red monkey" and stoned by the inhabitants of Gbungbaliga, a village in southern Dagbon. The Germans used this as a suitable pretext to turning their very loose presence in Togo into permanent occupation. They sent a punitive expedition to Dagbon under Lieutenant von Massow. The relations between the Germans who used to pass Bimbilla in very small groups and at irregular intervals and the Nanumba were, until that time, tolerable, if not friendly. Therefore, the news of the approach of a heavily armed column created a serious dilemma for the Bimbilla Naa, Abalsi. An oral tradition kept by *lunsi*, the tom-tom beaters, testifies that he, his elders (*nayilkapamba*), and other important chiefs reasoned in the following way: If we let the Germans pass and they beat the Ya Naa (chief of Yendi) they will later come back and subject us by force. Alternatively, if the Dagbamba win, they will never forgive us for betraying them and letting the Germans pass and they will probably punish us. So we have no choice but to fight the Germans.

This they did and on November 30, 1896, the Germans easily defeated the forces of the Nanumba in the battle of Bimbilla. Characteristically, the battle had three phases. First the cavalry and musketeers of the Bimbilla Naa attacked the Germans, who were established in the Naa Abalsi's vacated palace. Then came the forces of the Dakpam Naa, who was the most powerful pretender to the Bimbilla skin, from the Banyili or bangle house. And finally came the attack from the forces of the Nakpaa Naa, chief pretender from the Gbugmayili or lion's house.

What is significant in this first violent confrontation between two different principles of political order is not that the Nanumba could not stand a chance against the German-led column armed with modern weapons, but the remarkable fact that Nanumba forces were divided into three sections. Besides the paramount chief, the Bimbilla Naa, there were two divisional chiefs, potential pretenders to the Bimbilla *naam* after the Bimbilla Naa's death, who also had their own cavalry and musketeers. In fact, even less important Nanumba chiefs had their own warriors. They would coordinate their forces against an external enemy only, whereas for the purposes of internal politics, the Dakpam Naa, Nakpaa Naa, and other major chiefs would be relatively autonomous. The oral traditions collected show that this military autonomy sometimes led to violent internal conflicts, especially when succession to the Bimbilla *naam* was involved. The case introduces at once a fascinating aspect of Nanumba political culture. On the whole, the Nanumba network of *naam* was a much looser political order than that which the invading Germans brought with them. One of the shocks the Nanumba elders never forget to mention was that the Germans forced the Nanumba chiefs and people to work as overnight builders, porters, or cotton farmers. Forced labor was evidently completely unknown to the Nanumba. There was slave or captive labor, but the extent of the latter was very small in Nanun, as my data show. Moreover, chiefs, commoners, and dependent people worked predominantly in subsistence agriculture, whereas the Germans forced them to do work that was entirely different from anything they were used to. Today some elders praise the Germans, saying the Nanumba were lazy and had to be forced to work, which was good. They even contrast "German work" to "British work," referring to the latter as "*nyama-nyama*," meaning lousy, of bad quality. But they echo the disorders in Ghana's economy rather than the feeling of the Nanumba toward the Germans.

What is remarkable in this account is that the chiefs did not have any efficient means to compel anybody to work for them. Symbolically, some categories of the population, such as young warriors and other commoner youth, were expected to work for the village chief on his farms once a year. Warriors and followers were obliged by custom to erect the palace of the newly installed Bimbilla Naa or some village *nanima*. Coercion by physical force or threats was unknown in relations between the Nanumba chiefs and the rest of the people of Nanun.

Another shock came when the Germans on some pretext detained the Bimbilla Naa, Salifu, in Krachi around 1909 and later banished him to his native village of Nasamba, just south of Bimbilla. No Nanumba chief can be "deskinned," and no word exists for such a demotion. What the Germans did was completely abhorrent to the customary Nunumba rules of *naam*. The elders concluded that as the chief was not dead and no ritual funeral (*naakuli*) had been performed, which is the only condition for succession, the customary alternation between the two chiefly houses was not permissible. Instead, a relative of Naa Salifu from within the same line, Banyili, was made a provisional Bimbilla Naa. He was Naa Mahimi, who died soon after his installation. Once the Banyili incumbent (though provisional) of the Bimbilla skin really died, the pretender from the other ruling line, Gbugmayili, was eligible to the Bimbilla skin. He was Naa Harruna. With the beginning of the Great War in 1914, the British pushed the Germans out of Nanun. One of the measures the new colonial power took in Nanun was the restoration of Naa Salifu. But it was only after Naa Harruna died (cf. Amherst 1931) that Naa Salifu returned to Bimbilla (in 1917). This case shows that the characteristic system of alternating succession has been preserved despite great pressure from the Germans.

Succession has always been a difficult issue in Nanun, and it became even more so under the colonial and postcolonial regimes. While there was no quarrel about the principle of alternation of the two chiefly houses in Bimbilla, all four successions to the Bimbilla *naam* since Naa Salifu's death in 1929 have been marked by competition between the incumbents of the nominally highest, so-called gate *naam* (which is Dakpam *naam* for Banyili and Nakpaa *naam* for Gbugmayili) and the incumbents of less important *naams* who, however, were senior to the other pretender(s). This is explained by the two customary rules: 1) *naam* must be won in a competition; 2) the most senior of pretenders has greater chance. These rules were suppressed by the colonial and postcolonial administrations and replaced by written stipulation that left little doubt about succession procedure. (See Nanumba Customary Rules and Regulations 1969.) Usually, there was no doubt between the two lines or houses about the right of the succession. In all recent cases of succession a considerable degree of intervention on the part of colonial or postcolonial state was deemed necessary. The modern regimes failed to eliminate altogether the principle of competition for the *naam*.

Nevertheless, Nanun, in sharp contrast to Dagbon, presented a picture of relative order and stability, because the conflicts between different lines were in fact nonexistent. The alternation of two houses worked quite well. No conference of chiefs and colonial administrators was necessary as a prelude to the introduction of the system of Native Authority in the early 1930s, known in the literature as "indirect rule." A report about the constitution of Nanun was compiled in 1931 by a British deputy district commissioner, Amherst, and this alone was deemed sufficient (Amherst 1931). The Native Authority system was clearly based on the existing system of the *naam* in Nanun. The latter was provided with a modern bureaucratic appendix in the form of a Native Authority clerk. The judicial procedures and financial transactions, including revenues and taxes, were to be registered forthwith in books and reports to be controlled by the higher authority, the district commissioner (DC), who resided in Yendi.[5] The first clerks of Native Authority in Bimbilla were Mr. E. F. Tamakloe, an Ewe, who is known as the author of the first history of Dagbon (Tamakloe 1931).

Nanun was otherwise left more or less intact. There were a few signs of change: six boys, sons of chiefs, were sent to basic schools in the late 1930s, and some very modest steps at introducing modern amenities were undertaken. Nonetheless, the Native Authority system meant a certain degree of active incorporation of chieftaincy into the global colonial system. It also meant that the Nanumba were more closely involved in the economic life of the new country created by European conquest. When transport by lorry came into operation, the export of yams to the south commenced. Yam cultivation subsequently made Nanun famous all over the Gold Coast–Ghana. Manufactured goods of western origin reached Nanun, and some men worked in the south, in mines or on cocoa plantations. On the whole, however, there was not such a high degree of migration from Nanun as from other parts of the then Northern Territories of the Gold Coast or Upper Volta. The introduction of the colonial system and Native Authority system has on the other hand facilitated the influx of new people into Nanun. They were southern traders with manufactured goods, some transport owners and artisans.

Nanun in Independent Ghana: Development and Frustration

The awakening of the southern Gold Coast and the subsequent struggle for independence, which was led by Nkrumah from 1949, had an impact on Nanun in a very specific way. The chiefs led by Banyili Bimbilla Naa Natogmah adopted the policy of support for the Convention People's Party (CPP), and one of the first six literates, Bimbilla Naa Natogmah's brother, Natogmah Attah, was elected to the new legislative assembly. He remained an M.P. until the coup in 1966. This fact probably influenced Ladouceur's view of Nanun as Attah's personal fief (1979:230). Although Attah was a skillful politician, he had to respect the wishes of his brother while the latter was paramount chief, and later could not antagonize his successor, Bimbilla Naa Dasana, from the Gbugmayili house. Eventually, after Attah's second brother, Abarika Attah, became the Bimbilla Naa in 1983, the former was enskinned as a chief of the village of Tuu and thus became the only literate chief in the two chieftain houses.

Particularly during the period of Gold Coast's autonomy, 1951–57, which coincided with the last years of the reign of Naa Natogmah, various development projects were started in Nanun, which had now become a separate Nanumba District within the Northern Territories. Schools, a water station, a health center, and public buildings such as the district court and council buildings were raised in that period. The role of Naa Natogma in these efforts must not be underestimated. We can see this more clearly when comparing it with how little was achieved during the twenty-two-year reign of Naa Dasana (1959–81).

When Naa Dasana became the paramount chief, i.e., he "drank the *naam*" (*namdibo*) of Bimbilla, several projects remained to be completed in Nanun. These included the reconstruction of the water station and especially the building of a number of dams near larger villages. When these were finished, in the early 1960s, the funds of Ghana were exhausted, and so, too, it seemed were the imagination and interest of the paramount chief in further development of his traditional area.

Unfortunately for Nanun and its inhabitants, the independence of Ghana, proclaimed in 1957, brought with it an increase in the centralization of the government. In practice it meant that the Nanumba lost their district and were once again administered from Yendi. The change occurred at the time of the interregnum following the death of Naa Natogmah, when there was nobody in Nanun (Attah then in Accra engaged in state politics) who would defend local interests before the higher authorities. The political vacuum slowed down the introduction of those Western innovations that the Nanumba welcomed and saw as positive.

After the proclamation of independence, the then powerful Ghanaian state tried to suppress the chieftaincy and denounce the characteristics of it that the modernizing elite disliked. The Nkrumah government made a far-reaching decision to reduce the judicial powers of the chiefs to arbitration only. The magistrate's court was to take over all the criminal and civil cases that could not be solved by arbitration by the chiefs. In practice, most cases were still brought before the chiefs because the majority of people was illiterate and did not trust the Ghanaian judicial institutions headed by often corrupt lay magistrates. By the mid-1960s it seemed that the role of the chiefs, even in Nanun, was nearing its end. Nkrumah won with a one-party state in which chiefs were relegated to a merely decorative status (Göhring 1979:194–238; cf. Ladouceur 1979:157–211).

The abrogation of chieftaincy was one of the factors that led to the overthrow of Nkrumah in February 1966. The National Liberation Council (NLC) regime has proclaimed its support for the "traditional institution of chieftaincy." Even though NLC and subsequent Busia democratic governments did not really mean to give more powers to the chiefs, in the north it was understood as a signal of a revival—especially in Nanun, where chieftaincy was the only stronghold through which people could channel their rights, because almost everything "modern" was embodied by people other than the Nanumba. So the chiefs raised their voices. In 1969 they called for the reestablishment of a separate district administration for Nanun by the Busia government,[6] but to no avail. They and the people of Nanun succeeded only in 1974, after another military regime came to power in Accra, that of I. K. Acheampong (1972–78), whose populist program included a reform of the local government system. This exemplifies once again how the Nanumba chiefs succeeded in finding a specific role for themselves in the planned social change, such as the introduction of modern innovations in the administration and economy. The revived Nanumba District came into being on July 1, 1974, and even though most of its officers have been so far of non-Nanumba origin, the voice of the Bimbilla Naa and other chiefs seems to be respected more than before. From the monthly reports that the office of the district chief executive was obliged to send to Tamale, the capital of Northern Region, it is evident that practically no visit to Bimbilla by a regional or central officer, including the head of state or ministers, could avoid a courtesy call on the Bimbilla Naa. As a result of the Ghanaian government's failure to decentralize, the strict hierarchical order prevented the district administrators from raising problematic issues without consulting the regional administration in Tamale. Thus the most serious problems were never solved, because they "disappeared" in state bureaucracy. Factors of increasing corruption, general irresponsibility and helplessness, and a virtual lack of resources in the later years of Acheampong's regime must not be underestimated.

Unlike the district administrators, paramount chiefs like the Bimbilla Naa and others, by virtue of their exceptional status as "traditional rulers," could raise questions and demand action directly from the government and the head of state, bypassing district and regional administration. Unfortunately for Nanun, the increasingly senile though willful leadership of the Bimbilla Naa, Dasana, has rarely used this special privilege for benefit of Nanun and its inhabitants. Naa Dasana often mentioned to distinguished visitors that the town of Bimbilla and the whole district had no decent water supply, that roads were in a deplorable state of disrepair, that goods were missing from shops, and that he and the Nanumba skin should receive state support in their claim for the territory of Kpasaland across the Oti River. His will and energy, however, were not sustained enough, so that promises usually obtained from visiting dignitaries of the Ghanaian state, including Acheampong himself (who visited Bimbilla in January 1978), were never brought to fruition.

One of the reasons was that Nanun, unlike any other traditional area (paramountcy) in Ghana, has an extremely low number of literates among the chiefs. Only one chief among dozens had an English education, but he is of relatively minor influence on important matters. People who influenced Naa Dasana in his decisions were usually elders, his own relatives, chiefs, and untitled royalty, who were only marginally better than the chief himself in dealing with the external pressures of the modern state. This state of affairs could be related to the fact that when Western education was being introduced into Nanun in the late 1940s, Naa Natogmah tended to send only members of his own Banyili chiefly house to school. Thus the Banyili chiefs, though not educated themselves, had a number of educated younger people as their advisers. On the other hand, the thrust for education among the members of Gbugmayili started much later and the generation gap between the distrustful Naa Dasana and the young educated members of his house (his sons notably) resulted in his *not* using these literates as consultants.

The Kpasaland Dispute: Ethnicity Awakened

During the 1970s there was one issue where a concerted effort by all Nanumba people, from Naa Dasana down to simple villagers, resulted in success without the positive contribution or the opposition of the state administration. This is the Kpasaland dispute. It concerns fifteen hundred square kilometers of originally uninhabited hunting land between the Oti and Bonatje rivers, with the axis being the Kpasa River, traditionally considered to be in the sphere of influence of the Nanumba polity. Chiefs of Juali and Jimam on the Oti river were delegated by the Bimbilla *naa* to control those territories. The dispute started when Lake Volta flooded the existing main road connecting Bimbilla and Accra via Kete Krachi in the mid-1960s. The state built an alternative road through the Volta Region crossing the Kpasaland and reaching the Oti River at the present-day town of Damanku. A ferry over the Oti and a piece of new road then connected the new road with the old Yendi-Bimbilla-Krachi road.

Following the completion of the new road, people started to settle along it and exploited a good opportunity for farming there. Most of them were the Konkomba, coming either from Nanun or from their homeland around Saboba. Only when people settled in the area did a question of executive authority over them emerge. For a *naam*-centred polity an empty territory was hardly an issue for dispute. Therefore, only in the mid-1960s did the Nanumba fully realize that the administrative boundaries between the Volta Region and Northern Region followed the rivers Oti and Mo, thus placing Kpasaland under the administration of the Krachi District as part of the Volta Region. The causes of this almost unknown change of boundaries go back to the 1950s, when Krachi with Kpasa were a district in the Northern Territories. But Nkrumah's government decided that the Krachi people culturally belonged to the south and incorporated the Krachi-Nkwanta area into the then created Trans-Volta Togoland. Kpasaland was included and by 1960 became part of the Volta Region.

Quite characteristically, neither the Bimbilla Naa nor Nanumba literates knew at the time what was happening with Kpasaland. Perhaps if they knew, they even did not bother, because there were no people living permanently in Kpasaland in the 1950s. The Konkomba, who were the majority among the settlers in Kpasaland, became a decisive factor in the dispute. They initially recognized the authority of the Nanumba over Kpasaland, but when their leader, Konja, failed to secure a title from the Bimbilla Naa, they joined the side of the Atwode led by their paramount chief Osulewura (Shiarewura), who also claimed that Kpasaland belonged under his authority. Historically, he must have known that he was wrong, because there was no Atwode chieftaincy before the colonial conquest, Shiare being a center for worship of its powerful God and served by priests. But he found out that he could exploit existing administrative boundaries drawn from Accra, i.e., that Kpasaland legally belonged to the Krachi-Nkwanta District dominated in its eastern (Nkwanta) part by the Atwodes. The dispute lasted for about thirteen years before it reached a critical point in 1979.

In October 1979, the Stool Land Boundary Settlement Commission in Accra decided in favor of the Nanumba skin. The Osulewura allegedly made an appeal against the decision, but there was hardly any sign of it publicly. The Nanumba chiefs and people rejoiced at the judgment because the lengthy arbitration process cost them a lot in energy and resources, not to mention the potential risk of the loss of prestige should they have lost the case. Early in 1980 the Bimbilla Naa enskinned several new chiefs from both chiefly houses and posted them in various parts of Kpasaland. There was hardly any Nanumba population in Kpasaland and very few Nanumba followed the new chiefs. Dagbamba farmers who settled in Kpasaland welcomed the Nanumba chiefs, and some of them became councillors in their courts. The Konkomba of the Kpasaland, however, did not like the fact that they were now subject to Nanumba chiefs. They paid little, if any, allegiance to them.

Thus the Nanumba chiefs in Kpasaland functioned in a (sort of) social vacuum for little more than a year. The Ghanaian state failed to take any measures to support the efforts of the Nanumba chiefs and people to regain Kpasaland. These efforts were aimed not only toward traditional values, but also to incorporating Kpasaland within the Nanumba District's jurisdiction, i.e., under the Northern Regional administration. This would imply a change of regional and district boundaries. The constitution of the Third Republic of Ghana (1979–81), which was then in force, required that 80 percent of the population of the pertinent area expressed their wish to change boundaries between regions. The hostility of the Konkomba majority in Kpasaland with regard to the Nanumba sovereignty would indicate there was little chance of obtaining such a high percentage of support. At any rate, no effort at all was made on the part of the Ghanaian government to transplant the implications of the decision on traditional lands into the modern administrative domain. That meant a very peculiar situation pertained in Kpasaland under which, for example, tax revenues, police, roads authority, part of ministerial departments, et cetera, were administered from Nkwanta, whereas traditional matters, as well as some departments like the Ghana Education Service, would be managed from Bimbilla. The district chief executive in Bimbilla asked the Regional Administration in Tamale several times to expedite the transfer of Kpasaland into the Northern Region, but to no avail. The government was apparently not interested in fomenting any further problems on the political front at a time when a national economic crisis was already under way. That was, however, a miscalculation. The Nanumba ethnic consciousness was already activated and alerted to the insensitivity of the state and the growing enmity of the Konkomba.

The hostile attitudes between the Nanumba and the Konkomba have evolved gradually during the decades since 1940, when the relatively fertile lands of Nanun were settled by large numbers of Konkomba farmers. The Konkomba "subtribes," whose numbers were not even known to their student David Tait (1961), have fought one another until recently. Their oral history indicates that they were pushed farther to the east from their original territories by the invading Dagbamba. The British allowed the Dagbamba to dominate the Konkomba by placing Dagbamba chiefs in Konkomba territories. When one or two Konkomba subtribes came into conflict with the Dagbamba in the late 1930s and killed one of these chiefs (Zogberi Naa and his family), the British sided with the Dagbamba chiefs and did not prevent them from seeking revenge. This prompted some Konkomba groups to move to the south, especially to Nanun. They were well received, because Nanumba chiefs believed that it was a good sign and a blessing to have a substantial number of followers. At that time the Konkomba leaders accepted the condition of the Nanumba chiefs that they should pay allegiance to the latter. They were expected to supply annual labor for chiefs' farms, they had to bring their cases to the chiefs' judicial courts, and they were obliged to bring a hind leg from the first animal slaughtered at funerals or killed in hunts. The same rules applied to the native Nanumba and other settlers of foreign origin. The arrangement worked quite well for several decades during which the Konkomba, although treated as second-class people in Nanun, became prosperous farmers. What is even more important for later developments, their numbers grew rapidly.

The results of the 1960 census of Ghana showed that there were 21,160 Konkomba compared with 18,730 Mole-Dagbane speakers. Of the latter about two-thirds could have been Nanumba. No ethnic statistics were taken since, and it can be reasonably presumed that the Konkomba: Nanumba ration has changed even more in favor of the Konkomba. Contemporary estimates mention a 125,000 strong population in Nanumba District, and I suggest that at least two-thirds are Konkomba. One can logically conclude that since 1960 at least both Nanumba and Konkomba leaders know that in Nanun the Konkomba are more numerous than the Nanumba. That fact must then be seen against the continuing situation within which the Konkomba were tolerated as guests in Nanun, a settler population whose position within the ethnic grouping of the district was evidently the lowest. Few of their young people attended schools. Although Konkomba farmers were successful and hardworking, their prosperity in terms of income was hardly expressed in any apparent change of lifestyle. Not only in Nanun, but all over Ghana the Konkomba were viewed as savages, uncivilized "bush people" who were either feared or despised. The Nanumba certainly did not fear the Konkomba; they rather looked upon them with condescension.

Prelude to Conflict

The 1970s, especially with the reestablishment of the Nanumba District in 1974, saw the emergence of a small, modern Konkomba elite in Nanun. One was a successful businessman, another a clerk in the teacher training college, a third was attached to the office of the Ghana National Reconstruction Corps, et cetera. These young literates founded a district branch of the Konkomba Youth Association (KOYA). This organization, among others supported by Christian churches and the Ghana Institute of Linguistics, set out to promote literacy in the Konkomba language and to teach villagers how to overcome their general backwardness and fragmentation. KOYA became the primary factor in the Konkomba emancipation movement within Ghanaian society (cf. Yakubu 1986).

In Nanun, the Konkomba were in a peculiar situation because they were expected to obey Nanumba customs and regulations even though they constituted a clear majority in the district. Soon this disproportionality became an issue in the activities of the KOYA. One of the fields where the Konkomba were at the mercy of the Nanumba chiefs and subsequently the district magistrate's court was marital cases. As indicated previously, the Konkomba marriage custom prescribes intergenerational marriage, which implies betrothal of a young man to a baby girl. The man has to work for the father of the girl until she becomes of nubile age. Then the de facto marriage begins. The man by then is almost in his forties, and it often happens that in contemporary "open society" the young woman shows little enthusiasm for living with a man one generation older than herself. She rather prefers a young lover, and if pushed by her parents and the husband into obedience, she often chooses to elope. This has serious socioeconomic consequences, as the husband has worked for many years to deserve his wife and the parents feel greatly indebted to the husband. The marriage custom is an extremely serious affair among the Konkomba, and it is therefore not surprising that such breaches lead to arbitration and judicial treatment.

In Nanun the monopoly of arbitration has traditionally been in the hands of the Bimbilla Naa, his elders, and other chiefs. The Konkomba were expected to come with their marital disputes to the Nanumba chiefs and elders before going to the district magistrate's court. In both instances the authorities were not really familiar with the intricacies of the Konkomba marriage custom, but they knew very well that the Konkomba were eager to solve their disputes. This was used to the advantage of the arbitrators, who usually demanded material remuneration (in money or kind) from both sides in the dispute. According to some informants, a large source of income for the court of the Bimbilla Naa came in those years from such "arbitrations." Similarly, the lay magistrate took bribes from all, often without really solving the dispute to any side's satisfaction. One of the magistrates became notorious when he married a Konkomba woman who was the subject of a dispute between two Konkomba men, leaving both of them empty-handed!

KOYA leaders pointed out the exploitation involved in judicial treat-ment of marital disputes and proposed two measures: first, to reform the marriage custom itself by abolishing the betrothal; second, to establish their own arbitration of marriage disputes, which would be based on the expertise of the Konkomba themselves, and to reduce the known number of cases of which the KOYA members felt increasingly ashamed. The first proposal was evidently quite difficult for the older Konkomba to accept, as well as those already in the process of working for the parents of their future wives. But the second proposal was much more acceptable. By the late 1970s the KOYA started Konkomba arbitration in marital disputes under the chairmanship of Ali, the Konkomba elder/headman (*onikpel*) of Bimbilla. The Nanumba public saw in the Konkomba arbitration a flout-ing of Nanumba sovereignty, and a complaint against "secret tribunals" was lodged with the district administration.

The Bimbilla Naa, supported by both traditional leaders and Nanumba literates, demanded that the "tribunals" stop at once and later asked the government (via district administration) to evict the leaders of the KOYA and especially Ali from his traditional area, i.e., Nanumba District. The state, represented by the then district chief executive, tried to resolve the conflict by talking to both sides and asking for calm and reconciliation. In January 1980 an action followed, led by the district chairman of the then ruling People's National party, in which Ali was seized, conveyed on a tractor trailer, and dumped six miles from Bimbilla. There he was forced to board a truck for Yendi and ordered never to return. The Bimbilla Naa dissociated himself from this brutal action. Ali could return to Bimbilla, but the seed of discord was already firmly planted. By 1980, the KOYA's existence was believed by the Nanumba to be the main reason for Konkomba disobedience in respect of their customary duties towards the Nanumba chiefs. What caused even more indignation on the side of the Nanumba public was that the Konkomba ceased to sell their yam produce to Nanumba middlewomen. Instead they started to organize an alternative marketing of yams, which climaxed in the establishment of their own marketplace in Accra. Both the Nanumba chiefs and traders felt the consequences of the Konkomba boycott.

The 1881 Armed Confrontations

The situation grew more acute toward the end of 1980, but the regional administration did not do much about it. In February 1981, the monthly report to the Regional Administrative Officer by the district chief executive, Bimbilla, summarized the gravity of the situation:

> A new dimension of chieftaincy disputes is however about to rear its head in the Nanumba Traditional Area. I will call it a tribal dispute. This is between the Konkombas and the Nanumbas. This misunderstanding between the two tribes started two years ago when the Konkombas started to form a Youth Association with the aim of educating their tribesmen to do away with some of their outmoded customs. One would look at the aims and objectives of this Association to be laudable but certain activities of these people have been viewed with great suspicion by the Nanumbas. It is alleged that the Konkombas have on several occasions flouted the authority of the chiefs of the villages where they live with impunity. The Nanumbas being the land owners do not want to take kindly to this insubordination. For example it is alleged that Konkomba have refused to pay the customary traditional homage to Nanumba chiefs. They no longer take their cases to the chief for settlement. They have even refused to pay any tax for the land they are using. It is also alleged that some Konkomba tribesmen have instituted their own Secret Tribunals to try cases where heavy fines have been imposed on culprits. The Bimbilla-Na in particular is not happy about these developments . . .

> This conflict has to be given serious attention, if not it may explode one day. There are deep undercurrents of dissatisfaction and tension which will soon become manifest. Certain issues have to be explained to both sides to exercise the great restraint. It has been decided to summon the recalcitrant Konkombas concerned to the Regional Office on 31st March, 1981, to meet the Deputy Regional Minister to settle some of these issues. This will go a long way to reduce a lot of tension in the area.

Unfortunately, the DCE's predictions were only too accurate. Before the date of the meeting mentioned above, there were two other meetings in Bimbilla. At one of them, the Nanumba Traditional Council decided on March 17, 1981, to banish three Konkomba Youth Association leaders from the Nanumba Traditional Area (i.e., from the Nanumba District). At another meeting, Nanumba and Konkomba Youth Association leaders met on March 23. The two delegations parted with expressions of goodwill and hopes of achieving a reconciliation. There is no further evidence about a meeting scheduled for March 31, 1981, between the Konkomba Youth Association's leader and Mr. Baba (himself a Nanumba!), who was then the deputy regional minister in Tamale. It never took place. The Northern Regional Administration underestimated the explosive potential of the conflict. On the evening of April 23, 1981, an open clash broke out in Bimbilla between the Nanumba and Konkomba in which the personal secretary and interpreter of the Bimbilla Naa was shot dead and several other Konkomba and Nanumba were killed. One of them was a son of a Konkomba leader from Kpasaland. As a result of the clash and subsequent looting and burning of Konkomba houses in Bimbilla, all Konkomba left the town and have never returned. The Nanumba youth and warriors were mobilized and attacked a nearby Konkomba section of Kabuliya village, which they burnt to ashes. When the Kpasaland Konkomba learned about the clash in Bimbilla and Kabuliya and especially about the death of a literate son of one of their leaders, they started to attack all Nanumba and Dagbamba residents in Kpasaland. Even though the news about fighting and killing reached Bimbilla almost instantly, the Bimbilla police were not able to restore order on the other bank of the Oti River, because it is officially part of the Volta Region and thus comes under the control of the Kpasa police station. The message sent to the Ghana Police in Volta Region from Bimbilla via Tamale and Ho regional police headquarters reached Nkwanta and Kpasa days after the massacre was over. By then four Nanumba chiefs and an unknown number of other people were killed. (One oral report mentioned a full lorry of corpses.) Hundreds of people fled to neighboring Togo or tried to return to Nanun proper via lands north of the Mo River that belong to the Nanumba.

The incident in Bimbilla was publicized as minor (eight deaths), but the major clash in Kpasaland was completely hushed up by Ghanaian authorities. Again no adequate measures were taken to prevent any further outbreak of hostilities. Among the reasons for this were executive weakness of state apparatus and lack of communication and technical support, including lack of arms and fuel for the police. State officials failed to realize that the inclusion of Kpasaland within the orbit of Nanumba Traditional Area could lead to armed incidents in the new area despite regional boundaries between Nanun proper and Kpasaland. The police were unable to suppress the conflict. It was an evident failure to recognize that the "traditional" in contemporary context always has a "modern" dimension. The shortsighted outlook of state officials in terms of the opposition between "traditional" and "modern" is an important contributory factor to the conflict. The whole Kpasaland issue documents it clearly. The fact that both police and state executive administrators had been neither of Nanumba nor Konkomba origin and thus considered the conflict an alien, "tribal" anomaly was also a significant factor. These state agencies tended to stay away from the conflict, partly because they feared possible repercussions for themselves and their families.

As I have written the full story of the Nanumba Konkomba conflict (Skalník 1986a), I shall only briefly recapitulate the main points of further development of the conflict, with special reference to those moments relevant to the theme of this paper. The Ghanaian state underestimated the "modern" dimension of the "traditional" issues and continued to underplay the conflict. Its officials have not understood that "traditional" issues are in fact modern and play an important role in the life of the Ghanaian people, including that of the Nanumba and Konkomba. This ignorance and negligence gave both parties in the conflict time to arm themselves. The Nanumba could never forget the cost they had incurred in gaining Kpasaland, and so they intended to reconquer it from the Konkomba, who after April 1981 seized full control of this area. Rumors that the government considered giving Kpasaland to the Konkomba as their own district within the Volta Region fuelled the Nanumba's determination to regain Kpasaland as soon as possible. Various external factors contributed to the polarization of the forces in the conflict. Konkomba and Nanumba literates who occupied various positions in the civil service or military forces of Ghana have allegedly tried to help in the organization of the armed forces on both sides. This included money, training, and weaponry.

The Nanumba were, however, apparently divided on the issue of a military action against the Konkomba. The Bimbilla Naa was under severe psychological strain. Experienced Nanumba ex-politicians counseled against any armed conflict. But young, influential leaders of the Nanumba Youth Association were very belligerent. After the Bimbilla Naa Dasana and the Kpatihi Naa, his closest councillor and skinmaker, suddenly died under strange circumstances during the night of May 30/31, 1981, the young radical faction prevailed.

Finally, a tragedy occurred late in June 1981. After a meeting between the Nanumba and Konkomba youth leaders, which was convened by the Regional Administration in Tamale, the Nanumba forces, formed from revived traditional warriors and armed youth, crossed the Oti River at

Salnayili and tried to push the Konkomba out of the Chichagi area, which would then enable them to cross the Mo River into Kpasaland. The Nanumba miscalculated their opponents' strength, got bogged down in the Chichagi area, and were surprised by the well-organized Konkomba warriors in Wulensi in central Nanun, where they happened to be almost defenseless at the time. Ghana police failed completely in Wulensi, only throwing some smoke bombs and evacuating the Wulehe Naa from his palace, which was under the Konkomba attack. Several hundred died in Wulensi; some sources mentioned up to two thousand dead in the whole conflict. The Ghana army-cum-police managed to stop the fighting only two days later when Bimbilla itself was in danger of being taken by Konkomba forces organized in small guerrilla groups.

After the shocking news from Nanun, the conflict became for a while a national issue. The government realized that such a conflict arose from deep-rooted causes. In fact, seventeen cases of blood confrontation were registered during the Limann administration (1979–81) in the Northern Region only. The Nanumba-Konkomba war, as it came to be known, was the largest. The literate Ghanaian public seemed to be on the side of the Konkomba, even though it was clear that the Konkomba did not suffer major losses in either lives or material. The reason was that they detested old-fashioned ("feudal") Nanumba customs. The Nanumba, on the other hand, lost a considerable number of people, hundreds of heads of cattle, and other material wealth. Thousands of mainly Nanumba and Dagbamba refugees flooded Bimbilla, Yendi, and other places.

Ethnic War or Outwitting the Weak Modern State?

The Konkomba had visibly humiliated the Nanumba. The latter had no recognized leader, the regent, the eldest son of the deceased Bimbilla Naa, being a weak person with little if any authority. In villages with a large Konkomba population or where the Nanumba fled, ad hoc Konkomba chiefs *(oxbor)* were installed without the approval of the Nanumba. This especially aggrieved the chiefs of Nanun. Most of them became convinced that the aim of the Konkomba was to destroy the Nanumba and take their land from them. It was even alleged that documents existed about a secret plan to install Batu, the leading Konkomba businessman in Bimbilla (whose house was burnt in April 1981), as a new Bimbilla Naa. The president of Ghana, Limann, traveled to Bimbilla in July 1981 and even spent a night there, which is rarely done in areas where no proper modern amenities exist. He tried to ensure the reconciliation of the two parties. In the absence of a commonly recognized leader among the Nanun-based Konkomba, Nana Nandi, a Konkomba leader from the Krachi District, was brought to Bimbilla and made to shake hands with the Bimbilla regent as a sign of peace. This act was generally felt to be of no consequence and validity. Later the regional minister, who was believed to be taking sides in the conflict and by underestimating the real dimensions of the conflict to have caused the failure of the state to prevent the war, was made to resign. The real causes of the conflict remained, however, unrevealed. Journalists pointed out the outmoded, "feudal" customs of the Nanumba as the major cause. Others believed rather in the inherent belligerence of the Konkomba. But many agreed upon the almost total incompetence of the state agencies.

The point, however, lies elsewhere. My view is that the imported state with its administrative and coercive agencies, which imposed colonial "peace" and stopped "tribal" and other wars, failed to solve old problems and created new ones. The colonial and postcolonial state in Gold Coast/ Ghana made possible the free movement of population. This was motivated by the economic needs it brought with it. The Konkomba migration into Nanum is one of the effects of colonial policy of "divide and rule." Many planned and unplanned innovations were made possible and were welcomed on many sides as long, and only as long, as the imported state and colonial capitalist system functioned well. When it ceased to do so, as in Ghana in the 1970s, the old conflicts were revived and new ones added. This happened commensurate with the destruction of "traditional" pre-colonial structures and their replacement by "modern" shortcut solutions, introduced by the state bureaucracies. In the case of the conflict under discussion, local competing ethnic feelings won over the almost defunct state nationalism. The Nanumba and the Konkomba, by taking the differences into their own hands and ignoring the state, have thus outwitted it.

Some chiefs thought that Nanumba chieftaincy was betrayed by the Ghanaian state. They believed that they were protected by the state because they had been a natural ally of the state as centralized people organized around their chieftaincy, unlike the Konkomba. The Nanumba were outraged by the public support of the Konkomba and especially the manner in which newsmen reported the conflict. They accused President Limann of contributing to the conflict. Limann visited Nanun in February 1981, on the eve of the outbreak of hostilities. The Bimbilla Naa complained about subversive activities of "some aliens" in Kpasaland, meaning the Konkomba there. The president replied that nobody was alien in Ghana. The Nanumba felt unjustly treated at the time, while the Konkomba were encouraged by the speech. The president failed to advise that respect should be paid to the customary regulations of the Nanumba. It was the constitution of the Third Republic of Ghana that for the first time in the modern history of Gold Coast/Ghana recognized that land tenure is vested in the ethnic groups and their authorities that happen to be historically dominant in any particular area. Previous modern legislation did not recognize the ultimate rights over the land where no private land-ownership existed (which was the case in the whole Ghanaian north). The colonial and postcolonial state held that the land is under the custody of the state, which gave the state unchecked powers to undertake any public projects without consulting the people living on the land designated for the project. The Nanumba-Konkomba conflict may have been stimulated by this constitutional recognition of "traditional" land rights.

For some time the war strained the relationship between the Nanumba and the Konkomba. Most of the chiefs and a large section of the Nanumba public demanded from the Ghanaian government that if not all, at least those Konkomba who organized the war should be expelled from Nanun. The commission of inquiry formed by the government received a long list of names of Konkomba "war criminals." The situation was further compli-cated by the fact that the only Nanumba-enskinned Konkomba chief, the Kanjo Naa, was fully on the side of the Nanumba but had little support from KOYA members and more recent Konkomba settlers in southwestern Nanun. Both parties in the conflict, unable to enter into direct negotiations as a result of a lack of recognized leadership on both sides, awaited the findings of the commission of inquiry. This commission tried hard. Before it completed its work, the Rawlings takeover on December 31, 1981, took place. Work of the commission was suspended indefinitely, and a new situation of fear of the military regime set in. Rawlings, in one of his first speeches, pointed out the shameful weakness of the previous Limann ad-ministration, which allowed major bloodshed in Nanun. But he did not do anything to solve the conflict. From official documents it was apparent that chieftaincy was not a favorite of the Rawlings regime. As a demonstration of its confidence in its deterrent might, the new regime withdrew armed forces stationed in the Nanumba District from June 1981.

It was expected that the new Bimbilla Naa would be installed within a year of the death of the previous one, and many hopes were pinned on this. It was expected that the most likely candidate, the Dakpam Naa, Abarika, would provide strong leadership backed by the advice of realistic literates from the Banyili house. It was known that he might seek reconciliation with the Konkomba even though he himself and his village, Dakpam, suffered major losses in the war, second only to Wulensi. Various reasons, including the detention of the strongest candidate for the function of Kpatihi Naa, without whom no new Bimbilla Naa could be enskinned, and tensions between the vacating Gbugmayili and ascending Banyili delayed the funeral of Naa Dasana and the subsequent election of the new Bimbilla Naa until January-February 1983.

The new paramount chief, Abarika Attah, was able to unite the Nanumba for a new modus vivendi with the Konkomba. Since 1983 the Nanumba Youth Association had few meetings with the Konkomba Youth Association. By 1986 it appeared that all Konkomba in Nanun agreed on their need to have their own chiefs who would, however, be part of the Nanumba *naam* system. It was again apparent that the youth associations did not have enough authority to work out this modus vivendi. The Bimbilla Naa and his traditional council rejected the proposals of the Konkomba Youth Association. The Rawlings government changed its negative policy into positive approval of the chiefs in order to legitimize its power. Proposals were now made to include the chiefs in decision making at state level. The Ghanaian state, which managed to secure international financial aid from the mid-1980s, got stronger. Its new co-optation policy vis-à-vis chieftaincy was perceived by the chiefs as a sign of victory, a recognition of the importance of the institution. The regime, in search of a lasting domestic political model, turned to chieftaincy as its legitimizing instrument. It remains to be seen whether there will be power sharing between "commoner" leaders and chiefs. In Nanun the commoner leadership, now almost entirely Nanumba but lacking connection with the Banyili house,[7] could not secure any particular following. It is for the *naam* to lend its support to the regime, get its own candidates into modern district administration, and devise a lasting solution with Konkomba residents in Nanun.

The Rawlings regime seemed initially to be content with the freezing of the conflict, giving the impression that it was better not to open old wounds and to try to forget. The commission of inquiry led by Justice Lamptey was never asked to complete its work. I believe this weakness of the state might foster a new wave of hostilities, should the current regime collapse. Until 1984, economic measures taken by the Rawlings government did not give much hope for an economic recovery and the whole country had a distinct tendency to fall into viable local economies and political units. Meanwhile, measures such as the formation of the People's Defense Committees (later renamed Committees for the Defense of the Revolution, or CDRs), which at least in Nanun are composed out of marginal people, show that there has been an attempt to relegate chieftaincy to the relics of the past and simultaneously to make the powerful Ghanaian civil service an auxiliary body with no decision-making power. Rawlings also considered a special legislature about the land, and rumors circulated that perhaps he might nationalize all land. The new district council (led by district secretaries) which was to be elected by popular vote at the end of 1988 will be composed of two-thirds elected individuals (not representatives of any party) and one-third nominated members from traditional dignitaries. So longed-for "decentralisation" and "people's power" should finally be put into practice. This will be limited, however, to district level only. For the purpose of the district elections Ghana was divided in 1987 into 110 new districts. Some observers expect that CDRs may disappear in the process.

Conclusion

I have tried to demonstrate from the example of the Nanun that the institution of chieftaincy is not a "survival" doomed to disappear but a viable factor in modern local, district, and national politics. It is a sensitive indicator of tendencies in the country that signals the weaknesses and strengths of the imported modern system of government. The armed conflict that broke out in Nanun in 1981 between the Nanumba, united around their *naam*, and the Konkomba settlers, mobilized by their emancipation movement, is mainly a result of the mismanagement of social forces born as a result of the introduction of a Western political model into a society based on entirely different principles, such as the *naam* of the Nanumba and the "regulated anarchy" of kinship and locality of the Konkomba. The modern state with its nationalist ideology without nation (cf. Skalnik 1987b) does not live up to the expectations of ordinary people, the common citizens of Ghana. It seems to have taken on itself, through the colonial masters and their postcolonial apprentices, a heavier load than it can carry. In the absence of a well-functioning modern nation-state, the values and organizational principles that the Nanumba or the Konkomba evolved themselves, as a result of their historical experience, reemerge and dominate. Ethnicity[8] is their tool for solving questions that the modern state failed to face and solve. Although they seem to handle the leftovers of Western civilization in different ways, both the Nanumba and the Konkomba realize in the process that their mutual interests overlap more than they do with those of the state. The Nanumba, in the illusion of alliance with the state, underestimated the seemingly weaker Konkomba. "Tribal" ethnic hostilities flared for a while. Eventually, however, both parties in the conflict had to recognize their vested interests and the value the (neo-)traditional institutions have for both of them. As the "modern" imported state further disintegrates or incorporates neo-traditional values, it will be the indigenous political culture of people like the Nanumba or Konkomba that will combine and integrate until it will eventually form a new synthesis that will suit people better than the dictates of an alien state power.

Notes

1. Fieldwork in Ghana (1978–86) was made possible by the grants from the Netherlands Foundation for Tropical Research and the Harry Oppenheimer

Institute for African Studies. The major burden of financing it had, however, been carried by me. The University of Leiden and the University of Cape Town are to be thanked for granting me research leaves while paying me. The University Research Committee at Cape Town made grants possible for writing up the results and presenting them at various scholarly meetings. In Ghana I was assisted by the Centre for Development Studies at the University of Cape Coast and the Tamale Institute for Cross-Cultural Studies and their directors, Drs. Eddie Amonoo and Jon Kirby. In Nanun M. A. Adam, Y. Adam, K. Wujangi, A. Iddi, N. Attah, and Alhaji Yunusah were of particular help to me. My sincere thanks go to the participants in the XIth ICEAS symposium on responses of indigenous/local systems of authority to imported patterns of state power, where the paper was originally presented. Julia Segar, Robert Thornton, and namely Anne Sarzin have kindly edited the text.

2. *Political culture* is used here in the meaning of a matrix of attitudes, sentiments, and cognition characteristic of political life of a particular society or a specific group within it. Political culture is that set of rules and behavioral patterns that makes one polity different from all others even though they may be classified into one type, like democracy. In this sense phrases like *British democracy* and *French democracy* refer to differences in political culture in Britain and France.

3. By *polity* is here understood a territory with a population following a government or authority emanating from one or more centers. *Polity* is a working term used in order to avoid using concepts such as the "state" in places where "state-like" would be more appropriate.

4. *Articulation* is understood as a way of joining together two or more social orders or their parts. In political anthropology one can use the term *articulation* to describe the method whereby two or more kinds of political culture combine in one territory.

5. The district commissioner in Yendi, seventy kilometers from Bimbilla, was a British colonial officer. Soon after 1957, Ghanaians of non-Dagbamba origin were appointed as DCs. In Bimbilla, between 1974 and 1982 the DCs were either of Gonja or Dagarti ethnic origin.

6. Dr. Kofi A. Busia was a sociologist and anthropologist, author of an influential book, *The Position of the Chief in the Modern Political System of Ashanti* (1951). As prime minister of Ghana (1969–72), Busia was known for his pro-chieftaincy stance. The Nanumba chiefs demanded restoration of the district because they sensed a good chance of Busia coming to power. The Nanumba Customary Regulations and Procedures were also approved in 1969 in conjunction with the new chieftaincy policy of the Busia government.

7. The Banyili house, supporter of Nkrumah and his Convention People's Party, was almost automatically considered supporter of the Limann regime. The Limann regime claimed that it was a continuator of policies of the late Nkrumah.

8. *Ethnicity* is used here in the sense of political ethnicity, as it is nothing more and nothing less than the use of cultural symbols for political aims.

References

Amherst, H. W. 1931. *Report on the constitution, organisation and customs of the Nanumba people*. Ghana National Archives, Tamale.

Göhring, Christina. 1980. *Chief und Präsident: Strukturanalyse traditioneller und moderner Herrschaft in Ghana.* Arbeiten aus dem Institut fur Völkerkunde der Universaität zu Göttingen, Band 16. Hohenschäftlarn: Klaus Renner Verlag.

Ladouceur, Paul. 1979. *Chiefs and politicians: The politics of regionalism in Northern Ghana.* London: Longman.

Skalník, Peter. 1983. Questioning the concept of the state in indigenous Africa. *Social Dynamics* 9(2): 11–28.

_____. 1986a. The Nanumba-Konkomba War: A study of local politics in Northern Ghana. An unpublished B. A. (Hons.) dissertation, University of Cape Town.

_____. 1986b. Nanumba chieftaincy facing the Ghanaian state and Konkomba "tribesmen": An interpretation of the Nanumba-Konkomba war of 1981. Pp. 89–109 in *State and Local Community in Africa,* ed W. van Binsbergen, F. Reyntjens, and H. Hesseling. Brussels: CEDAF/ASDOC.

_____. 1986c. The December 31 revolution in Ghana: Countrywide and district levels. Unpublished paper presented to the Anthropology Seminar of the University of Cape Town.

_____. 1987a. On the inadequacy of the concept of the "traditional state" (illustrated with ethnographic material on Nanun, Ghana). *Journal of Legal Pluralism* 25 and 26: 301–25.

_____. 1987b. Why Ghana is no nation-state. Unpublished paper presented at the International Conference on Minority Situations and Problems of Identity, Rabka, Poland.

Tait, David. 1961. *The Konkomba of Northern Ghana.* Edited by J. Goody. Oxford: Oxford University Press for the International African Institute.

Tamakloe, Emmanuel F. 1931. *A brief history of the Dagbamba people.* Accra: Government Printer.

Yakubu, Bukari. 1986. The youth and inter-ethnic conflict in Northern Ghana since the wake of the June 4th uprising. The case of the Nanumba/Konkomba conflict. Unpublished manuscript.

About the Contributors

Peter Skalník is a senior lecturer in social anthropology at the University of Cape Town. He was born in Czechoslovakia. He studied at Prague and Leningrad and received his Ph.D. in African studies and anthropology from Charles University at Prague. He has done fieldwork in Ghana, European mountain communities, and Tuva (Central Asia). Before coming to Cape Town, he taught at universities in Czechoslovakia, the Netherlands, and Switzerland. With Henri J. M. Claessen he is the editor of *The Early State* (1978) and *The Study of the State* (1981).

Glenn Petersen is a professor of anthropology at the Graduate Center and Baruch College of the City University of New York. He received his Ph.D. from Columbia University. He has done extensive field research on agriculture and politics on Ponape in the Caroline Islands, Micronesia. He is the author of *One Man Cannot Rule a Thousand* (1982).

Jérôme Rousseau is an associate professor of anthropology at McGill University, Montreal. He had done fieldwork among the Kayan of Sarawak and specialized in the study of peoples of Borneo. He took his Ph.D. at the University of Cambridge. He is the editor of *The Peoples of Central Borneo* (1974). His book on the societies of central Borneo is in press and he is presently writing a book on Kayan religion.

William D. Wilder is a senior lecturer in social anthropology at the University of Durham. He has done fieldwork in Malaysia. His Ph.D. in anthropology is from the University of London (London School of Economics). He is the author of *Communication, Social Structure and Development in Rural Malaysia* (1982).

Joseph M. Hiatt is a consulting anthropologist based in Washington, D.C. He has conducted fieldwork among the bedouin in Jordan. He received his Ph.D. from the University of Pennsylvania in 1981 with the dissertation titled "Between Desert and Town: A Case Study of Encapsulation and Sedentarization among Jordanian Bedouin."

Colin Scott is an assistant professor of anthropology at McGill University, Montreal. He did fieldwork among the Cree Indians of James Bay. He took his Ph.D. at McGill University. He is the author of *Modes of Production and Guaranteed Income in James Bay Cree Society* (1979).

David Z. Scheffel teaches anthropology and sociology at Cariboo College, Kamloops, B.C. He has done fieldwork among the Inuit of Labrador and the Russian Old Believers of Alberta. He received his Ph.D. from McMaster University, Hamilton, Ontario. The research with the Old Believers has led to the making of a documentary film by the National Film Board of Canada.

Lucien R. Bäck, until recently a senior expert in the International Labour Office specializing in advising African and Asian countries about rural development, works for ETC Consultants in the Netherlands. He has done fieldwork in Rwanda, Niger, Cameroon, and Chad. He took his Ph.D. in ethnology at the Free University, Berlin.

Index

Alhazai, 7; wealth accumulation, 138–39, 141, 142; influence in cooperatives, 140
Allah, 134
Amherst, H., 150
Amman, A., 112
Andaya, B., 55
Animation rurale, 124, 135
Anthropology, x, 2, 18, 19, 25
Antichrist, 110–11, 117–18
Archaic polities: accepted classifications, 3–4; and outwitting, 13, 17–18
Association des Femmes du Niger (AFN), 124
Athens, S., 23
Authority: conceptualized (Skalník), 8; people's authority, 17–20; Ponapean concepts of, 24, 25; of community, 35; tribal authority (Kreisha), 73–78
Avoidance: in outwitting, 11; semi-avoidance, 114
Avvakum, 112
Azerbaidzhan, vii

Bäck, L., 6, 121–43
Bailey, F., 79
Bedouin Control Board, 71
"Beggars democracy," vii
Belloncle, G., 127
Belshaw, C., ix
Benda, V., 19
Berlin, I., 25
Bernart, L., 24
Bock, C., 43, 47, 48
Braroe, N., 85
Braudel, F., ix
British Mandate Commission (1921), 70–71, 72, 75–76
Brunei, Sultanate of, 62
Bureaucracy, 18; Ponapean, 30–34; Ghanaian, 153
Burridge, K., 61

Busia, K., 167

Caisse de Crédit de Coopération Economique (CCE), 126
Caisse Nigérienne de Crédit Agricole (CNCA), 138, 141
Call, P., 110, 113
Capitalism: and virtue, 34; accumulation, 94; welfare capitalism, 98
Carneiro, R., 12
Carrère d'Encausse, H., 20
Caste, 1, 56
Castles, L., 55
Central Borneo: as "ethnic groups," 42–43; and slavery, 43–44; trade, 43–46; relation with Malay Sultanates, 46–48
Chakaapaash, 87–88
Champion, T., viii
Charlick, R., 124, 130–31
Cherniavsky, M., 110, 111, 112
Chiefdoms, 8; and early state, vii–ix; in Ponape, 4, 11–12, 23–40; models of, 12; and power, 23, 29, 30
Chiefs: and honor (Ponape), 4, 23–27; Hausa, 6–7; in Lesotho, 13–14; in Central Borneo, 42–43 (trade), 44–48; in Niger, 122, 127, 132–33; in Nanun, 145–46, 147, 149, 166; and independence, 151–52, 163; under Nkrumah, 152–53; Konkomba, 162; Nanumba/Konkomba relations, 164–65
Chrysostomus, J., 112
Claessen, H., vii–xi, 12
Class: in modern Kelantan, 56–61; in Hausa society, 138–39
Clastres, P., 3, 8, 28
Cohen, R., 2
Colonialism: in Ponape, ix–x, 28; European, 1; and the State, 3; in Borneo, 10, 41–50; Dutch in Borneo, 46–49; colonial transformations, 48–49; and state formation,

171

WIDENER UNIVERSITY
WOLFGRAM
LIBRARY
CHESTER, PA